Robert E. Swindle, Ph.D., is a professor of Business Administration at Glendale Community College in Arizona and has taught at both the college and university level since 1969. He has written several books on business, including *The Business Communicator,* published by Prentice-Hall.

THE CONCISE BUSINESS CORRESPONDENCE STYLE GUIDE

ROBERT E. SWINDLE

PRENTICE HALL PRESS

New York   London   Toronto   Sydney   Tokyo

Published in 1987 by Prentice Hall Press
A Division of Simon & Schuster, Inc.
Gulf + Western Building
One Gulf + Western Plaza
New York, NY 10023

Originally published by Prentice-Hall, Inc.

PRENTICE HALL PRESS is a trademark of Simon & Schuster, Inc.

Library of Congress Cataloging-in-Publication Data

Swindle, Robert E.
  The concise business correspondence style guide.

  Includes index.
  1. Commercial correspondence.   I. Title.
HF5721.S85   1983   808'.066651021   82-16537
ISBN 0-13-166652-5
ISBN 0-13-166645-2 (pbk.)

Manufactured in the United States of America

10 9 8 7 6

CONTENTS

Preface, *vii*

I
GETTING READY TO COMMUNICATE, 1

1   Mastering a Few Mechanics, *3*
2   Punctuating Correctly, *16*
3   Choosing the Best Words, *37*
4   Forming Sentences and Paragraphs, *57*
5   Communicating Naturally, *72*

II
MEMOS, LETTERS, AND TELEGRAMS, 79

6   Writing Interoffice Memos, *81*
7   Adopting a Letter Style, *93*
8   Minimizing Letter Writing, *120*
9   Communicating Electronically, *129*
10 Word Processing Methods, *138*

III
LETTER-WRITING TECHNIQUES, 151

11 Responding to Routine Correspondence, *153*
12 Delivering Good News, *162*
13 Softening Bad News, *167*
14 Using Persuasion, *176*
15 Asking for Money, *186*
16 Special Communications, *194*

IV

BUSINESS REPORTS, 199

17 Planning the Study, *201*
18 Researching the Topic, *209*
19 Preparing Graphic Illustrations, *220*
20 Writing the Report, *230*

V

EMPLOYMENT COMMUNICATIONS, 263

21 Creating Resumes, *265*
22 Writing Application Letters, *278*
23 Preparing for Interviews, *291*
24 Follow-up Letters, *301*

Index, *309*

PREFACE

The Concise Business Correspondence Style Guide is an information-packed guide to the creation of effective communications for the modern world of business. I begin by helping you establish a solid foundation in the rules of writing, knowledge that is essential to everyday communications in business. Subsequent sections of the book introduce you to the intricacies of memos, letters, and telegrams—including current methods of communicating electronically and exciting developments in word-processing systems.

An entire section is devoted to various psychological techniques that you may use to motivate others to respond in the desired manner. The final two sections of the book instruct you in the preparation of business reports, résumés, and employment letters. Other outstanding features are included:

S*T*A*R guidelines which emphasize a natural approach to writing, a style that is reflected throughout the book.

Concise grammar and usage sections that eliminate confusing terminology and focus on results.

Periodic self-checks interspersed throughout the mechanics and grammar section to test your comprehension.

Beginning-of-chapter flowcharts that show you how to plan different types of business letters.

Models show you how to fashion effective communication.

Step-by-step examples of opening, middle, and closing sections of letters—showing you how to write effectively, rather than just describing the process.

Many, many sample letters.

Strong emphasis on "doing."

End-of-chapter checklists which provide specific guidelines for completing a wide variety of written communications.

GETTING READY
TO COMMUNICATE

Which words should be abbreviated, and which should be capitalized? Should you use the word or the figure when writing numbers? Where do you need commas, semicolons, and colons? What about quotation marks, apostrophes, and dashes? Which words are "in," and which ones should you avoid? How long should you make sentences and paragraphs? The following four chapters provide you with definitive answers to these types of questions, and Chapter 5 concludes the section by introducing some valuable tips for communicating in a natural manner.

1

MASTERING
A FEW MECHANICS

The word *mechanics* as used here refers to decisions we must make concerning when to (or not to) abbreviate words, to capitalize the first letter of words, or to use figures, symbols, or words. This first chapter contains much detail, but the fact that you already know some of the rules will make the materials relatively easy for you to handle. You need deal with only those elements with which you are unfamiliar.

ABBREVIATIONS: USE THEM SPARINGLY!

The human animal generally seeks the path of least resistance, including the abbreviation of many words that should be written in their complete form. Some abbreviations may be used in business correspondence but only when you are confident that the reader will understand them.

Business terms
(some with periods and some without)

CEO (chief executive officer)
C.O.D. (collect on delivery)
COBAL (Common Business Oriented Language)
e.o.m. (end of month)
F.O.B. (free on board)
FORTRAN (FORmula TRANslation)
GNP (Gross National Product)
memo (memorandum)
No. (number, when followed by a figure)
Inc. (Incorporated)

Government agencies
(do not follow the letters with periods)

CAB (Civil Aeronautics Board)
DOT (Department of Transportation)

EEOC (Equal Employment
Opportunity Commission)
FAA (Federal Aviation
Agency)
FCC (Federal
Communication
Commission)
FDIC (Federal Deposit
Insurance Corporation)
FHA (Federal Housing
Administration)
FPC (Federal Power
Commission)

FRB (Federal Reserve
Board)
FTC (Federal Trade
Commission)
ICC (Interstate Commerce
Commission)
OSHA (Occupation Safety
and Health
Administration)
SEC (Securities and
Exchange Commission)

Names of states (in mailing addresses only)

Examples: IN (Indiana), SC (South Carolina), and CA (California). See page 96 for a complete listing.

Time expressions
(use small letters, except in telegrams)

Examples: 9:30 a.m., 2:45 p.m.

Do not use a.m. or p.m. unless preceded by figures.

(no) I'll see you in the A.M.
(yes) I'll see you tomorrow morning.
(yes) I'll see you at 8:30 a.m.

Titles with names

Dr. Mary Beth Hughes (only one space following the period)
Mr. Ronald P. Scheider (only one space following each period)
Harry M. Pfitzer, D.B.A. (Doctor of Business Administration)
Ms. Diane Washington (regardless of marital status)

Company names

Solomon Bros., Inc. (when abbreviated in the company's
letterhead)

Metric prefixes and units (no periods required)

k (kilo), h (hecto), da (deka), d (deci), m (milli), m (meter),
g (gram), l (liter), C (Celsius)

Although many abbreviations are used with business forms, you
should *not* abbreviate the following words in letters, memos, or
reports:

Days, months, and holidays

(no) Employees will return from the Xmas holiday on Mon.,
Dec. 30.

(yes) Employees will return from the Christmas holiday on Monday, December 30.

Geographic areas

(no) L.A. is located on the W. Coast.

(yes) Los Angeles is located on the West Coast.

Person's name

(no) Let Geo. do it.

(yes) Let George do it.

School subjects

(no) I took college classes in acctg. and econ.

(yes) I took college classes in accounting and economics.

Words in addresses

(no) The shipping address is 1612 W. 27th Ave.

(yes) The shipping address is 1612 West 27th Avenue.

Now try to determine what, if anything, is incorrect about the sentences in the following self-check.

SELF-CHECK: ABBREVIATIONS

Slide a piece of paper downward as you read, exposing the correct sentences and explanations only after you have studied the test sentences.

1 Congress recently raised the interest rate on F.H.A. loans.

Congress recently raised the interest rates on FHA loans.
Do not place periods after each letter in the abbreviation.

2 You are to begin work on Mon. at 8:30 am.

You are to begin work on Monday at 8:30 a.m.
Do not abbreviate days of the week.
Periods must follow a and m.
Notice that the period following m also ends the sentence.

3 Turn west when you reach 24th St.

Turn west when you reach 24th Street.
Do not abbreviate street.

4 We will hold the conference in San Jose, Calif., the week after Xmas

---

We will hold the conference in San Jose, California, the week after Christmas.

Do not abbreviate California or Christmas.

5   Robert Snyder Sent a COD shipment to 2318 N. 22nd Ave.

Robert Snyder sent a C.O.D. shipment to 2318 North 22nd Avenue.

Do not abbreviate Robert, North, or Avenue.
Place periods after each letter in C.O.D.

CAPITALIZATION: YOU MUST HAVE A REASON!

People who are uncertain of which words to capitalize sometimes overcapitalize, beginning every important word with a capital letter. To write correctly, and to make our communications attractive, we must follow these rules:

Days, months, and holidays (first letter of each word)

Example: Independence Day falls on the first Tuesday in July.

Historical events (first letter of each word)

Example: We have had continual inflation ever since World War II.

Example: Nearly half the labor force was jobless during the Great Depression.

Important documents (first letter of each significant word)

Example: The Bill of Rights is an important part of the Constitution.

Significant words include all words except articles (a, an, the), conjunctions (and, but, or, nor, for), and prepositions (of, for, in, through, between, as, with).

Directions (only when referring to specific regions)

Example: Many companies are moving from the Midwest to the South.

Example: The company is located at 1203 West 16th Street.

Otherwise, directions (west, east, north, south) are not capitalized.

6

Addresses (first letter)

Capitalize *street, boulevard, avenue,* and *drive* only when referring to a specific street, boulevard, avenue, or drive.

> Example: Please deliver the order to 1710 North 103rd Street.

> Example: They are located on one of the boulevards.

> Example: They are located on Glendale Boulevard.

Family relationships (when substituted for a name)

> Example: Will you please hand the check to Mother?

We capitalize *mother* because we could substitute the mother's name (let's say, Olga) for the word *mother* so that the sentence would read, "Will you please hand the check to Olga?"

> Example: His father is president of the company.

To substitute *John* for *father* would give us: "His John is president of the company," which obviously doesn't work. Therefore, we do not capitalize *father.*

Stated another way, we *do not* capitalize words denoting family relationships when those words are preceded by possessive words such as *his, my, your, her, their, our, Jack's.*

Person's title and name (first letter only)

> Example: Ms. Rhonda E. Norton

> Example: Mr. William R. Rogers

> Example: Dr. Jose P. Ortega

Occupational positions
(when following person's name; otherwise optional)

> Example: Mr. James Mitchell, Executive Vice-President

> Example: Ms. Martha Jamison, Comptroller

> Example: Martha Jamison is the new comptroller.

Titles of articles and publications
(first letter of each significant word)

> Example: An article titled "The Success and Failure of the Glasser Corporation" appeared in the June issue of *Business Week.*

> Example: Every business executive should read the *A to Z Office Handbook.*

College courses and languages
(first letter only of languages and specific courses)

> Example: She is studying English, algebra, French, and psychology.

Example: He is enrolled in Intermediate Accounting.

Direct quotations (first letter of first word)

Example: She then commented, "We expect to hire several college grads."

Complimentary closes (first letter of first word)

Example: Very truly yours

Example: Yours very truly

Example: Very sincerely

Word relating to numbers immediately following (first letter only)

Example: Mr. and Mrs. Baldwin will arrive on Flight 261.

Example: Those figures are in Section 4 of the report.

Example: Will you send two copies of your Invoice 26133?

SELF-CHECK: CAPITALIZATION

Slide a piece of paper downward as you read, exposing the correct sentences and explanations only after you have studied the test sentences.

1   Jeannie's Father is the President of the Corporation.

Jeannie's father is president of the corporation.

Do not capitalize <u>father</u> because it cannot be replaced by the person's name and because it is preceded by the possessive word <u>her</u>.

No reason to capitalize <u>president</u>, because it does not follow a person's name.

No reason to capitalize <u>corporation</u>, because a specific corporation is not referred to.

2   Many Businesses will be closed on monday, Labor day.

Many businesses will be closed on Monday, Labor Day.

No reason to capitalize <u>businesses</u>.

Must capitalize days of the week and holidays (both words here).

3   The truck, which is owned by some company in the east, was traveling west on 65th avenue.

The truck, which is owned by some company in the East, was traveling west on 65th Avenue.

Use <u>East</u>, <u>West</u>, <u>North</u>, and <u>South</u> (capitalized) only when pre-

ceded by <u>the</u>, denoting a specific and sizable geographic location.
Capitalize <u>avenue</u> (<u>street</u>, <u>drive</u>, <u>boulevard</u>, <u>road</u>) when it is a specific avenue.

4   Our professor of History spent a lot of time discussing the industrial revolution.

Our professor of history spent a lot of time discussing the Industrial Revolution. .

Capitalize historical events.
Do not capitalize <u>history</u>, because it is not the complete name of a college course.

5   Ms. Springer, who is arriving on flight 211 at 3:20 p.m., will discuss her new book, *The Life and Death of Socialism.*

Ms. Springer, who is arriving on Flight 211 at 3:20 p.m., will discuss her new book, *The Life and Death of Socialism.*

Capitalize <u>flight</u>, because it relates to the number immediately following.
Capitalize only the significant words in the names of publications, including the first word (<u>the</u> in this instance).

NUMBERS: WORDS OR FIGURES?

When you write letters, memos, telegrams, and most other types of business communications, you will generally be dealing with numbers. Follow these rules when deciding whether to spell out the number or give it in its numeral form:

Beginning a sentence: Use words
    Example: Sixteen employees earned merit increases.
    Example: Thirty percent of our employees have more than ten years seniority.

Ages of people: Use words
    Example: This applicant is not yet twenty-one years of age.

Fractions standing alone: Use words
    Example: The price of the stock declined by one quarter of a point.
    Example: Nearly one half of our employees are union members.

Periods of time: Use words

Example: Our contract is for a thirty-second commercial.
Example: The commercial will be aired every sixty minutes.

Amounts of money: Use figures

Example: The net amount of the invoice is $450.25.
Example: Your check for $215 has now been processed. (not $215. or $215.00)
Example: Our balance-of-payments deficit was $27 billion.
Example: The Chairman of the Board at Dow Chemical Co. received compensation for one year of more than $1.6 million.
Example: Tomatoes are selling for $23.00 per case, compared to $22.50 last month. (Zeros used for cents position in first figure only because second figure includes cents.)

Credit terms: Use figures

Example: Terms on the invoice are 2/10, n/30.
Example: The terms on our household items are 3/10 e.o.m.

Days and years: Use figures

Example: If you order today, payment will not be due until February 15.
Example: The transaction was finalized October 15, 1981.

Do not place the day before the month (15th of February or 15 October 1981).

Use ordinals with dates
only when they are not preceded by month

Example: We expect to receive the merchandise by the 24th.
Example: We expect to receive the merchandise by June 24.

Number of units: Use figures

Example: We ordered 16 No. 3610 circuit breakers.
Example: The truckload includes 1,310 cases of applesauce.

Percentages: Use figures
(except at beginning of sentence)

Example: Our net income increased 15 percent over last year.
Example: Sixteen percent of our inventory was lost.

Do not use percent sign (%) except in tabulated materials.

Time of day: Use figures

Example: If we begin the meeting at 9:00 a.m., we should finish by 2:30 p.m.

Addresses: Use figures

Example: Please send the order to our warehouse at 1610 West 7th Avenue.

If you encounter a situation where none of these rules apply, or if you cannot recall the applicable rule, spell numbers of ten or lower and use figures for those that are greater than ten.

SELF-CHECK: NUMBERS

Slide a piece of paper downward as you read, exposing the correct sentences and explanations only after you have studied the test sentences.

1   500 people attended the convention.

   Five hundred people attended the convention.
Do not begin a sentence with figures.

2   Joyce earned forty-five dollars for only 16 hours of work.

   Joyce earned $45 for only sixteen hours of work.
Use figures and dollar signs for quantities of money.
Spell periods of time such as <u>sixteen</u>.

3   We mailed our first notice to Apex Corporation on the 21st of March 1981.

   We mailed our first notice to Apex Corporation March 21, 1981.
Place the day after the month.
Do not use ordinals with dates unless month not shown.

4   Yes, we can give you the 7% discount on a purchase of sixteen units.

   Yes, we can give you the 7 percent discount on a purchase of 16 units.
Use figures for percentages, except at beginning of sentence.
Use percent sign only in tabulated materials.
Use figures for number of units.

5   They requested delivery at 16001 West twenty-Second Street by noon.

They requested delivery at 16001 West 22nd Street by noon.
Use figures for street numbers.

6 Our annual sales totaled three million dollars.

Our annual sales totaled $3 million.
Use dollar sign and figures for dollars in millions and billions, except at beginning of sentence.

SYMBOLS:
WORDS OR SIGNS?

Use the dollar sign freely in all types of business communications, but all other symbols (such as @, #, ¢, and &) may be used only in tables, invoices, and other tabulated materials.

SPELLING:
PERSISTENCE AND A GOOD DICTIONARY

Grade school textbooks provide many rules for spelling, but few people can remember them all. We discard these rules at an early age because we find they are unreliable; there are too many exceptions to the rules.

Fortunately, we can spell most words by sounding them out because they are spelled the way they are pronounced. We also spell many words, especially those that are spelled differently than they are pronounced, through sight—by taking a mental picture of the words.

Unfortunately, no one can spell all words. When you know you can't spell a word, or when you are in doubt, check it in a recently published dictionary. Even people who are good spellers rely on dictionaries—at home, at school, and at work—to check the spelling of words as they use them and to expand their vocabularies by checking the meanings of newly encountered words.

As you progress in business, many business terms will become a permanent part of your standard vocabulary. Correspondingly, you will routinely spell such words as *personnel, management, executive, corporation, demographics, laissez-faire, free rein, merchandise, mortgage, oligopoly,* and *subsidization.* You may save a lot of time, effort, and possible embarrassment, however, by studying the following list of words frequently misspelled in business communications. As an added precaution, you might want to mark this section with a paper clip and refer to the list when in doubt.

absence	bulletin	despair	guarantee
accelerate	bureau	develop	guidance
acceptable	business	difference	handling
acceptance	calendar	disappearance	happiness
accessible	cancel	disappoint	harass
accidentally	cancellation	disastrous	height
accommodate	candidate	disbursement	hurriedly
accompanying	career	discipline	immediately
accomplish	catalog	discussion	immensely
accumulate	category	dissatisfaction	impossible
accurate	certain	distribute	incidentally
achievement	changeable	divide	incredible
acknowledgment	chargeable	efficiency	independent
acknowledging	collectible	efficient	indispensable
acquaint	column	eighth	inevitable
across	commission	either	influence
advantageous	committed	eligible	install
advisable	committee	eliminate	intelligence
aggravate	commodities	embarrass	intelligent
aggressive	comparatively	encouraging	intentionally
allege	competent	endeavor	interfere
allowance	competition	enforceable	interrupt
analysis	conceivable	enthusiastic	irrelevant
analyze	confidence	entirely	judgment
announce	confidentially	environment	knowledge
apologize	consent	equipment	labeled
apparatus	controlled	equipped	laissez-faire
apparent	conscience	equivalent	legible
appealing	conscientious	erroneous	legitimate
appearance	conscious	especially	leisure
appreciate	consistent	exceed	license
approach	conspicuous	excellent	lightning
appropriate	continuously	existence	likable
argument	controlling	existent	lying
arrangement	convenient	expense	maintenance
assistant	convincing	experience	management
association	courteous	explanation	manual
attendance	criticism	facilities	manufacturer
attorney	criticize	familiar	meant
automatically	deceive	feasible	millionaire
available	deductible	February	miniature
bargain	defendant	finally	minute
beginning	deferred	financially	miscellaneous
belief	deficiency	forward	mischievous
believe	definite	freight	monotonous
believing	dependent	generally	moral
beneficial	describe	government	morale
benefited	description	grammar	mortgage
budget	desirable	grateful	movable

necessary	policies	representative	sympathize
neither	practical	requirement	temperature
noticeable	practically	research	temporary
obstacle	precede	resistance	tendency
occasion	predictable	restaurant	thorough
occupant	predominant	ridiculous	through
occur	prefer	sacrifice	totaled
occurred	preference	safety	toward
occurrence	preferred	schedule	transferring
offered	prevalent	secretary	tremendous
omission	privilege	seize	typical
omitted	probably	separate	unanimous
operate	procedure	severely	undoubtedly
opinion	propaganda	signature	unnecessary
opportunity	proportion	significant	unusual
originally	psychology	similar	useful
paid	pursue	simultaneous	usually
pamphlet	quality	sincerely	valuable
parallel	quantity	source	various
particularly	questionnaire	strenuous	vegetable
perceive	realize	succeed	vice versa
permanent	receipt	success	voluntary
permissible	receivables	suffered	Wednesday
perseverance	receive	sufficient	weather
personnel	recognize	superintendent	weight
persuade	recommend	supersede	whether
pertain	refer	supplies	writing
pertinent	referred	suppress	write
physically	reference	surely	written
pleasant	repetition	surprise	yield

You cannot take the time to look up all words in a dictionary, of course, and you won't have this list available at all times. After studying it, therefore, consider the words in the following self-check to see if you can identify which ones you should check in the dictionary (or list). Then, if you are dissatisfied with your performance, spend some additional time studying the list of words.

SELF-CHECK: SPELLING

Cover the column at the right side until you have identified the column or columns containing words that may be misspelled.

	A	B	C	D	Answers
1	changable	committee	apearance	finally	A, C
2	knowlege	receipt	source	competent	A
3	supplies	reccomend	judgement	obstacle	B, C
4	assistent	controlled	cincerly	safty	A, C, D

#					A, B, C, D
5	recieve	analyse	compitition	devide	A, B, C, D
6	approach	impossible	gratful	government	C
7	Wedesday	intelligent	writting	typical	A, C
8	yield	suprise	Febuary	freight	B, C
9	representative	quantity	questionaire	precedure	C, D
10	opinion	weight	unanomous	uneccesary	C, D
11	proportion	apealing	changable	supplies	B, C
12	recomend	opportunity	maintnance	schedule	A, C
13	association	continously	decieve	managment	B, C, D
14	opinion	writen	nether	morgage	B, C, D
15	comission	develope	thorough	appologize	A, B, D

2

PUNCTUATING CORRECTLY

Have you ever heard anyone say anything nice about traffic signals? Probably not, because we tend to view them as a necessary evil—something that we must contend with if we are to avoid accidents and traffic citations. But imagine the hassle of driving through a large city without such devices. The trip would be time consuming and extremely hazardous.

Similarly, some people view commas, semicolons, and other forms of punctuation as useless and bothersome. But consider the difficulty we would experience without these essential writing aids. Placing punctuation in the wrong places is like putting traffic signals in the middle of city blocks rather than at intersections, causing readers to become just as confused as drivers would be. To make our written communications effective, therefore, we must learn the functions of all forms of punctuation and know when we should or should not use them.

COMMAS ,,,,,,,,,,

Except for the period, which will be discussed later in this chapter, the comma is a writer's best friend. Commas enable writers to separate or join words, phrases, clauses, and sentences; and they tell the reader when to pause or (through their absence) when to read full speed. Correspondingly, commas enable us to express ourselves on paper in much the same way we express ourselves in person.

Set off dependent phrases and clauses at beginning of sentences

Clause: *Because he acted foolishly,* a reprimand seems advisable.

Phrase: *Under these circumstances,* a reprimand seems advisable.

16

Unlike a phrase, a dependent clause has a subject (he) and a verb (acted).

When we add a dependent phrase (or clause), such as "Under these circumstances," at the beginning of an already complete sentence "A reprimand seems advisable," we must set off the dependent phrase (or clause) from the rest of the sentence with a comma.

Connect sentences

Example: I like the work, but the pay is too low.

When we combine two complete sentences into one with the use of connecting words *and, but, or, nor,* or *for,* we must place a comma at the end of the first sentence.

Separate parts of a series

Example: Please return the first, third, and fourth copies.

Example: We must increase productivity, reduce costs, and minimize taxes.

Yes, the comma preceding the connecting word (*and,* in both of these examples), although omitted by many writers, is recommended for increased clarity.

Separate descriptive words

Example: The program turned out to be a long, profitless undertaking.

In effect, we are using the comma to replace the word *and* in this sentence. Either way is correct, with the choice of a comma or the word *and* depending on which seems more natural to you.

Introduce a direct quote

Example: The department manager shouted, "I want to know just who you think is in charge here!"

Set off descriptive phrases

Example: Miss Smith's memo, which is twelve pages, outlines the program very effectively.

Example: Joe James, our acting superintendent, is a very valuable employee.

The phrases set off with commas were added to already complete sentences to tell the reader something about the length of the memo and exactly who Joe is. All such phrases must be set off from the rest of the sentence with commas.

Set off direct addresses

Example: Okay, Joe, we will make the corrections.

Example: Leslie, your education and experience are very impressive.

Example: Your education and experience are very impressive, Leslie.

When we write as though we are talking with others, we set off their names with commas.

Set off added phrases which question what was just said

Example: We are going to accept their offer, aren't we?

Set off added phrases which have the opposite meaning of what was just said

Example: We are seeking applicants with talent, not just coursework.

Example: The boss is interested in results, not excuses.

Set off words such as "yes" and "no"

Example: Yes, we can deliver your order by the 24th.

Example: No, we are not interested in extending the contract.

Set off name of state when used with name of city

Example: Your shipment passed through Kansas City, Missouri, on June 12.

No commas are required when only the city or the state is used.

Example: Your shipment passed through Missouri on June 12.

Set off the year when used with month and day

Example: June 1, 1945, is the date the company was founded.

Example: June 1 is the due date.

Example: Your first payment will be due in March, 1982.

Use of a comma in the final example is optional.

Set off qualifying words

Example: We can meet the deadline, perhaps, by working overtime.

Example: No one returned our phone calls, however.

Example: However, no one returned our phone calls.

Notice that *perhaps* and *however* are *not* being used as connecting words in these examples.

Specify quantities in groups of three digits

Example: More than 32,000 consumers responded to the survey.

Example: Our net income for the year was $3,216,011.32.

SELF-CHECK: COMMAS

Slide a piece of paper downward as you read, exposing the correct sentences and explanations only after you have studied the test sentences.

1   After receiving many inquiries the office manager decided to reply.

After receiving many inquiries, the office manager decided to reply.

Set off the dependent phrase with a comma.

2   We wanted to fill the order but we were out of stock.

We wanted to fill the order, but we were out of stock.

Use a comma when connecting two complete sentences with and, but, or, nor, or for.

3   They sell toys nationwide with the assistance of agents brokers and wholesalers.

They sell toys nationwide with the assistance of agents, brokers, and wholesalers.

Use commas to separate parts of a series.

4   Pam is an experienced dedicated employee isn't she?

Pam is an experienced, dedicated employee, isn't she?

Separate descriptive words with commas.
When an added phrase questions what was just said, set it off with a comma.

5   Purchase orders received today and there are several should be included.

Purchase orders received today, and there are several, should be included.

Use commas to set off descriptive phrases and clauses.

6   We must begin production today not next month.

We must begin production today, not next month.

Use commas to set off phrases which have the opposite meaning of what was just said.

7   That package however was forwarded from Columbus Ohio last week.

That package, however, was forwarded from Columbus, Ohio, last week.

Set off qualifying words such as <u>however</u> (when not used as connecting words).
Set off name of state when used with name of city.

8   Yes shipment was made October 4 1981 from New York City.

Yes, shipment was made October 4, 1981, from New York City.

Set off words such as <u>yes</u> and <u>no</u>.
Set off the year when used with both month and day.

SEMICOLONS ;;;;;;;;;;

We use semicolons in much the same way that we use commas, but semicolons are more powerful than commas; we might even think of them as "supercommas."

Join sentences without connecting words

With: Government spending was at a record high, *and* a tax increase soon followed.

Without: Government spending was at a record high; a tax increase soon followed.

So how do you know when to use a connecting word and when not to? The choice is yours. You must decide which way sounds better. For variety, you may use connecting words in some sentences and only semicolons in others. Two thoughts must be closely related, of course, to combine them into a single sentence.

Join sentences with words other than
<u>and</u>, <u>but</u>, <u>or</u>, <u>nor</u>, or <u>for</u>.

Example: We like the style, but we question the price.

Example: We like the style; however, we question the price.

We must use the semicolon-comma combination with connecting words such as *however, therefore, consequently, moreover, nevertheless, whereas, otherwise,* and *for example.*

In the preceding example, the word *however* is read with the second part of the sentence (however, we question the price). If, instead, you wish the connecting word to be read with the first part of the sentence, you reverse the semicolon and comma.

> Example: We have a major problem, however; the price is much too high.

In this sentence, the connecting word *however* relates more closely to the first part of the sentence. The option of reversing the semicolon-comma combination in this manner enables us to express our thoughts more accurately.

When using semicolons, place them after closing quotation marks

> Example: The supervisor said, "Let's apply a little psychology in our labor relations"; he soon resumed his autocratic ways, however.

We use a semicolon here to join two complete sentences without the use of a connecting word.

Replace commas with semicolons when commas are used elsewhere

> Example: We place a high value on fast express service by trucking companies, because we do not like to keep excessive amounts of merchandise on hand; but we are also concerned with rate levels, claim ratios, and equipment availability.

When we have competing commas in a sentence, we use a semicolon (supercomma) with the connecting word. The semicolon helps readers spot the major break in the sentence, the place where two sentences are connected.

Separate parts of a series when commas are used within the parts

> Example: Absenteeism has been extensive: Joe missed six days; Jim, nine days; and Judy, seven days.

Instead of stating that Jim missed nine days and that Judy missed seven, we use commas to show that the word *missed* has been deleted. Having used commas in this manner, we must use semicolons to show readers where the main divisions are located.

COLONS ::::::::::

We sometimes treat colons like commas, but they are not commas; and we sometimes treat them a little like periods, but they are not periods. In this unique role, colons provide us with added flexibility in expressing our thoughts on paper.

Announce a following list or series

> Example: The workers are seeking three benefits: increased wages, shorter hours, and improved fringes.

We use a colon here because it introduces a following list. We may use a colon in this manner only when it is preceded by a complete sentence.

> Example: The three benefits the workers seek are increased wages, shorter hours, and improved fringes.

A colon following the word *are* would not be preceded by a complete sentence; therefore, we continue into the following series without any introductory punctuation.

When a complete sentence follows the colon, we capitalize the first letter of the first word.

> Example: One point is obvious: We must invest more money.

Announce a descriptive clause

> Example: This department is under the direction of just one person: James P. Culligan.

A colon has the effect of emphasizing whatever words follow it—the person's name, in this instance.

If we wanted to deemphasize the person's name, we would replace the colon with a comma.

Separate hours and minutes

> Example: The second shift of workers begins at 3:30 p.m.

Announce a direct quotation

> Example: Ms. Rochester then made the following statement: "Beginning next month, all overtime will be allocated strictly on the basis of seniority."

Notice that the colon is preceded by a complete sentence; otherwise, we would use a comma in its place.

SELF-CHECK: SEMICOLONS AND COLONS

Slide a piece of paper downward as you read, exposing the correct sentences and explanations only after you have studied the test questions.

1   Business was good this year revenues next year should be even better.

Business was good this year; revenues next year should be even better.

Semicolon used to connect two complete sentences.

2   At the price suppliers are charging we cannot make a profit on resale but we must meet the price of our competitors.

At the price suppliers are charging, we cannot make a profit on resale; but we must meet our competitors' prices, terms, and services.

Set off dependent clause with a comma.
Use a semicolon to connect the two complete sentences because of competing commas.

3   Stock prices are at a yearly low therefore we cannot afford to sell now.

Stock prices are at a yearly low; therefore, we cannot afford to sell now.

Use the semicolon-comma combination with connecting words such as <u>therefore.</u>

4   All had been big sellers breakfast cereals which totaled $3 million coffee $2 million and cat food $1 million.

All had been big sellers: breakfast cereals, which totaled $3 million; coffee, $2 million; and cat food, $1 million.

Use a colon to introduce a series preceded by a complete sentence.
Use semicolons in a series that also contains commas.

5   The four elements of marketing are price product place and promotion.

The four elements of marketing are price, product, place, and promotion.

We cannot use a colon after the word <u>are</u> because it would not be preceded by a complete sentence.

6   They promised to deliver the merchandise by 530 pm.

They promised to deliver the merchandise by 5:30 p.m.

Use a colon to separate hours from minutes.
Place periods after the <u>p</u> and the <u>m</u>, with no spacing in between.

APOSTROPHES '''''''''''

We use apostrophes to relate possessions, characteristics, and behavior to specific individuals or groups.

Show possessive for words that can be either singular or plural

Example: The wrecking firm moved the employee's car from the company parking lot.

Example: The wrecking firm removed the employees' cars from the company parking lot.

The reader knows that we are speaking of only one employee in the first example, because we have placed the apostrophe before the *s*.

We place the apostrophe after the *s* in the second example because we are speaking of more than one person.

Show possessive for words that are distinctively plural

Example: We now produce 33 different types of children's toys.

Example: Will you please send us three gross of men's handkerchiefs?

Unlike the word *employees,* the plural of words like *children* and *men* does not end in *s*. Therefore, we add an *s* after the apostrophe.

Show possessive for proper names ending in "s"

Example: Mr. Jones's report was very comprehensive.

Example: Ms. Harris' department had the greatest increase in productivity.

We add *'s* to the first sentence because *Jones* is a one-syllable word.

   We add only an apostrophe to the second sentence because *Harris* has more than one syllable.

Avoid assigning possessives to inanimate objects

(no)   The building's exterior is badly in need of paint.

(yes)   The exterior of the building is badly in need of paint.

Show possessive for time

Example: When may we expect to receive last month's reports?

Better: When may we expect to receive the reports for March?

Use possessive words preceding "ing" words when the words refer to people

Example: Tom's arriving late slowed the entire assembly line.

Example: Our calling all employees by their first names has improved morale noticeably.

Other examples of possessive words are *their, your, his, her,* and *my.*

Use apostrophes for contractions
of the words "it" and "is"

> Example: It's going to be a long bargaining session.
>
> Example: The building is old; when will its roof need replacing?

The second example uses the possessive form of *it,* which does *not* require an apostrophe. Adding an unnecessary apostrophe to the possessive form *its* is one of the most common errors in English.

SELF-CHECK: APOSTROPHES

Slide a piece of paper downward as you read, exposing the correct sentences and explanations only after you have studied the test sentences.

1 Managers should consider the workers feelings. (several workers)

Managers should consider the workers' feelings.

Place an apostrophe after the s̲ to show that we are writing about the feelings of more than one worker.

2 We check each persons productivity once every hour.

We check each person's productivity once every hour.

Place an apostrophe before the s̲ because writing about just one person.

3 Today is Jones day off, but tomorrow is Adams rest day.

Today is Jones's day off, but tomorrow is Adams' rest day.

We add 's̲ to Jones (one syllable) to form the possessive and only an apostrophe to Adams (two syllables).

4 This computers functions are quite limited.

The functions of this computer are quite limited.

Do not assign possessive to inanimate objects.

5 The retailer raising the price resulted in fewer sales. (one retailer)

The retailer's raising the price resulted in fewer sales.

Use possessive form for words preceding ing̲ words (raising) when the words refer to people (retailer).

6   Its going to extend its useful life.

It's going to extend its useful life.

Use apostrophe for contraction of it and is, but not for the possessive form its.

QUOTATION MARKS " " " " " " " "

We use quotation marks to enclose the exact words of other people. But quotation marks may be used for several additional purposes.

Enclose direct quotes of others

Example: The sales manager stated emphatically, "This sales campaign is essential to the survival of the company."

Always capitalize the first letter of the first word in a quote. Always place periods before closing quotation marks.

Example: "Go ahead and make the refund," he said, "or we may lose the account."

In effect, we are setting off *he said,* which is not part of the quote, with commas.

Notice that we do not capitalize the first letter of the first word where the quote is continued.

Use only one set of quotation marks to enclose a multiple-sentence quote.

Example: The customer commented as follows: "The bill is correct. We agree. More time is what we need."

Use apostrophes in place of quotation marks to identify a quote within a quote.

Example: The speaker then stated, "The term 'social responsibility' has many meanings."

Discuss words and define terms

Example: I disagree with your definition of the word "success."

Example: The term "negotiable instrument" may be defined as "a written obligation that can be transferred from one person to another."

Enclose slang expressions and nicknames

Example: I view the entire proposal as a lot of "bunk."

Example: This letter is to introduce our new production manager, Winnie "Sledgehammer" Johnson.

Cast doubt on something

Example: What does our marketing "team" have to report this month?

This questions whether the marketing people are functioning as a team.

Example: What does our "marketing" team have to report this period?

This suggests that the marketing people may be some kind of team other than a marketing team.

Enclose titles of articles

Example: The information is from an article entitled "Eastern Airlines Stakes Its Rebound on a Bid to Buy European Craft."

Notice that only the significant words in the title are capitalized and that the closing period precedes the closing quotation marks.

SELF-CHECK: QUOTATION MARKS

Slide a piece of paper downward as you read, exposing the correct sentences and explanations only after you have studied the test sentences.

1   The personnel manager replied we should reward employees on the basis of merit not tenure.

    The personnel manager replied, "We should reward employees on the basis of merit, not tenure."
    Precede the quote with a comma, capitalize the first letter in the quote, and place a period before the closing quotation marks.

2   We will ship the order she said as soon as we verify their credit standing.

    "We will ship the order," she said, "as soon as we verify their credit standing."
    Set off she said, *placing the first comma before the closing quotation marks. Do not capitalize* as, *because it is only the first word in a continuation of the interrupted quote.*

3   My definition of the word arbitrator is one having the power to decide.

My definition of the word "arbitrator" is "one having the power to decide."

When referring to a particular word, set it off with quotation marks.

Also enclose definitions with quotation marks.

4   The credit manager said can you hold just one minute: John is on the other line. I'll be right back.

The credit manager said, "Can you hold just one minute? John is on the other line. I'll be right back."

Place all three sentences within one set of quotation marks.

5   The magazine article was titled How to Read Stockmarket Indicators.

The magazine article was titled "How to Read Stockmarket Indicators."

Place titles of articles within quotation marks.

HYPHENS ----------

Some words are spelled with hyphens. We also use hyphens to combine words that describe other words, to write numbers, and to divide words at the end of lines.

Spell some words with hyphens

Example: Our company president is a self-educated person.

Example: She is the first woman within this corporation to attain the position of vice-president.

Most words beginning with *self* are hyphenated.

In recent years, most internal hyphenations of words after prefixes (such as re-, pre-, sub-, co-, de-, and others) have been dropped. For example, the word "cooperation" was once spelled "co-operation."

Example: Top management has decided to deemphasize television exposure this year.

So how are you supposed to know which form to use? Consult a recently published dictionary when in doubt.

Join some descriptive words

Example: George, this is certainly an up-to-date report.

Example: Such under-the-table practices are quite common.
Example: Joyce sent a three-page letter to them.

The hyphenated words describe the words immediately following.

Example: Will this be a two- or a three-page letter?

We use the word *page* only once, near the end of the sentence, to avoid needless repetition.

Do not hyphenate words ending in "ly"

Example: The newly formulated plan appeared incomplete.

The word *newly* describes the word *formulated* (not the word *plan*); therefore, we do not connect the two words.

Hyphenate fractions
only when they describe the word immediately following

Example: Nearly two thirds of our employees voted for union representation.
Example: The union received a two-thirds majority of the votes cast.

The fraction in the first example does not describe the word immediately following (of); whereas the fraction in the second example does describe the word immediately following (majority).

Avoid misinterpretation

Example: Many businesses are experiencing a small shipment problem.
Example: Many businesses are experiencing a small-shipment problem.
Example: Many businesses are experiencing a small shipment-problem.

In the first example, the reader cannot determine whether the problem concerns small shipments or whether a shipment problem is of small dimensions. The second example specifies that a problem exists with respect to small shipments, and the third example refers to a shipment problem that is not very significant.

Hyphenate spelled numbers greater than twenty

Example: twenty-one, thirty-three, ninety-five

Divide words at the end of lines

Example: eval·u·a·tion

We may split the word *evaluation* in any of three places, as shown in the dictionary. Rather than dividing the word between the first and second syllables or the second and third syllables, however, we should keep single-letter syllables with the first part of the word, carrying only the syllable *tion* to the following line.

Do not divide one-syllable words

> Example: through, serve, charge

Do not divide words with fewer than seven letters

> Example: letter, report, detail, active

Do not divide a word at the end of a page

Include the entire word on the first page or carry the entire word to the following page.

Do not hyphenate the names of people

> (no)   Ron-ald, Mr. Dickin-son

Instead, carry the undivided name forward to the next line.

DASHES — — — — — — — — —

On a typewriter, dashes are two hyphens—back to back—with no spaces on either side. We generally use them to emphasize a word or phrase that follows.

> Example: Their product entry—the winning one—is still on display.
>
> Example: The corporation maintained a secret account of over $10 million, most of which was distributed among politicians in hidden donations—to presidents, presidential candidates, congressmen, and lesser officials.

To have used a comma here in place of the dash would confuse the reader because of competing commas elsewhere in the sentence. Dashes enable us to include additions to sentences that would otherwise make the sentences too long.

UNDERSCORE _____

We use the underscore on a typewriter to specify that words should be in italics, including foreign words and the names of publications. We also use the underscore to emphasize important words.

Identify words as foreign

Example: A common business expression is <u>caveat emptor</u> (let the buyer beware).

If this sentence were in a book or magazine, the two Latin words would appear in italics as *caveat emptor*.

Identify names of publications

Example: The timely article appeared in the February 22 issue of <u>Business Week</u>.

Example: The title of the book is <u>Business Math Basics</u>.

Notice that the underscore is continued between words.

Emphasize important words

Example: We do <u>not</u> want a replacement for the damaged <u>machine</u>.

ELLIPSES . . . . . .

We use the ellipsis to tell the reader that some words have been omitted from a quotation.

Example: Mr. Randolph made the statement, *"The Wall Street Journal* is the most widely read publication among business people . . . in addition to extensive financial information, the weekday newspaper carries summaries of important national and international news events."

The three dots, which are separated from one another by one space, indicate that words which the writer considers unimportant to the meaning of the sentence have been omitted from Mr. Randolph's original statement.

Example: Ms. Spriggs stated, "The Dow Jones Industrial Average is computed on the basis of the closing prices of the same stocks each day: 30 industrial stocks, 20 railroad stocks, and 15 public utility stocks. . . ."

When we use an ellipsis at the end of a quote, we add an extra dot to serve as a period.

SELF-CHECK: HYPHENS, DASHES, AND UNDERSCORES

Slide a piece of paper downward as you read, exposing the correct sentences and explanations only after you have studied the test sentences.

1   The airline has government authority to operate around the world flights.

The airline has government authority to operate around-the-world flights.

Connect the three words with hyphens to describe the word immediately following.

2   The assistant manager appears very self sufficient.

The assistant manager appears very self-sufficient.

Words beginning with self are usually hyphenated.

3   Frank Babbit bought a one half interest in the company.

Frank Babbit bought a one-half interest in the company.

Hyphenate fractions when they describe the word immediately following.

4   I suggest that you read The Decline of Unionism in the current issue of Forbes.

I suggest that you read "The Decline of Unionism" in the current issue of Forbes.

Place title within quotation marks, and underscore the name of the publication. Notice that no comma is required before the first quotation marks, because this is the title of an article, not a quote.

5   The highly priced Fiat is a prestige automobile.

Correct as shown.

Highly describes priced, not Fiat; therefore, no hyphen is required.

6   When the clerk has scanned all the products, the computer categorizes each item meat, produce, canned goods, and bakery products.

When the clerk has scanned all the products, the computer categorizes each item—meat, produce, canned goods, and bakery products.

We use a dash here, rather than a colon, because we are adding words of explanation to the sentence, rather than announcing the words that follow.

PARENTHESES (((((()))))))

When we find that our communications are overladen with punctuation, we may switch to parentheses for clarification. The word *parenthesis* (with a lone *i*) is singular, and the word *parentheses* (with an *e*) is plural. Parentheses are also handy for numbering lists and parts of a series.

Use when there is too much competing punctuation

(no)   As citizens were displaced in primary industries, agriculture, fishing, and mining, they found jobs in secondary industries, manufacturing. Then, as businesses automated their factories, displaced workers were absorbed into tertiary industries, service jobs.

(yes)   As citizens were displaced in primary industries (agriculture, fishing, and mining), they found jobs in secondary industries (manufacturing). Then, as businesses automated their factories, displaced workers were absorbed into tertiary industries (service jobs).

Set off parenthetical remarks

Example: The auditors studied the balance sheet (this is when the trouble began) before deciding to recheck their original computations.

When an entire sentence is enclosed within parentheses and placed within a sentence, it should neither be capitalized nor ended with a period. Exceptions are short exclamations, as in the following example:

Example: As soon as they received the news (if only we had known in time!), they canceled the order.

Example: The auditors studied the balance sheet before deciding to recheck their original computations. (This is when the trouble began.)

When an entire sentence is placed within parentheses, apart from the text, it is capitalized and punctuated in the usual manner—all within the parentheses.

Defining organizations and agencies with acronyms

Example: The Organization of Petroleum-Exporting Countries (OPEC), composed of Arab oil-producing countries and Venezuela, joined forces in the early 1970s to establish common prices for their petroleum. Having a virtual monopoly on this form of energy, OPEC countries raised petroleum prices dramatically.

Once we have related the organization or agency to the identifying letters, using parentheses, we may use just the letters, without parentheses.

Number the parts of a series or listing within a sentence

Example: A charter is a written agreement between (1) the corporation being formed and the stockholders and (2) between the corporation and the state in which the charter is secured.

Enclose figures in legal and quasilegal documents

Example: The contractual amount is three million dollars ($3,000,000).

PERIODS, EXCLAMATION MARKS, AND QUESTION MARKS .....!!!!!?????

We all know when to use periods, exclamation marks, and question marks, so let's discuss the spacing required with their use and their placement with quotation marks.

Use two spaces at the ends of sentences

Example: Here is an important direction! You are to fill all orders in the same sequence as they are received. Do you anticipate any problems in complying with this order? If so, please notify your immediate supervisor at once.

Space only once after periods in abbreviated titles

Example: Who submitted the order, Dr. Messor or Mrs. Fulbright?

Do not space following periods in single-letter abbreviations

Example: They authorized us to ship the order C.O.D.

Notice that the last period also ends the sentence.

Do not space following abbreviated time designations

Example: You may expect our telephone call at exactly 12:10 p.m.

Place periods before closing quotation marks

Example: She commented, "This is my final warning."

Place exclamation marks before closing quotation marks

Example: The manager yelled, "Come on, let's get back to work!"

Analyze the situation for question marks

Example: She then asked, "Which copy should I return to the buyer?"

Example: Did she ask, "Which copy should I return to the buyer"?

The quote in the first example contains the question, so we place the question mark within the quotation.

Because the entire second sentence is a question, we place the question mark after the closing quotation marks. Note that this custom applies only to question marks; not periods, which always fall inside the final quotation marks.

As a matter of courtesy, we often state commands as questions, in which case we use periods instead of question marks.

Example: Since payment is now eight days past due, will you please send your check to us for the full amount of the bill.

Example: After completing your sales campaign in Portland, will you concentrate your efforts on our Boston market.

SELF-CHECK: PARENTHESES, EXCLAMATION MARKS, AND QUESTION MARKS

Slide a piece of paper downward as you read, exposing the correct sentences and explanations only after you have studied the test sentences.

1   Three government agencies regulate transport companies: Interstate Commerce Commission, Civil Aeronautics Board, and Federal Maritime Commission. (Number each part of the series.)

Three government agencies regulate transport companies: (1) Interstate Commerce Commission, (2) Civil Aeronautics Board, and (3) Federal Maritime Commission.

Place the last number after the conjunction <u>and</u>.

2   The director asked whom do you recommend?

The director asked, "Whom do you recommend?"

Because the quote is the question, we place the question mark before the closing quotation marks.

3   Did the director ask whom do you recommend?

Did the director ask, "Whom do you recommend"?

Place the question mark after the closing quotation marks because the entire sentence is a question.

4   She then yelled into the phone we won't pay your bill until we receive a corrected invoice!

She then yelled into the phone, "We won't pay your bill until we receive a corrected invoice!"

Place the exclamation mark within the quote, where the yelling takes place, preceding the closing quotation marks.

3

CHOOSING THE BEST WORDS

As an employee, you will experience superior-subordinate relationships—sometimes as the superior, sometimes as the subordinate, and sometimes playing both roles simultaneously. You will also communicate with other employees within your particular company and with such diverse groups outside the company as consumers, retailers, wholesalers, shareholders, suppliers, and government representatives.

Much of our success in dealing with these people depends on our choice of words. We must choose words that other people will understand, but without talking down to them. If we are to capture and maintain their interest, we must use words that reflect our sincerity and objectivity; and, equally important, we must make certain that we are using words correctly.

So where do we begin? An important first step in sharpening your language skills is to read this chapter carefully and work with the self-checks until you know the materials thoroughly. But that is only the beginning of the required effort. If you are to broaden your choice of words, you must constantly strive for improvement. Ask acquaintances to help you on a day-to-day basis, if they are qualified to do so. Read a daily paper regularly, one or two weekly magazines, and an occasional book. A lot of work, yes, but is there any skill more important in business, or in life generally, than communicating effectively? Certainly not!

CHOOSE THE SIMPLER WORD

Are we trying to impress people with our high level of intelligence, or are we trying to communicate with them? Most of us want to impress others favorably, but we should not burden the reader (or listener) with complex words when more commonly used substitutes are at our command. The following list helps to illustrate this point:

Replace the complex word with	*a simpler one*
Government aid *alleviated* the impact of the flood.	lessened
What *alternatives* do we have?	choices
We do not *anticipate* any problems.	expect
When is the sales promotion to *commence?*	begin
Transistors are important *components*.	parts
Why don't we *consolidate* our efforts?	combine
See if they will *convert* the freight charges from collect to prepaid.	change
The high rate of returns *denotes* an increasing degree of customer dissatisfaction.	reflects or suggests
When can you *effect* delivery?	make
When did they *initiate* the program?	begin or start
This product represents our *initial* attempt to enter the market.	first
Be sure to *inquire* about their credit terms.	ask
What *precipitated* the decrease in profits?	caused
Will you please send us a *remittance* for $25.	check
We *utilized* their services twice last month.	used
The shipment was quite *voluminous*.	bulky
Will you please *expedite* delivery.	rush

But what about all those big words you worked so hard to master? The complex word is still appropriate when it (1) enables you to express your thoughts more precisely, (2) replaces several other words, or (3) avoids repetition. Before opting for the big word, however, be certain that you are not communicating at too high a level for the other person.

SELF-CHECK: CHOOSING THE SIMPLER WORD
Cover the right column until you have chosen substitutes for the italicized words at left.

1	They did not *apprise* us of their spring sale.	inform
2	We will *compensate* you well for the effort.	pay
3	When was the letter *forwarded*?	mailed or sent
4	Shall we *interrogate* our employees about it?	ask or question
5	I think that we should *terminate* the program.	end
6	Do you have *verification* of payment?	proof

USE SINCERE WORDS

We should avoid expressions of certainty when we are only assuming what the reactions of others might be.

(no)   We are confident that you will rest well on your new waterbed.

(yes)   We believe that you will rest well on your new Sleepeze waterbed.

(no)   Considering the age of your toaster, we know that you will be pleased with a $10 adjustment.

(yes)   The number of years that the toaster has been in use was a primary consideration in our decision to offer you a $10 adjustment.

For all the writer knows, the reader of the first sentence may become seasick on the waterbed; and there is no way that the writer of the second sentence can anticipate the reader's response to the $10 adjustment.

Keeping in mind that broad assumptions such as these tend to irritate and offend, we should word our communications to suit others, not ourselves.

Expressions of surprise are usually nonproductive

(no)   We were very surprised to hear that you are unhappy with your new typewriter.

(yes)   We were distressed to learn of your experiences with our Model 1612 electronic typewriter.

(no)   We have never received a complaint quite like yours.

(yes)   Your comments caught us a little off guard, because most of our customers have expressed satisfaction with this product.

The first statement indirectly questions authenticity of the customer's complaint, implying that customer dissatisfaction with the product is practically unheard of. The second statement suggests that the customer is unique—even weird, maybe.

We should avoid statements that cast doubt on the integrity or normalcy of others, because the response will almost always be negative.

Qualify your statements to avoid broad generalities

(no)   Everybody in Congress is opposed to the new energy bill.

(yes)   Almost everybody in Congress is opposed to the new energy bill.

When, if ever, did all members of Congress agree on any substantive issue? Use words such as *seems, almost, appears, usually,* and *gener-*

ally to qualify your remarks when absolute certainty does not exist. We could improve the sentence further by providing precise numbers of congressional members who oppose the bill.

SELF-CHECK: USING SINCERE WORDS

Improve each sentence before reading the suggested wording that follows.

1   Shipment was delayed three days by floods in the Midwest, of which you are no doubt aware.

Shipment was delayed three days by floods in the Midwest.

2   We were shocked to learn of your dissatisfaction with the Model X16 calculator.

We have considered your comments on our X16 calculator.

3   You still have not made payment on the earlier purchase.

We have no record of your having paid for the earlier purchase.

BE TACTFUL

In being sincere in our communications, we must be careful to avoid damaging blows to the other person's ego. For best results, we must be tactful.

(no)   Of all the applicants who took our employment test, you scored the lowest.

(yes)   Your score on our employment test was not high enough to qualify you for the position.

(no)   We find that the requested loan would represent too great a risk for us at this time.

(yes)   The extensiveness of your current debt structure makes it impractical for us to make the requested loan at this time.

(no)   Your typewriter ribbons are of inferior quality.

(yes)   Your typewriter ribbons do not meet our specifications.

SELF-CHECK: BEING TACTFUL

Improve each sentence before reading the suggested wording that follows.

1   We cannot understand your reasoning.

    How did you arrive at that conclusion?

2   You failed to show our purchase-order number on the invoice.

    Will you please list our purchase-order numbers on all future invoices.

3   You still have not made the first payment.

    We have no record of your having made the payment that was due on January 15.

USE OBJECTIVE WORDS

Most business people emphasize the favorable attributes of their products and services, and they deemphasize any unfavorable characteristics. This is the name of the game, right? In doing so, however, they should minimize their use of *est* words (such as *best, greatest, cheapest, largest, fastest, newest*) unless they can support their claims with factual data. Although exaggerated business claims may be viewed as harmless "trade puffery," people soon respond to the overuse of such words with scepticism and mistrust.

We should also avoid the careless use of flowery words such as *tremendous, wonderful, fabulous, spectacular, superb,* and *super* because they tend to confuse. For example, the reader's interpretation of the following sentences may differ drastically from the intended messages:

(no)   This mattress is our deluxe model.

(no)   The new employee's performance has been superb.

The reader (or listener) of the first statement may think that the retailer is talking about a top-of-the-line mattress, only to discover later that the best mattress is labeled "*super* deluxe." Similarly, the word *superb* in the second sentence could have several meanings, depending on how freely the person making the statement uses such words. It's a matter of economics: Complimentary words are worth considerably more when they are scarce (used sparingly).

Another way to increase your objectivity is to use precise terms.

(no)   We plan to complete construction of the building soon.

(yes) We plan to complete construction of the building by June 13.

The word *soon* could mean next month to the builder but next week to the buyer.

(no)   John can type very fast.

(yes)   John can type 65 words per minute.

Typing very fast might mean 65 words to one person but 80 or more to someone else. To be even more precise, we might indicate the length of the test taken and the number of errors made.

SELF-CHECK: USING OBJECTIVE WORDS

Improve each sentence before reading the suggested wording that follows.

1   The purchase of this house would be the best investment you could make.

The purchase of this house would be a wise investment.

2   Sales for 1981 were outstanding.

Sales for 1981 increased 15 percent over the previous year.

3   This is our high-speed printer.

This unit prints 10,000 lines per minute.

EMPHASIZE THE POSITIVE

Rather than stating a thought in a negative way, why not emphasize the positive?

(no)   We cannot process your claim until you complete and return the enclosed form.

(yes)   We will adjust your account as soon as you complete and return the enclosed form.

Instead of telling customers what we cannot do, we tell them what we can do. Avoid negative words such as *cannot, mistake, failure, delay, fault, excuse, cheap, dispute, complaint, blame, reject, claim, sorry,* and *inconvenience*. Words that accuse, scold, or express anger cause people to react defensively to our communications; and we are trying to make friends in our business transactions, not adversaries.

If certain words irritate others, why not replace them with euphemisms? Euphemisms are relatively pleasant words and phrases, or, as one person described them, "sugar-coated words."

(no)   You had better have a good *alibi* this time.

(yes)   You had better have a good *reason* this time.

(no) Maybe they would be interested in our *cheaper* model.

(yes) Maybe they would be interest in our *less expensive* model.

(no) We took action immediately upon receipt of your *complaint*.

(yes) We took action immediately upon receipt of your *inquiry*.

Select the "sugar-coated" word when you can do so without distorting the intended message.

SELF-CHECK: EMPHASIZING THE POSITIVE

Improve each sentence before reading the suggested wording that follows.

1 We are not arriving at the airport until 7:45 p.m.

We will arrive at the airport at 7:45 p.m. on TWA Flight 333.

2 I gave her a serious lecturing.

I discussed the problem with her.

3 We disputed their claim that prices are lower this year.

We questioned their statement that prices are lower this year.

USE FRESH TERMINOLOGY

When young people in the 1960s approved of something a speaker said, they would yell, "Right on!" It was a clever and effective expression at first, but so many people began using the term that it became a cliché (a trite phrase). How would you react today, for instance, if you heard someone say, "Right on!" Wouldn't you think of the person as rather corny?

Other examples of phrases that have recently become clichés are "have a good day," "at this point in time," and "the bottom line." When you hear phrases (or words) repeated often, avoid using them.

Many of the following phrases, all of which should be avoided, were outdated even before the 1960s:

do not hesitate to contact me	as per your letter
is to acknowledge receipt of	at an early date
as regards to	attached hereto *or* herewith
	attached please find

by and large
will you kindly
due to the fact that
enclosed please find
please be advised that
we trust that
pursuant to our
   conversation
regret to advise
said (the said invoice)
same (regarding same)
thanking you in advance
the writer *or* undersigned

the above captioned
under separate cover
believe you me
few and far between
in connection with
in receipt of
of the above date
last but not least
we remain (at end of letter)
afford us the opportunity to
due to the fact that
in accordance with

But how can we remember all these trite phrases so that we can avoid using them? It's easy; simply write as you talk. We don't use such phrases when we are talking; so why should we resort to them when writing?

Some clichés may be classified as "golden oldies": *hit the nail on the head, beating around the bush, a dime a dozen,* and many others. Avoid using these dated expressions, especially when their use might confuse the person with whom you are communicating.

SELF-CHECK: USING FRESH TERMINOLOGY
Improve each sentence before reading the suggested wording that follows.

1   We wrote to you on December 15 with reference to employment.

    We wrote to you on December 15 about (concerning, regarding) employment.

2   Please do not hesitate to contact us if we can be of further service to you.

    Please let us know if we can help you further.

3   We are today in receipt of the merchandise.

    We received the merchandise today.

DESEX YOUR COMMUNICATIONS

In the past, when we referred to a worker, an executive, or a member of almost any group, we conveniently used the pronouns *he* and *him.* But with women now constituting nearly half the work force, it is inappropriate to continue this pattern. The most practical way to overcome this deficiency in our communications is to speak and write in the plural form. Rather than referring to an individual, we speak and write in terms of more than one person.

(no) The *auto worker* receives considerably more money than workers in most other industries because *he* belongs to a powerful union.

(yes) *Auto workers* receive considerably more money than workers in most other industries because *they* belong to a powerful union.

All auto workers are not males, as implied in the first statement; therefore, we avoid making a distinction between male and female workers by referring to auto workers as a group.

SELF-CHECK: DESEXING YOUR COMMUNICATIONS
Improve each sentence before reading the suggested wording that follows.

1 Businessmen who are in business for themselves work many hours each week.

Most people who are in business for themselves work many hours each week.

2 If an investor believes that market prices are going to decline, he sells; if he believes prices are going to rise, he buys.

If investors believe that market prices are going to decline, they sell; if they believe prices are going to rise, they buy.

EMPLOY JARGON SELECTIVELY

The word *jargon,* in the modern sense, refers to terminology that is understood only by members of a particular group. Truckers carry on radio conversations that, until recently, only made sense to truckers. Musicians have a language that is exclusively their own, and the same can be said for mathematicians, geologists, psychologists, sociologists, accountants, and many other groups. When outsiders listen to members of these disciplines conversing with one another, it is similar to overhearing people speaking a foreign language.

The use of jargon isn't necessarily bad. It is more efficient for data processing employees to speak or write to one another of CRTs, CPUs, and IOCs, for example, than to take the extra time that would be required to use nontechnical language. We should always keep the receivers of our communications in mind, however, avoiding terminology that may be "foreign" to them.

Jargon is sometimes defined as slang, and we can usually improve our communications by replacing slang words with more precise ones:

(no)   Our trucks are *eating* a lot of gasoline
(yes)   Our trucks are *using* a lot of gasoline

(no)   Their *necks* are *on the line* this time.
(yes)   Their *careers* (*jobs, futures*) are *in jeopardy* this time.

Also avoid word fillers. When we cannot think of the correct words, we sometimes fill the air with such "nonwords" as *and such, and that sort of thing, and what not, etc.,* and the repetitive *ya know, ya know, ya know.* If you catch yourself using word fillers, slow your talking speed to allow time for a better choice of words.

Other words that may be categorized as slang are *get, got, real, really, feel,* and a variety of swear words. Improve your communications by replacing *get* with a more precise word:

(no)   He is trying to *get* a spare part for the machine.
(yes)   He is trying to *find* (or *locate*) a spare part for the machine.

(no)   Prices are *getting* very high.
(yes)   Prices are *increasing* significantly.

You don't even have to replace *got* with another word: simply delete it from your sentence:

(no)   You have *got* every product that we offer.
(yes)   You have every product that we offer.

(no)   Unions have *got* one important advantage, leverage.
(yes)   Unions have one important advantage, leverage.

Improve your communications by replacing *real* and *really* with more acceptable words, or with no word at all:

(no)   Her sales presentation was *really* impressive.
(yes)   Her sales presentation was extremely impressive.

(no)   That was *really* nice of them.
(yes)   That was nice of them.

Avoid words that suggest we are relying more on emotion than on intellect:

(no)   We *feel* that we will be able to do a better job for you.
(yes)   We *believe* that we will be able to do a better job for you.

(no)   We *feel* that Plan C will be best.

(yes)   We *have determined* that Plan C will be best.

To avoid the possibility of offending, never use swear words in your business communications.

SELF-CHECK: EMPLOYING JARGON SELECTIVELY

Improve each sentence before reading the suggested wording that follows.

1   Extended unemployment can wipe out a worker's savings.

Extended unemployment can deplete a worker's savings.

2   Many businesses have gotten hit by the recession.

Many businesses have suffered from the recession.

3   That is one item they ain't got.

That is one item they do not (don't) have.

ECONOMIZE ON WORDS

To avoid cluttering our communications with useless words, we should not combine words that have identical meanings:

Instead of stating	*Use only*
basic fundamentals	basics or fundamentals
but nevertheless	but or nevertheless
carbon copy	carbon or copy
component part	component or part
each and every	each or every
free gift	free or gift
if and when	if or when
rules and regulations	rules or regulations
sum total	sum or total
thought and consideration	thought or consideration
true facts	truth or facts

We may also streamline our communications by replacing wordy phrases with one or two words:

Instead of stating	*Use only*
afford us an opportunity to	permit us to
we are in agreement	we agree
at the present time	presently or now
are in a position to	can
for the purpose of	for
How come?	Why?
give consideration to	consider
in the amount of $25	for $25
in the event that	if
in the neighborhood of	about
in order to	to
in order for	for
in view of the fact	because
subsequent to	after
with reference to	about or concerning

Finally, we should avoid the use of needless prepositions:

(no)   Joyce is sorting *out* the files.
(yes) Joyce is sorting the files.

(no)   Set it *down* on the counter, please.
(yes) Set it on the counter, please.

(no)   I wish that they would do a better job of cleaning *up* this office.
(yes) I wish that they would do a better job cleaning this office.

(no)   When are you going *down* to our plant in Puerto Rico?
(yes) When are you going to our plant in Puerto Rico?

(no)   The hardware store was the last place I worked *at*.
(yes) The hardware store was the last place I worked.

SELF-CHECK: ECONOMIZING ON WORDS

Improve each sentence before reading the suggested wording that follows.

1   We have asked them to recheck their figures again.

We have asked them to recheck their figures.

2   We wrote a letter in order to establish a written record of our conversation.

We wrote a letter to establish a record of our conversation.

3   We are flying over to Houston tomorrow.

We are flying to Houston tomorrow.

USE THE CORRECT WORD

One of the worst offenses we can make in our communications is to use a word incorrectly. Let's examine several sets of words that are commonly misused:

Accept/except

When we *accept,* we receive; when we *except,* we exclude.

> Example: Did the new employee *accept* your advice?
>
> Example: All employees *except* Jose are members of the union.

Advise/advice

Advise is something that we do, and *advice* is something the we give or receive.

> Example: Be sure to *advise* her of her rights.
>
> Example: The personnel manager gave us some good *advice.*

All ready/already

All ready describes a mutual state of readiness or preparedness; *already* (one word) means *prior to a specified time.*

> Example: The members were *all ready* to begin the meeting.
>
> Example: The purchasing manager had *already* placed the order.

All together/altogether

All together refers to a group as a whole, and *altogether* means completely.

> Example: The machine parts were *all together* on the shop floor.
>
> Example: The marketing manager developed an *altogether* different approach for introducing the new product.

Affect/effect

To *affect* means to influence; it is an action word that acts upon (influences) a word or words that follow.

> Example: The mistake will *affect* (influence) her chance for promotion.

49

Effect is the result or outcome of something, and it is followed somewhere in the sentence by the word *on.*

> Example: What effect (result) will the mistake have *on* your promotion?

We can also use *effect* as an action word meaning to *bring about* or *cause to happen.*

> Example: We can *effect* delivery immediately.

Balance/remainder

Use *balance* in an accounting sense, when referring to money that is owed or left over, and use *remainder* for anything other than money that is left over.

> Example: The San Jose Bottling Company owes a *balance* of $135.
>
> Example: The *remainder* of the work can be left until morning.

Better/best and other ter/est words

Use *ter* words when comparing two people or things and *est* words when comparing more than two.

> Example: Jan is a *better* (faster) typist than Jim.
>
> Example: Jan is the *best* (fastest) typist in the office.

Between/among

Use *between* when discussing two people or things and *among* when discussing more than two:

> Example: Divide the bonus *between* the two employees.
>
> Example: Divide the bonus *among* all 15 employees.

Cite/sight/site

To *cite* means to present; whereas *sight* refers to vision and *site* to location.

> Example: Employees *cited* Article 34 of the union contract as grounds for their action.
>
> Example: They will check your *sight* to make certain that it is perfect.
>
> Example: This land is the *site* for our new assembly plant.

Compliment/complement

Use *compliment* (with an *i*) to praise someone and *complement* to discuss things or people that go well together.

> Example: The boss *complimented* Martha on a job well done.

Example: The new files *complement* the office decor.

Continuous/continual

Anything that is *continuous* is without pause; something that is *continual* occurs regularly but with interruption.

Example: The roar of the machine was *continuous*.

Example: The ringing of the phone was a *continual* irritation.

Capitol/capital

Capitol is the name for the main government building; *capital* refers to the main city of a state, province, or country, or to possessions of monetary value, including money.

Example: He will be at the *capitol* building all day tomorrow.

Example: Edmonton is the *capital* of Alberta.

Example: Business properties such as vehicles and machinery are called *capital* goods.

Example: She invested nearly all of her *capital* (money) in the common stock of IBM Corporation.

Datum/data

Datum is singular for *data,* but it is seldom used. Many business people erroneously use *data* as a singular word, but most writers of business magazines, textbooks, and newspapers use it correctly.

(no)   Is this the data you requested?

(yes)   Are *these* the *data* you requested?

(no)   This data is incomplete.

(yes)   *These data* are incomplete.

Each other/one another

Use *each other* in connection with two people, places, or things, and *one another* when discussing more than two.

Example: Make certain that the *two deliveries* do not conflict with *each other*

Example: Make certain that the *three deliveries* do not conflict with *one another*.

Eager/anxious

A person who is *eager* has pleasant expectations; someone who is *anxious* is suffering from a degree of anxiety or fear.

Example: Ted was *eager* to begin his three-week vacation.

Example: Doris was *anxiously* awaiting a reply from the Internal Revenue Service.

Farther/further

Farther (beginning with *far*) pertains to distance, and *further* concerns degree or anything other than distance.

> Example: How much *farther* is it to the airport?
>
> Example: Let's discuss the proposal *further,* shall we?

Imminent/eminent

Imminent is something that is threatening to occur, whereas *eminent* refers to a prominent or distinguished individual or situation.

> Example: A steelworkers' strike appears *imminent.*
>
> Example: Jan's promotion places her in a very *eminent* position.

Imply/infer

To *imply* something is to make an indirect suggestion; whereas to *infer* is to interpret.

> Example: His questions seemed to *imply* that he is interested in our new product line.
>
> Example: What did you *infer* from his comments?

In/into

In deals with location, and *into* involves action.

> Example: The files are *in* the bottom drawer.
>
> Example: Jamie tossed the files *into* the bottom drawer.

Later/latter

Later means some time in the future, and *latter* refers to something that occurred more recently.

> Example: We will inform them *later.*
>
> Example: The *latter* of their two proposals appears acceptable.

Lay/lie

Lay is the present tense verb for the placement of an object, and the past-tense verb for the positioning of a person (see *lie* below).

> Example: *Lay* the contract on his desk right now.
> She *laid* the contract on his desk yesterday morning.
> She had already *laid* the contract on his desk.

Lie is the present-tense verb for the positioning of a person.

> Example: Why don't you *lie* on the couch until you feel better?

He *lay* on the couch for almost an hour this morning.

He has *lain* on the couch for a few minutes each morning.

Loose/lose/loss

Loose is something that is not restrained or right. *Lose* is when something is misplaced or taken away. *Loss* is a state resulting from something of value that is no longer accessible.

> Example: Competitors may benefit from any *loose* talk concerning our new product offering.
>
> Example: The cylinder came *loose* from the frame.
>
> Example: Did she *lose* the Sale?
>
> Example: The bankruptcies of two major suppliers represent quite a *loss* to this company.

Number/amount; fewer/less

Use *number* and *fewer* when discussing anything that can be counted, and use *amount* and *less* for anything that cannot be counted.

> Example: A great *number* of *people* responded to the questionnaire.
>
> Example: Roger has an enormous *amount* of *energy*.
>
> Example: Our new catalog contains *fewer* product *offerings*.
>
> Example: Consumers seem *less enthusiastic* about our new products.

On/onto

On specifies position; whereas *onto* specifies movement.

> Example: The file is *on* her desk.
>
> Example: The speaker walked *onto* the stage.

Oral/verbal

Because the word *verbal* may be applied to either written or spoken communications, the word *oral* is used when referring to spoken words.

> Example: Margaret's *verbal* skills are well illustrated in this six-page report.
>
> Example: The audience applauded his *oral* report.

Principle/principal

Principle refers to a law or an assumption; *principal* can refer either to the head of a high school, to something that is most important, or to money.

Example: A general *principle* of business management is that each employee report to only one superior.

Example: Ms. Prescott is *principal* of West High School.

Example: Profit maximization is our *principal* (major) objective.

Example: The payments are $250, including *principal* and interest.

Pronouns I/me, he/him, she/her, they/them, we/us, who/whom

We use *I, he, she, they, we,* and *who* as subjects for our sentences—as the person, place, or thing that is the center of discussion (usually at the beginning of the sentence).

Example: *I* will be there.

Example: Tom and *I* will be there.

Example: *We* plan to take immediate action.

Example: *They* have guaranteed delivery by 2:00 p.m.

Example: *Who* issues the contracts?

We also use these words with *is, are, was,* and *were.*

Example: This *is she.* (when answering the telephone, perhaps)

Example: If it *were I* making the decisions, things would be different.

We use *me, him, her, them, us,* and *whom* in all other situations (usually at the end of the sentence or clause).

Example: Did you phone *him?*

Example: Hand the letter to *her,* please.

Example: The agreement was between *him* and *me.*

If *who* and *whom* still give you trouble, here is an easy rule to follow: If you can substitute either *he* or *she,* you should use *who.*

Example: *Who* is responsible for petty cash? (*She* is responsible.)

The sentence makes sense if we replace *who* with *he* or *she,* so we use *who.* If the word can be replaced with *her* or *him,* on the other hand, use *whom.*

Example: You are waiting for *whom?* (You are waiting for *him.*)

If we replaced *whom* with *he* or *she,* the sentence wouldn't make sense, but *him* or *her* fits nicely; therefore, we use *whom.*

The distinction between *who* and *whom* is becoming less important each year, so when in doubt, use *who.* Similarly, when we are confronted with a choice between *whoever* and *whomever,* current practices dictate that we use *whoever.*

Self/selves

These affixes help us form reflexive words. The decision of whether to use *me* or *myself,* for example, depends on the first part of the sentence.

> Example: Will *you* tell them something about *me?*
> Example: May *I* tell you something about *myself?*

To use a word with *self* or *selves,* we must be referring to the same person or persons mentioned elsewhere in the sentence. We use *me* in the first example because *me* and *you* are not the same person. We use *myself* in the second example, on the other hand, because *myself* and *I* are the same person. Also consider the following examples:

> (no)   *I* like *me.*
> (yes)   *I* like *myself.*
>
> (no)   Why don't *you* take a closer look at *you?*
> (yes)   Why don't *you* take a closer look at *yourself?*
>
> (no)   *They* (children) don't always do what is best for *them.*
> (yes)   *They* don't always do what is best for *themselves.*

Who/which/that

Who refers only to people, and *which* refers only to things or animals. *That* is more flexible, applying to persons, things, or animals.

> Example: Rhonda is the employee *who* (that) received the award.
> Example: Is this the machine *that* is broken?

SELF-CHECK: USING THE CORRECT WORD

Cover the words in the column at right until you have decided on the correct word.

1	How will the transfer (affect/effect) her future?	affect
2	Which approach would be (better/best), dividing the overtime (between/among) Janet and Rod or (between/among) all three employees?	better between among
3	A large (number/amount) of customers appear (anxious/eager) for our spring sale to begin.	number eager
4	Randy is (continuously/continually) (complimenting/complementing) employees on the quality of their work.	continually complimenting
5	There is one envelope for (you/yourself) and one for (me/myself).	you me

6	The argument is strictly between Jack and (I/ me).	me
7	To (who/whom) did you say to hand the report?	whom
8	Yes, Mr. Prentiss, it was (they/them) who called.	they
9	He is the employee (that/which) we hired last week.	that
10	Will shipping our products from a plant that is (farther/further) away have a significant (af-fect/effect) on our costs?	farther effect
11	We encourage all of our managers to co-operate with (each other/one another).	one another
12	An economic crisis appears (imminent/ eminent).	imminent
13	The president's reserved personality causes many employees to (imply/infer) a general disinterest in their performance.	infer
14	The (later/latter) suggestion gained wide ap-peal among members of the board.	latter
15	When you complete the letters, please (lay/lie) them on my desk.	lay

4

FORMING SENTENCES AND PARAGRAPHS

If we were to think of writing as a puzzle, which many people seem to do, we would find that we have already familiarized ourselves with important parts of the puzzle: mechanics, punctuation, and word choice. Now all we have to do is put the parts of the puzzle together to form interesting sentences and paragraphs.

SENTENCE STRUCTURE

Let's begin by making sure that we know a complete sentence when we see one. To be complete, a sentence must have a person, a thing, or an event (the subject of the sentence) that is described or involved in some kind of physical or mental activity (the predicate or action part of the sentence).

> (no)   Believed that stock prices were going to decline.
> (yes)   John believed that stock prices were going to decline.

The first example is a *sentence fragment* because it doesn't have a subject; it doesn't tell us who believed that stock prices were going to decline. The second example is a *complete sentence* because we have added *John* as a subject, as someone who performs the mental action that follows.

> (no)   The size and shape of the office and the amount of protection needed.
> (yes)   The size and shape of the office and the amount of protection needed are two important considerations.

The first example is a fragment because it is without a predicate. Adding the phrase *are two important considerations* to the second example gives us a complete sentence.

Predicates must contain verbs such as *is, are, was, were, wrote, said, spoke, studied, am going to, have written,* and *will try to.* The subjects in the following examples are underscored once, and the predicates are underscored twice.

Example: Sales for this month were high.

Example: Small investors pay higher brokerage fees than large ones do.

Example: Are you going to request a stock certificate?

Example: Investors do not need to pay cash for the total amount of their investments.

Example: The idea gained popularity very quickly.

Example: The most that investors can lose in the stock market is the amount that they originally pay for the stocks.

Example: Check the price of wheat when you talk with them.

We assume the subject of the final example to be *you,* even though it isn't shown. Why? Because we sometimes talk and write in this abbreviated or imperative manner.

When we add words like *although, because,* and *since* to the beginning of a complete sentence, the sentence sometimes becomes a fragment.

Complete: Most people who join informal work groups do so for increased security.

Fragment: Since (because, although) most people who join informal work groups do so for increased security.

Both examples include a subject and a predicate, but the word *since* (because, although) makes the second sentence incomplete. By itself, the statement doesn't make sense. So why do we add such words to our statements? We do so when we are going to combine them with other sentences.

Complete: Since most people who join informal work groups do so for increased security, management may dissuade employees from joining such groups by helping them feel more secure in their jobs.

Adding the word *since* changed the first part of the sentence into a dependent clause (a fragment if used alone), which we added to an independent clause (a complete sentence in itself). The resulting statement is a complex sentence.

There are three structural types of sentences. We may use either simple, complex, or compound sentences in our communications, or a combination of all three types. The preceding examples (except for the last one) are *simple sentences* because they contain only one subject and only one predicate. When we add a dependent clause (a fragment) to a simple sentence, we refer to the resulting combination as a complex sentence.

Fragment:	Since three weeks are required for delivery.
Simple:	The purchasing manager starts the reordering process a month in advance.
Complex:	Since three weeks are required for delivery, the purchasing manager starts the reordering process a month in advance.

We bring the dependent clause (fragment) and the simple sentence together to form one complex sentence. Could we have added the dependent clause to the end of the simple sentence rather than at the beginning? Certainly!

Example:	One manager handles all personnel problems *in most small companies.*

The way you form a sentence depends on which way sounds most natural to you, and the choice generally depends on what you have said or written just before.

Notice that no comma is required when we place the dependent clause at the end of the sentence, because it reads well without one.

A dependent clause (fragment if used alone) is placed within the following simple sentence, rather than at the beginning or end of the sentence:

Example:	The manager, breaking with tradition, permitted a new employee to make the bank deposit.

If you question the need for commas to set off the dependent clause, try reading the sentence without pausing where the commas are now placed.

We form *compound sentences* by combining two complete sentences:

Complex:	While applicants are talking, interviewers usually record the answers to important questions.
Simple:	Applicants should use care when responding to questions.
Compound:	While applicants are talking, interviewers usually record the answers to important questions; therefore, applicants should use care when responding to questions.

(If you do not know why we used a semicolon and a comma with the connecting word *therefore,* you should review these forms of punctuation on page 20.)

So what kinds of sentences do we use—simple, complex, or

compound? We use all three types of sentences, while avoiding the overuse or underuse of any one pattern. The following paragraph helps to illustrate this important point:

> We received your order this morning. The credit manager approved your request. We are receiving a new supply of 24/8 oz. peaches tomorrow. We will ship your order as soon as the peaches are received. Consolidated Freightways will deliver the order to you in about four days.

Try reading the paragraph aloud. When we use too many simple sentences, we irritate our readers. We don't talk in this choppy fashion, so why should we write that way? Streamline your writing by combining some of your thoughts into complex and compound sentences. Doesn't the following paragraph read much better than the previous one?

> The credit manager approved your request, which we received this morning; and we will ship your order tomorrow, immediately upon receipt of a new supply of 24/8 oz. peaches. You may expect delivery by Consolidated Freightways in about four days.

This is not to suggest that you avoid simple sentences entirely; they are just as important as complex and compound sentences. We use all three types of sentences so that we may write naturally, the same way we talk. We may even combine simple and complex sentences or two complex sentences into one, so long as we do not permit the sentence to become too long or too complicated.

SELF-CHECK: SENTENCE STRUCTURE

Before looking at the answers in the column on the right, determine whether the statements are fragments or simple, complex, or compound sentences.

1 If department managers judge an employee's performance to be inadequate, they should dismiss the employee.　　complex

2 A much more effective practice, however, is to choose an employee within the department to show the new employee around.　　simple

3 The business concepts of planning, organizing, leading, and controlling.　　fragment

4 Government guidelines for questions that may and may not be asked job applicants are lengthy.　　simple

5	Some employees are paid hourly wages; others participate in incentive programs.	compound
6	Although she is usually responsible for arranging insurance coverage for employees.	fragment

SUBJECT-VERB AGREEMENT

We must keep our subjects and verbs in agreement, and we can easily do so by keeping our subjects firmly in mind.

Example: The production manager was at the meeting.

Example: The production manager and his assistant were at the meeting.

The production manager is the singular subject of the first example, which requires the singular verb *was. The production manager and his assistant* (joined with the word *and*) is the plural subject of the second example, which requires the plural verb *were.*

When we have the connecting words *or* or *nor* in the subject, rather than *and,* we pick a verb to agree with the part of the subject that follows the word *or* or *nor.*

Example: Either Mr. Brown or his employees are responsible for the overcharge.

Example: Neither the employees nor their supervisor is responsible for the overcharge.

In the first example, the plural verb *are* agrees with the plural part of the subject *his employees.* In the second example, the singular verb *is* agrees with *their supervisor.* You wouldn't say "His employees *is* responsible" or "Their supervisor *are* responsible.

When we place a dependent phrase or clause between the subject and the verb, we must be especially careful to choose the correct verb.

Example: Mr. Brown, not his employees, is responsible for the overcharge.

Example: The success of all the programs depends on teamwork.

The verb *is* in the first example relates to *Mr. Brown,* and the verb *depends* in the second example relates to *success,* not *programs,* even though the word *programs* is placed next to the verb.

Although we may be thinking of an entire group of people when we use the words *each, everyone,* and *everybody,* we must match them with singular verbs.

Example: Each employee is responsible for his or her own timecard.

Example: Everyone at the meeting was in agreement.

Example: Everybody at the meeting was pleased with her presentation.

The word *none* presents a special problem. We treat it as a singular word in formal communications and as a plural word in informal communications.

Formal: None (no + one) of these problems is insurmountable.

Informal: None of these problems are insurmountable.

Which form should you use? We recommend the formal wording only when writing term papers for college courses; rely on the informal usage at all other times.

We must also pay special attention to our use of the word *number*. Treat the word as singular when it is preceded by *the,* and make it plural when preceded by *a.*

Example: The number of employees who are qualified for the position is insignificant.

Example: A large number of employees are qualified for the position.

We must make certain that the action part of our sentences relates to the intended subject.

(no)   Hundreds of thousands of jobs will become available each year because of the need to replace those who die or retire.

(yes) Hundreds of thousands of jobs will become available each year because of the need to replace employees who die or retire.

The first sentence suggests that the jobs will die or retire. We avoid confusion by replacing the word *those* with *employees.*

Also consider the following statement written by a grocery store employee:

(no)   I alerted the manager, and he was caught trying to leave the store without paying.

(yes) I alerted the manager, and he caught the person trying to leave the store without paying.

The first statement suggests that the manager was caught stealing, which was certainly not the intended message.

To avoid repeating words, we often use word substitutes. When doing so, we must make certain that the substitutes agree with the words they are modifying.

(no)   If a <u>creditor</u> violates truth-in-lending laws, <u>they</u> are subject to a $10,000 fine.

(yes)   If a <u>creditor</u> violates truth-in-lending laws, <u>he or she</u> is subject to a $10,000 fine.

(yes)   If <u>creditors</u> violate truth-in-lending laws, <u>they</u> are subject to fines of $10,000.

By using a plural subject (*creditors*), a plural verb (*are*), and a plural substitute (*they*) in the final example, we can avoid a gender preference (*he, she*).

When we begin sentences with the word *there* and *it,* which should be done sparingly, we must know what they relate to before deciding which verb to use.

Example: <u>There is</u> (or <u>There's</u>) <u>a new employee</u> in the accounting department.

Example: <u>There are</u> <u>several items</u> on the agenda today.

We can use *There is* or *There's* in the first example because we are discussing only one of something (a person, in this instance). We must use *There are* in the second example, rather than the widely misused *There's,* because we are discussing more than one of something.

Similarly, we must keep our tenses straight. Rather than discussing past, present, and future events interchangeably, we must decide which time frame we want to use and stick with it.

(no)   When employees *are* unionized, they usually *began* the grievance procedure with complaints to their union representatives.

(yes)   When employees *are* unionized, they usually *begin* the grievance procedure with complaints to their union representatives.

The first example switches from the present (*are*) to the past (*began*). To keep the tenses parallel in the second example, we relate the present (*are*) to the present (*begin*).

Try to maintain this consistency within each of your paragraphs, changing tenses from one paragraph to another only when there is an obvious need to do so.

SELF-CHECK: SUBJECT-VERB AGREEMENT

Determine what, if anything, is wrong with each sentence before looking at the correct version.

1   Everyone is asked to contribute their time to the cause.

<u>Everyone</u> is asked to contribute <u>his or her</u> time to the cause.

2   Which one of the employees are responsible for the error?

Which <u>one</u> of the employees <u>is</u> responsible for the error?

3   The chairman of the board and his assistant are planning the
     meeting.

Correct as shown, using a plural verb with a plural subject.

4   A large number of adjustments is involved, but none of them is
     very complicated. (*Assume that the communication is
     informal.*)

<u>A</u> large <u>number</u> of adjustments <u>are</u> involved, but <u>none</u> of them
<u>are</u> very complicated.

5   While discussing the problem with my supervisor, the idea oc-
     curred to me.

The idea occurred to me while I was discussing the problem with
my supervisor.

*(First sentence suggests that the idea was discussing the prob-
lem with the supervisor.)*

6   ◦ More females attain management positions in personnel depart-
     ments than she does in any other area of business.

More <u>females</u> attain management positions in personnel departments than <u>they</u> do in any other area of business.

7   There's several reasons for responding promptly to inquiries.

There <u>are several reasons</u> for responding promptly to inquiries.
(or)
The <u>reasons</u> for responding promptly to inquiries <u>are</u> . . .

PARALLEL CONSTRUCTION

Other parts of sentences, beside subjects and verbs, must agree with
one another to maintain *parallelism* in our speaking and our
writing.

Avoid *double negatives;* rather than accompany negative
words such as *aren't, isn't, won't,* and *cannot* with the negative
words *none* or *nothing,* use the positive words *any* or *anything.*

(no)   We *aren't* going to send *none* of them to San Francisco.

64

(yes)   We *aren't* going to send *any* of them to San Francisco.

(no)   I *don't* have *nothing* to do with setting company policy.

(yes)   I *don't* have *anything* to do with setting company policy.

Similarly, be certain to accompany the word *hardly* with positive words.

(no)   We *can't hardly* wait until the new supplies are received.

(yes)   We *can hardly* wait until the new supplies are received.

Also avoid contradicting yourself by including a word that doesn't agree with what you have already said.

(no)   There is *absolutely no way* we can complete the order today *unless* we work overtime.

(yes)   The only way we can complete the order today is by working overtime.

Finally, we must maintain parallelism among the elements of a series.

(no)   The assistant personnel manager is responsible for hiring employees, training an employee, promotions, and to discipline employees.

(yes)   The assistant personnel manager is responsible for hiring, training, promoting, and disciplining employees.

(yes)   The assistant personnel manager's responsibility is to hire, train, promote, and discipline employees.

One element of the first example refers to *employees* (plural) while another refers to *an employee* (singular). Two elements begin with *ing* words, and one is an infinitive (to discipline).

We achieve parallelism in the second example by using *ing* in each element of the series and by using the word *employees* only once, at the end of the sentence; and we make the third example parallel by using infinitives (to hire, to train, etc.), but dropping the word *to* on all but the first element. Consider these additional examples of parallelism:

(no)   firstly, secondly, and third

(yes)   first, second, and third

(no)   (1), (2), finally . . .

(yes)   (1), (2), (3)

(no)   recruit applicants, test applicants, interviewing applicants

(yes)   recruit, test, and interview applicants

(yes)   recruiting, testing, and interviewing applicants

Determine what is wrong with each sentence, if anything, before looking at the correct version.

1   I handled payroll records, accounts receivable assistant, checking invoices, and some typing.

      I handled payroll records, assisted with accounts receivable, checked invoices, and typed letters.

2   They delivered 24 cases of peaches, but we didn't want none until next week.

      They delivered 24 cases of peaches, but we didn't want any until next week.

3   I don't believe that Jody should be given a raise, and that's final.

      Jody shouldn't be given a raise, and that's final.

4   First we must concentrate on increasing net sales. Secondly, we must search for ways to reduce costs and expenses.

      First, we must concentrate on increasing net sales. Second, we must search for ways to reduce costs and expenses.

INTERESTING SENTENCES

We can pump some life into our sentences by avoiding repetition, by using directive words, and by employing active construction. We often may eliminate repetition from sentences by simply deleting one or two words.

(no)   We hope that you will <u>reapply</u> with our company <u>again</u> next summer.

(no)   There are <u>at present</u> 300 million credit cards <u>now</u> in use.

Reapply and *again* are redundant, so one should be deleted; the same is true of *at present* and *now* in the second example.

    Rather than repeating the names of places or things, vary your word choice.

(no)   *Auditors* didn't have to contend with computers in the past; now *auditors* must be familiar with the operational characteristics of computer systems.

(yes)   *Auditors* didn't have to contend with computers in the past; now *they* must be familiar with the operational characteristics of computer systems.

(no) His behavior affects the *help* that he hires to *help* do the work.

(yes) His behavior affects the *people* that he hires to *help* do the work.

(no) Any way we do *it, it* will be costly.

(yes) Any way we do *it, the process* will be costly.

Therefore, similarly, accordingly, moreover, consequently, and *correspondingly* are examples of directive words. They inform the reader or listener of the direction of our thoughts—in this case, that our thoughts are continuing in the same direction as before. Directive words that inform others we are "shifting gears" by going in a different direction include *but, however, nevertheless,* and *whereas.*

Without: Jean Meadows related well to representatives of truck lines, rail carriers, and steamship companies. When she was chosen to replace the retiring traffic manager she did not perform as well as expected.

With: Jean Meadows related well to representatives of truck lines, rail carriers, and steamship companies. When she was chosen to replace the retiring traffic manager, *however,* she did not perform as well as expected.

Because we previously made a positive statement, the word *however* alerts the reader that we are switching to a negative result. Without the directive word, the reader would flounder.

Without: Many studies have illustrated that a manager's recognition of a job well done will motivate employees to work harder. We should observe and comment when employees perform well.

With: Many studies have illustrated that a manager's recognition of a job well done will motivate employees to work harder; *therefore,* we should observe and comment when employees perform well.

The directive word *therefore* provides continuity by guiding the reader (or listener) through a "because of *that,* then *this*" pattern of logic.

Although we may improve the flow of our thoughts with directive words, overusing them will make our communications sound artificial.

We may control the tone of our communications somewhat by placing directive words at different places within our sentences. The word *therefore* may be placed in any of three places in the following statement:

Example: *Therefore,* we should be hearing a lot more about wage and price controls.

Example: We should be hearing a lot more, *therefore,* about wage and price controls.

Example: We should be hearing a lot more about wage and price controls, *therefore.*

So where do we place directive words—at the beginning, middle, or end of our sentences? You must decide which arrangement sounds best. The first and third sentences sound natural, but the second sounds awkward. The positioning of directive words depends to a great extent on what has just been said or written.

Punctuation helps our readers, right? Of course, but punctuation also slows readers. Commas cause readers to pause, semicolons represent even longer pauses, and periods bring readers to an abrupt halt. When possible, therefore, we should form our sentences in ways that will minimize punctuation.

(no) *For example,* students may work toward four-year degrees, but they will usually perform better if they concentrate on just one semester at a time.

(yes) Students may work toward four-year degrees, *for example,* but they will usually perform better if they concentrate on just one semester at a time.

We need a comma before the connecting word *but,* so we place *for example* at that point; we slow the reader only once instead of twice by breaking the sentence with punctuation only one place in the sentence instead of two.

By placing the dependent clause at the end of a sentence rather than at the beginning, we can usually avoid slowing the reader with a comma.

(no) *To inform upper management of progress made,* accountants prepare charts and graphs every three months.

(yes) Accountants prepare charts and graphs every three months *to inform upper management of progress made.*

We may avoid slowing the reader with an unnecessary period by combining two sentences into one.

(no) Some managers make business the center of their lives. They spend many hours at work each week.

(yes) Some managers make business the center of their lives, spending many hours at work each week.

We converted two simple sentences to one complex sentence.

All well-written books, magazines, and newspapers are written in active voice. All you have to do to make your writing active is to use people, places, and things as the subjects of your sentences.

Passive: The program was coordinated by Miss Bassett.

Active: Miss Bassett coordinated the program.

| Passive: | The idea of divestiture, the "breaking up" of giant oil companies, is now being considered by Congress. |
| Active: | Congress is now considering the idea of divestiture, the "breaking up" of giant oil companies. |

Using active voice makes our writing more interesting to read. When we happen to be discussing a topic that is unpleasant, however, we can soften our statements by using passive voice.

| Active: | Mike made three serious errors in this income statement. |
| Passive: | Three serious errors were made in this income statement. |

Passive voice makes the sentence less accusatory. Rather than using the person's name as the subject of this negative message, we remove Mike from the sentence entirely.

Make your sentences more interesting by telling the reader what the catch-all word *this* actually stands for.

| (no) | This is expected to increase to $125 billion by 1985. |
| (yes) | This *amount* is expected to increase to $125 billion by 1985. |

| (no) | Everyone wants to be treated fairly; *this* is normal. |
| (yes) | Everyone wants to be treated fairly; *this reaction* is normal. |

A final way to make your sentences more interesting is to minimize the use of *it* and *there* at the beginning of sentences.

| (no) | It is suggested that we meet again on October 16. |
| (yes) | I suggest that we meet again on October 16. |

| (no) | There is an important reason for postponing the project, insufficient funds. |
| (yes) | The main reason for postponing the project is insufficient funds. |

You may, however, be unable to avoid such lackluster beginnings in some sentences, especially when writing without the use of personal pronouns (I, we, you) in formal reports.

SELF-CHECK: INTERESTING SENTENCES
Check to see how you would improve each sentence before looking at the improved version.

1   Since marketing employees make such an important contribution to profits, marketing employees should be paid more.

Since marketing employees make such an important contribution to profits, they should be paid more.

2   Employees must be able to respond to a wide range of questions. New employees participate in a two-week training session before actually beginning work.

Employees must be able to respond to a wide range of questions. <u>Correspondingly</u> (Therefore, Accordingly, Consequently), new employees participate in a two-week training session before actually beginning work. (*Could also combine into one sentence.*)

3   Mr. Davis, in a attempt to avoid a late charge, predated his check.

In an attempt to avoid a late charge, Mr. Davis predated his check.

or

Mr. Davis predated his check, in an attempt to avoid paying a late charge.

4   The $3,000 sale was made by Sylvia Blair.

Sylvia Blair made the $3,000 sale.

5   We must first identify the main selling points of our new product. This may help us convince customers to buy more.

We must first identify the main selling points of our new product. This <u>information</u> may help us convince customers to buy more.

or

We must first identify the main selling points of our new product, to help us convince customers to buy more.

6   It's going to be a very profitable year.

Profits will be very high this year.

PARAGRAPH STRUCTURE

You have been told to group related sentences into paragraphs, but this guideline doesn't mean that you must exhaust an idea before beginning a new paragraph. After writing two or three sentences, look for the slightest reason to end the paragraph and begin a new one: a new subject, a different time period, a change of mood, a new stage of development, a switch from a negative concept to a positive one (or vice versa). Why? Because paragraphs that are too long appear forbidding to the reader.

Notice that most newspaper and magazine articles begin with very short paragraphs, usually made up of only one sentence. This pattern exists because newspaper and magazine editors know that readers are more likely to read a particular article when the paragraphs are relatively short—especially the beginning paragraphs.

So just how short or long should you make your paragraphs? A paragraph in a letter may range anywhere from a single line to as many as 12 or 14 lines. A paragraph in a business report, on the other hand, may range from as few as 4 or 5 lines to as many as 18 or 20, with anywhere from 8 to 12 lines as a desirable average. The practice of continuing a paragraph for an entire page or more is no longer acceptable.

5

COMMUNICATING
NATURALLY

Getting ready to communicate? But, you ask, isn't that what I have been doing with the first four chapters? Yes, you have, and we will now build on that knowledge by showing you how to plan your messages and how to communicate naturally. Although this chapter is relatively brief, you may find it the most valuable section of the book. If you give the suggested methods of planning a try and follow the S*T*A*R guidelines, you will find that communicating well is a lot easier than you thought it was.

PLANNING THE
COMMUNICATION

Whether you are playing chess, striving for a touchdown, driving to work, or taking an essay examination, you need a plan. The same statement is true of business communications; before you reach for the telephone or begin pounding the typewriter, take a minute or so to plan the best strategy.

Identify the objective

What do you want to accomplish with the communication? What is the desired response? If your ultimate goal is to land a job, the immediate objective may be to secure an interview. When refusing credit to a potential customer, one objective may be to retain the person's goodwill. In responding to a routine inquiry about a product, your underlying objective will be to make a sale. Identify the objective of your communication and keep it your primary focus throughout the communicative process.

Select the medium

Once you have established the objective (or multiple objectives) of your communication, you must choose the best medium for transmitting the message. The different levels of communication media are illustrated in Figure 5-1.

Level 1 communications are one way, and a response (dotted line) may take anywhere from several hours (telegrams) to several days or weeks (letters, memos, and mailgrams). Both Level 2 and Level 3 media provide you with immediate feedback (notice that the arrows point in both directions), and Level 3 media add the extra opportunity to observe the other person's actions and reactions.

Your choice of the most effective medium for transmitting a message depends to a great extent on the content of the message.

Figure 5-1 Levels of communication media. (Dotted line represents delayed feedback.)

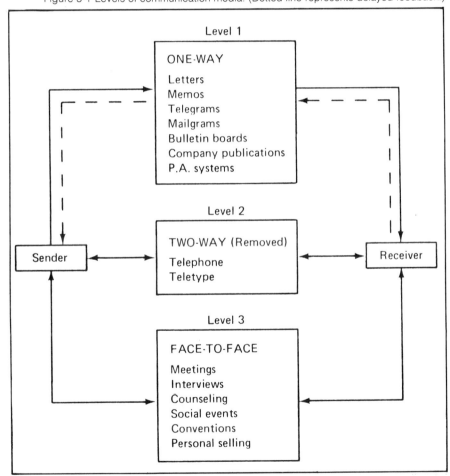

What is the length of the message? How important is it? What are the cost considerations? Is the message routine or urgent? How soon do you need a response? Is a permanent record of the communication needed? Which medium is most likely to motivate the other person to respond in the desired manner?

An intelligent choice of media requires a thorough knowledge of the characteristics of each medium and the exercise of good judgment. Although it may appear less costly to write or phone a customer instead of traveling to his or her place of business, a personal demonstration of your product might secure the sale where the letter or phone call would not. Similarly, issuing a bulletin to a group of employees may appear to be the least costly method of communication, but group meetings would provide invaluable feedback not realized with a bulletin.

However, two-way communications seldom eliminate the need for one-way, written communications. Telephone calls often require written records of the conversations in the form of letters and memos, and written records of meetings and interviews must be maintained. Teletype messages are unique in this respect, as explained in Chapter 9; in addition to being a form of either one- or two-way communication, they provide senders and receivers with printed records of their exchanges.

Organize the message

Many people start writing before deciding what they want to say or the order in which they are to say it. They are disorganized, and their communications show it. Rather than moving from one idea to the next in a logical sequence, they scatter their thoughts and their communications lack impact.

You may keep your thoughts on track by taking the time to organize your ideas—before you start communicating. Identify the key points to be made, and then organize them from past to present, from the most important to the least important or vice versa, alphabetically or geographically. Use whichever approach you judge to be most appropriate for the situation at hand, and then do your writing in a comparatively relaxed and systematic manner.

Time the transmittal

Timing is an important consideration with most of our communications. Do we have time to wait for a response to our letter, or should we phone? If we are writing to someone in a distant city, we can expect to wait anywhere from eight to ten days for a reply—assuming that the other person answers promptly. Telephone and teletype messages, on the other hand, can be instantaneous.

USING THE S*T*A*R APPROACH

Wouldn't it be great if we could follow some formula that would guarantee our success as business communicators? Although there is no such formula, we will communicate better by keeping four important guidelines in mind:

*Service
*Time
*Audience
*Reason

We may combine the first letters of these four words to form the word *STAR,* a convenient way of remembering the following guidelines.

Service

One company advertises that customer satisfaction is its most important product, and the managers of that company urge employees to adopt a service attitude in their business transactions. But is such indoctrination necessary? Don't employees realize that their companies would not exist without suppliers, wholesalers, retailers, and consumers?

Not always. When people work for a very large corporation, they sometimes think of the company as right at the center of everything important—that the rest of the world exists mainly for the corporation's benefit. Such an attitude should be avoided, of course, because it is erroneous and self-defeating.

Regardless of how strategic or nondescript your position within an organization, you will be more productive when you adopt a service attitude. When you approach business transactions with a "What can I do for you?" attitude, your communications will reflect a tone of consideration, courtesy, and helpfulness. Write and talk in terms of the other person's interest, rather than your own—relying more on the words *you* and *your* than on *I, my, we,* and *our.* Remember, employees have the responsibility of making friends for their companies and departments—not enemies.

Time

Whether you are speaking or writing, place yourself in a specific time frame. If you are discussing the past, try to imagine the action as it took place in the past. If you are discussing the present, place yourself in that situation. By identifying closely with the time frame you are discussing, you will avoid the tendency to switch tenses unnecessarily; you will be able to keep the verbs *is, are,* and *were* and their complements straight without having to give them much thought. Attention to these technicalities will be minimized, freeing you to write in a more natural style.

Audience

A similar approach works for picturing your audience, the people with thom you are communicating. Instead of writing to a government agency, a company, or a department within a company, try to imagine the specific person (or persons) who will read your correspondence. Pretend that you are in a face-to-face situation with your readers—sitting across the desk from them or enjoying a friendly coffee break together. When we write to inanimate objects such as departments, divisions, and companies, our correspondence tends to be cold and impersonal. Keeping a specific audience in mind helps us overcome the disadvantage of communicating at a distance.

Reason

Finally, we should keep the main purpose of our communication in mind. If the purpose of our letter or phone call is to answer a specific question the other person has asked, we should concentrate on answering the question and avoid introducing extraneous materials.

But what if the person has more than one point to make in the communication? There is no rule against covering more than one subject in a letter or during a telephone conversation, so long as the subjects relate specifically to the person with whom you are communicating. But do not expect the receiver of your letter to pass it to someone in another department when finished with it. Instead, send separate letters.

Keep the meaning of the letters S*T*A*R in mind for your personal communications and those in business. The S*T*A*R approach is helpful when you are planning your communications, during the time you are actually communicating, and in reviewing the effectiveness of your completed messages. Although this type of doublecheck does not guarantee that you will become a "star" communicator, the approach will encourage you to strive for improvement.

COMMUNICATING NATURALLY

In pretending that you are communicating directly with readers, write the same way you would talk with them. What? Use the same words and phrases I'd use if I were talking to someone in person? Exactly! A natural approach, using everyday language, is the key to good writing. Instead of switching to an artificial vocabulary for your written communications in an effort to impress, write to people exactly as you would talk to them. Your communications will improve dramatically, and writing in a conversational manner (your own style) is much easier than trying to imitate others.

A department manager included the following sentence in an interoffice memo: "In compliance with your directive of the 14th, all overtime work is being discontinued forthwith." Would he actually use such terms when speaking? Of course not! He would probably say something like this: "Beginning with today's afternoon shift, we are stopping all overtime work." So why doesn't he write like he talks? Clearly, this manager's effectiveness would increase significantly if he adopted a more natural approach to written communications.

Many people ask, "How do I begin the report?" and "What do I say in the letter?" Asked what it is they want to say, they are usually able to express it orally. To this my response is, "That's it; write it the same way you just said it." Follow this advice and you will be on your way to communicating "naturally."

COMMUNICATING PROMPTLY

The longer you postpone writing a letter or memo, the more difficult it is to write. As a matter of practice, *do it now!* Always have a pen (typewriter), paper, carbon paper, envelopes, and stamps at hand—at home and at the office—so that you are prepared to write.

If you put off writing a letter that should be written, the thought of having left something undone remains with you; it will take just as long to write the letter next week as it would today—and probably longer. Get in the habit of communicating promptly, while the details are fresh in your mind.

Don't strive for perfection at the beginning. After you have planned the main parts of your communication, try to get some words on paper. For most people, getting started is the most difficult part of writing. Once you have written a rough draft of whatever it is you are writing, you can improve your word choice, sentence structure, and other details. Eventually you will be able to do it right the first time.

Sometimes striving for perfection of the final communication can even be counterproductive, because people who dwell too long on a single communication soon view writing as a tedious task. Do the best you can without being overly critical of the results. Sure, a few years from now your efforts of today may seem primitive, but that's an indication that your writing has improved with time. And that's progress.

MEMOS, LETTERS,
AND TELEGRAMS

You should find this section of the book of particular interest, because we are now ready to deal with the specifics of interoffice memos and letters—the two most important forms of written business communications. After identifying some of the expenses related to the use of letters, we consider some available substitutes for letter writing. Subsequently, we explore the applications of teletype services and word-processing systems.

6

WRITING
INTEROFFICE MEMOS

A new employee's first encounter with written communications usually involves memos. Why? Because memos are generally less critical to the welfare of the company than letters are. Employees send memos to one another—not to customers, suppliers, or other groups outside the company. Unlike a letter, therefore, a memo that is poorly conceived or written cannot damage the company's public image.

Just because memos are circulated within the company, however, doesn't mean that you should give them casual treatment. Your superiors, your peers, and your subordinates will judge your performance to a great extent on the quality of these written communications. In fact, well-written memos can very well represent a crucial step toward a successful career in business.

PURPOSE OF MEMOS

But how do I decide whether to make a phone call or write a memo? To answer this question, let's consider the several purposes of a memo.

Convenience or economy?

Wouldn't it be easier to telephone another employee than to write a memo? Yes, a phone call would be more convenient and less costly than a memo—if you and the other employee work in the same geographic area. If the communication involves a long-distance call, on the other hand, a memo may be more economical and therefore more practical. We also rely on memos for transmitting highly technical communications rather than overwhelming others with detailed telephone conversations.

Multiple recipients

Although we might use the telephone to convey a message to one or two people, this approach would be impractical when several recipients are involved. Rather than visiting or calling each member of a committee regarding the agenda of an upcoming meeting, for example, we would outline the agenda in a memo and send a copy to each committee member. Similarly, we wouldn't phone individual employees to announce a change in company policy. Instead, we would write a memo and post it on strategically positioned bulletin boards. Or, if the communication were very important, we would circulate a memo and have employees acknowledge their receipt and understanding of the message by placing their initials on a copy of the memo and returning it to us.

Confirmations

Even when employees do communicate with one another in person or by telephone, some conversations must be confirmed with written communications. If several managers agree on a change of procedure, for example, they don't just shake hands on the agreement. One of them must record the agreement with a written memo as a way of avoiding future misunderstandings and conflict. Then, if one of the managers or anyone else should later question the exchange, the confirming memo provides a permanent record of the original agreement.

STANDARD MEMO FORMAT

Before reading further, take a minute or two to study the sample memo in Figure 6-1. Notice that in addition to the company name and the words "Interoffice Correspondence," the standard memo form carries several headings: DATE, TO, FROM, SUBJECT. These headings provide useful reminders to senders so that such detail is not overlooked, and they also make the message easier to understand. Instead of having to read the entire message to learn what it is about, for example, the receiver simply looks at the subject line.

Not only do we forego the formalities of salutations and complimentary closes, but memos are generally less formal in tone than letters. Memos should be relatively informal because they carry messages to members of the corporate group—not to outsiders.

Date line

Spell the month and show the date and year, without the use of abbreviations and without using hyphens or diagonals. In business communications, also avoid the date form used by the military.

A.D. SCHMIDT CORP.

DATE	January 27, 1983	COPIES TO	Joyce Randolph
			Rod Meecham
TO	Jim Rucker		Tom Yeager
FROM	Jossie Smeltzer		
SUBJECT	Warehouse Selection, Rochester, New York		

I have met with the managers of L&J Frozen Storage in Rochester, Jim, and they appear eager to handle our new pet-food line. Here are the main provisions of their facility:

1. Their main building is located in an industrial park just within the city limits (north side).

2. It is served by six major truck lines and two railroads (list attached).

3. They have ample space to accommodate our estimated monthly average of 4,500 cases, with adequate room for expansion.

4. Their monthly storage charge is 33 cents per case, including unloading, plus 35-cents-per-case charge for individual deliveries at the warehouse.

5. They have membership in the NAPW.

These provisions appear more favorable than those offered by the City Center facility, and, unlike City Center, L&J does not handle any competing brands of pet food.

If you agree with my assessment of these two options, please let me know right away, so that I may instruct Rod Meecham to make an in-person check of the L&J buildings sometime next week. If not, we will try to find another alternative.

ceh

Enclosure

Figure 6-1 Sample interoffice memo.

(yes)   February 2, 1983
(no)   2-2-83
(no)   2/2/83
(no)   2 February 1983 (military version)

Addressee line

Whether we show the addressee's title depends on the degree of formality within the organization. If everyone is on a first-name basis, you may omit titles before their names.

TO: Bill Miller, Comptroller
TO: Janice Walker, Accounts Receivable

If you are working in a more formal atmosphere, on the other hand, or if you wish to show special respect for the addressee, include the person's title and position.

TO: Mr. William F. Miller, Sales Manager
TO: Ms. Janice E. Walker, Assistant Traffic Manager

Sender line

The entry on the FROM line also depends on the degree of formality that exists within a company. If the atmosphere is relatively informal, you may use your first name or nickname and omit your middle initial.

FROM: Pat Morrison
FROM: Joe Quamma

Under more formal circumstances, or if the company is very large, list your full name and position or department.

FROM: Patricia Morrison, Traffic Coordinator
FROM: Joseph R. Patrick, Inventory Control

Note that we do not place a title before our own names. Others may refer to us as Mr. or Ms., but we do not use these titles of courtesy in connection with our own names.

We should sign or initial every business document we write, and most people place their initials on memos immediately following their names—as shown on the sample memo in Figure 6-1. Some business people place their initials or full signature at the very end of the message instead (Figure 6-2), as a deterrent to anyone who might add some comment to the memo without the sender's knowledge or permission.

Subject line

You should pay special attention to the subject line for two reasons. First, it specifies the nature of the communication, so that readers may determine the importance of the message and whether or not it is urgent. Second, the subject line provides a guide for filing.

Who usually does the filing of letters and memos? Quite often it is the most recently hired and least experienced person in the office, and this person usually decides where to file memos on the basis of the subject line. Therefore, the file clerk would probably place the memo in Figure 6-1 somewhere in the W's or in a special folder marked "Warehousing."

Body of the memo

Although there is nothing wrong with double-spacing a memo, especially if it runs several pages, most business people use single-spacing. Several pages? Yes, memos may take up only part of a page or they may be quite long. If your boss asks you to provide details of your trip to a company facility in another country, for example, you may have a difficult time confining the report to one or two pages.

You should allow at least 1 inch for your margins on both sides and at the bottom of the page. If your memo is longer than one page, use blank sheets (without the usual memo headings) for the following pages and allow at least 1 inch for the top margin. These additional pages should also reflect the name of the addressee, the current date, and the page number.

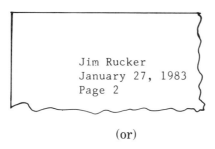

```
Jim Rucker
January 27, 1983
Page 2
```

(or)

```
Ms. Janice E. Walker          2          February  2, 1983
```

ICE lines

The letters I, C, and E form the acronym ICE, an easy way to remember what information (if any) should follow the message.

> I—identity of typist
> C—carbon copies
> E—enclosure

The letters "ceh" at the bottom of the memo in Figure 6-1 are the typist's initials. That's right, typists want to claim credit for their good work, and their bosses want to know who is responsible when something is typed wrong. If you type your own memos, you should omit the initials.

Typists usually place at the bottom of the page (below their own initials) the names of any employees who are to receive copies, but the memo form in Figure 6-1 designates a special place at the top of the page for this information. Three people received copies of the memo. So how many copies did the typist make? Four copies were required: one for each of the three people listed at the top right corner of the page and a copy for the sender's file. Keep copies of all written communications.

In writing the memo to Jim Rucker, Ms. Smeltzer included some traffic information (a list) relating to the warehouse. In doing so, she alluded to the enclosure in the body of the memo (at the end of item 2 in the listing), and added the word "Enclosure" at the bottom of the memo. This notation serves as a reminder to the sender to include the traffic information when mailing the memo, and it alerts the recipient to check for the additional information.

Short form

Rather than placing brief messages on a long memo form, an unattractive and wasteful practice, most businesses also have a short form. The short memo is usually 5½ inches long, compared to 11 inches for the long form, and both the long and short forms are the standard 8½ inches wide. Figure 6-2 illustrates the type of message typically communicated on a short form.

So why didn't Kim telephone this information to Sid? Because the memo provides a detailed record. If Sid forgets to phone Kim when the labels arrive, Kim possesses written evidence (a copy of the memo) that she instructed him to do so, and the blame will be on Sid. Sid probably likes the arrangement also, because the memo provides him with a reminder to take the required action when he receives the labels.

As with all written communications in business, we make an extra copy of memos for our files. With most memo forms, we must

```
DATE:    November 12, 1982          CULINARY CANNING COMPANY

  TO:    Sidney Starr, Label Room      INTEROFFICE MEMORANDUM

FROM:    Kim Peterson                 ─────────────────────────

SUBJECT: S&J Labels


San Francisco Printing Company is sending 24,000 S&J labels to us today

via UPS.  Will you please phone me immediately upon their arrival, Sid?

Thanks.
         Kim
```

Figure 6-2 Short-form memo.

use carbon paper and blank pages to make copies, but carbonized forms are also available. Memos are often some color other than white to distinguish them from other documents circulated within the company.

Round-trip forms

Many companies use multicopy reply memos similar to the one shown in Figure 6-3, which is a product of Diamond International Corporation. You, the sender, enter the name of the addressee, the date, and your brief message in the top half of the form—making sure to sign your name. You then detach the middle (yellow "originator" copy), which becomes your file copy. You mail the form, with the original (white) and bottom (pink) copy still attached to each other and with the carbons intact.

The addressee places his reply, if one is called for, in the bottom portion of the memo, along with your (the originator's) name,

REPLY MEMO SO-4

TO _____ DATE _____

_____

_____

_____

_____

_____

SIGNED _____

PLEASE REPLY HERE

TO _____ DATE _____

_____

_____

_____

_____

_____

SIGNED _____

REPLIER: RETAIN PINK COPY AND RETURN ORIGINAL (WHITE) TO ORIGINATOR.

ORIGINATOR: RETAIN MIDDLE COPY—FORWARD ORIGINAL (WHITE) AND TRIPLICATE (PINK) WITH CARBON INTACT.

Figure 6-3 Sample reply memo. (Courtesy Diamond International Corporation)

the date, and his signature. He then removes and discards the carbons, retains the pink copy for his file, and returns the original to you. Upon your receipt of the reply, you do not need to retrieve your file copy to see what you said at the beginning. The entire communication is before you: your message and the addressee's reply. These forms are available in different sizes—long or short, narrow or wide—and you may order them with the name of your company printed at the top. They are not inexpensive, as you may have surmised, but they save time. And when you save time in business transactions, you usually save money.

SOME GUIDELINES

As mentioned at the beginning of this chapter, our superiors, peers, and subordinates tend to judge us by our written communications, and since we use memos to correspond with these groups, it makes sense to try to write impressive memos. Just how can we impress others with our memos? We can do so by going directly to the main point of our message, by providing complete information, and by spelling out the action we are seeking.

Get to the point

If you want to "shoot the breeze" with other employees, give them a ring on the telephone; or, better yet, spend your coffee or lunch break with them. Although we do want to maintain a friendly tone in our interoffice communications, we don't want to waste our time or that of the reader by including unnecessary verbiage.

Notice in the memo in Figure 6-1 that the sender didn't make any small talk about the weather, the state of the economy, or her personal life. After establishing the purpose of the message in the subject line, she related every sentence to the subject—right on track.

Provide complete information

We should move directly to the point in our memos, but not to the extent that we omit important information. Include all pertinent data, and organize it in the clearest way possible. Again using the memo in Figure 6-1 as an example, notice that the sender aided the receiver by listing and numbering key points.

A useful guideline in checking the completeness of your information is to place yourself in the position of the receiver. Ask yourself if you could respond to the message on the basis of the information included. Remember, an incomplete message invariably results in additional communications.

Specify action

When your message requires action on the part of recipients, don't make them guess what you want them to do. Spell out the action; be specific. The sender of the memo in Figure 6-1 is seeking Jim Rucker's "go ahead" on arrangements with L&J Frozen Storage, and she requests his response "right away." For the best effect, position requests for action at the end of your communications.

The short memo form in Figure 6-2 illustrates all of these features. The sender moves right to the point, provides essential information, and asks for specific action—no fuss, no muss. Aren't memos handy? You can say what you have to and let it go at that, with absolutely no frills. In striving for brevity, however, don't spare words like *please* and *thanks*. Although your company may not have a rule about courtesy toward fellow employees, co-workers, like most people, generally respond favorably to considerate treatment.

INTEROFFICE MAIL

Much of the U.S. mail that arrives at the company mailroom consists of purchase orders for the firm's products (or services). Personnel in the mailroom must deliver these orders to the product distribution department. When people in the distribution department have secured credit approval from the credit department, organized the orders into shipments, and reserved the products with the inventory-control department, they send the papers to the traffic department. After selecting a transportation company, traffic personnel process the shipping papers and send them to employees in the shipping department. When personnel in the shipping department have forwarded the products, they return signed copies of the shipping papers to the traffic department, and the traffic people distribute copies to several areas of the company, including product distribution, data processing, and records. Get the idea? People in business don't just correspond with suppliers and customers; most of their communications are within their own organization.

Rather than running all over the place exchanging documents, employees of the different departments mail their communications in interoffice envelopes. The most commonly used envelopes are light brown and measure either 4 by 9½ inches (for folded pages) or 9½ by 13 inches (for unfolded documents). The front of the envelope usually reflects the company name, and the remaining space (front and back) is lined for addresses—as illustrated in Figure 6-4.

In this way one envelope can be recycled anywhere from 60 to 90 times, depending on its size. The user simply crosses out the last

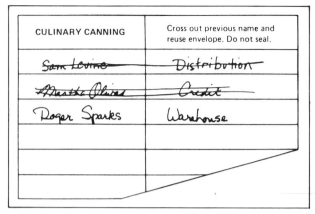

CULINARY CANNING	Cross out previous name and reuse envelope. Do not seal.
~~Sam Levine~~	~~Distribution~~
~~Martha Oliver~~	~~Credit~~
Roger Sparks	Warehouse

Figure 6-4 Portion of small-sized interoffice envelope.

name on the envelope, writes in the name and location of the next addressee on the following line, inserts the message, tucks in (but doesn't seal) the flap, and places it in the outgoing mail. Mailroom personnel usually collect and distribute interoffice mail among all departments several times each working day.

CHECKLIST: INTEROFFICE MEMOS

Is a memo the best medium for this message?

- Do we need a response?
- Can we wait for a mailed response?
- Would a telephone call eliminate the need for further correspondence?
- How many copies are needed, including one for your (the sender's) file?
- Which is more appropriate, the short or long form?
- Would a reply (round-trip) memo be more appropriate?

Did you complete the headings properly?

- Did you spell out the month and show the day and year?
- Is it advisable to show the addressee's title (Mr., Ms., Dr.) in this particular communication?
- Did you place your initials after your name or at the end of the message?
- Does the subject line provide an appropriate guideline for filing?

91

Is the body of the memo well organized and attractive?

- Are your ideas organized in some logical sequence?
- Did you list and number key points (if several)?
- Did you avoid unnecessary verbiage and get right to the point?
- If you used more than one page, did you include the addressee's name, the date, and the page number on all but the first page?
- Have you included all relevant information?
- Did you specify the desired action (if any)?
- Should you have included a deadline for the reader's response?
- Did you allow a margin of about 1 inch on both sides and at the bottom of the page?

Did you include all the necessary information at the bottom of the memo?

- Are the typist's initials shown (unless you typed it yourself)?
- Did you list the names of others (if any) who are to receive copies?
- Did you indicate that there are enclosures (if any)?

Did you check the communication for accuracy?

- Are dates, quantities, and other numbers accurate?
- Are all names spelled correctly?
- Are all words spelled correctly?

7

ADOPTING
A LETTER STYLE

The rules for writing business letters are undergoing rapid change for two reasons. Business people are becoming less formal in their communications, and they are finally acknowledging the fact that more and more women are participating in the world of business. What, more rules? Yes, there are certain conventions that you must follow if your letters are to be widely accepted in business, but isn't it easier to follow a few guidelines than to "play it by ear"?

PARTS OF A LETTER

You should familiarize yourself with all the parts of a letter before trying to combine the pieces into a final product. Consult the complete letter in Figure 7-1, however, as a guide when reading the following pointers.

Sender's address

Always make certain that your own address is shown on the letter. If you are writing on company stationery (letterhead), the name of the business is printed at the top, with the return address (and possibly the telephone number) listed either at the top or bottom of the page. For personal letters, as in Figure 7-1, you must place your return address above the date line.

Date line

Show the date of writing on all letters, spelling out the name of the month and avoiding ordinals (nd, rd, th).

  (no)   Nov. 26th, 1983
  (yes)   November 26, 1983

```
                        300 North Avenue  ⎫   Return address
                        Atlanta, GA  30313 ⎬
                        October 4, 1982   ⎭   Date


Mr. Frederick S. Perry   ⎫   Receiver's (inside) address
Ideal Mills, Inc.        ⎬
30 West Monroe Street    ⎪
Chicago, IL  60603       ⎭

Dear Mr. Perry:

Usually I am very pleased with Ideal utensils and pans, so I recently
purchased eight loaf pans to increase my supply.  I normally buy only one
or two items to determine whether the product is satisfactory.  In this
case, however, I felt that I could safely purchase all of the needed
items because of my previous satisfaction with your products.

I was very disappointed, therefore, when the pans proved unsatisfactory.
To bake any yeast-based dough, the temperature must be high (400-425
degrees) initially.  With the new pans, this temperature caused the
surface dough that was in contact with the pan to become extremely dark
and tough.  A similar situation occurred with cakes, even though the
temperatures were comparatively moderate.

I first spoke with the grocery store manager where the pans were purchased.
He referred me to your district manager, who, in turn, suggested that I
write directly to you.  I am enclosing the cash register receipt and
requesting a refund of $26.35.

                    Sincerely,      ⎧ Complimentary close

                    E. M. McIntyre  ⎨ Signature

                    E. M. McIntyre  ⎩ Typed name

Enclosure ⎬   The receipt that was included
```

Figure 7-1 Sample letter (on personal stationery).

94

Receiver's address

If you are writing to a specific individual, show the person's complimentary title and name on the first line of the address.

Example: Mr. John H. Rowden
Miss Pamela Rochester
Mrs. Rhonda Wells
Ms. Patricia R. Golden
Dr. S. E. Campella

If you know the position of the person within the company, place it directly after the person's name or on the next line—depending on which arrangement is more attractive.

Example: Miss Rita Cloister, Manager
The Sharpe Shoppe
Example: Mr. J. R. Remington
Assistant Personnel Manager
Smothers Manufacturing Co.
Example: Ms. Paula R. Scott, Assistant
Director of Customer Services
The General Instrument Corp.

The job title fits nicely on the top line of the first example and on the second line of the second example, but we used part of the first line and all of the second line for Ms. Scott's title in the third example. Each of these addresses is well balanced, with no very long lines and no extremely short ones. Notice that when we place all or part of a job title on the first line we separate it from the person's name with a comma. People are proud of their titles, so be sure to include them when known.

If you are writing to the person at a business address, place the name of the business on the second line. Use the next line for the street address, and the last line for the city, state, and zip code.

Showing the position

Ms. Paula R. Scott, Assistant
Director of Customer Services
THE GENERAL INSTRUMENT CORP.
17000 St. Claire Avenue
Cleveland, Ohio 44110

Position not known

Mr. Patrick R. Golden
Rolodex Corporation
P. O. Box 315
St. Paul, MN 55101

You may, if you wish, emphasize the company name by capitalizing all letters, as in the first example, especially for long inside addresses (more than four lines). Do not abbreviate directions, or the words *Street* or *Avenue*. The letters *P.* and *O.* in the address at the right are the abbreviation for *post office*. When you use a box number, place it between the company name and the last line (the city, state, and zip code) and omit the street address.

For letter (inside) addresses, as illustrated here, you may spell out the name of the state or use the appropriate two-letter code from Figure 7-2, whichever better balances the address. For envelope (outside) addresses, you should always use the two-letter codes. Avoid the use of periods with the state codes, and leave two blank spaces between the state codes and the zip codes. If you are answering another business letter, the zip code will be shown in the company's letterhead (the printing on the stationery). If it is not, you must find the number. Most large companies subscribe to the *National Zip Code Directory,* but you also may secure this information by phoning the post office and telling them the name of the city and the street address. Zip codes for local addresses are shown on a map near the back of your telephone directory.

Businesses may soon find it necessary to deal with the so-called "ZIP plus four," nine-digit codes. Although the Postal Service projects savings attributed to the expanded numbers of approximately $450 million per year, implementation and details of the program will depend on congressional action still pending.

Salutation

When business people direct letters to specific individuals, they usually follow the address with a salutation. We wouldn't think of calling other business people "Dear" when talking with them, but most of us continue to do so in letters. Some people, however, have

Figure 7-2 Two-letter state codes.

Alabama	AL	Illinois	IL	Montana	MT
Alaska	AK	Indiana	IN	Nebraska	NE
Arizona	AZ	Iowa	IA	Nevada	NV
Arkansas	AR	Kansas	KS	New Hampshire	NH
California	CA	Kentucky	KY	New Jersey	NJ
Colorado	CO	Louisiana	LA	New Mexico	NM
Connecticut	CT	Maine	ME	New York	NY
Delaware	DE	Maryland	MD	North Carolina	NC
Dist. of Col.	DC	Massachusetts	MA	North Dakota	ND
Florida	FL	Michigan	MI	Ohio	OH
Georgia	GA	Minnesota	MN	Oklahoma	OK
Guam	GU	Mississippi	MS	Oregon	OR
Hawaii	HI	Missouri	MO	Pennsylvania	PA
Idaho	ID				

Puerto Rico	PR
Rhode Island	RI
South Carolina	SC
South Dakota	SD
Tennessee	TN
Texas	TX
Utah	UT
Vermont	VT
Virginia	VA
Virgin Islands	VI
Washington	WA
West Virginia	WV
Wisconsin	WI
Wyoming	WY

dropped the word "Dear" from their salutations. Use whichever of the recommended forms you wish from the following list, but avoid the more flowery and sexist salutations in the *Not recommended* column.

Recommended	*Not recommended*
Dear Mr. Greenspan:	Sir:
Mr. Greenspan:	Dear Sir:
Dear Ms. Peters:	My Dear Sir:
Ms. Peters:	Gentlemen:
Dear Miss Randolph:	My Dear Mr. Powell:
Ms. Randolph:	To Whom It May Concern:
	Dear Madam:

Similar rules apply to correspondence with government officials.

Examples	*Examples*
Mr. President:	Governor Green:
Dear Mr. President:	Dear Governor Green:
Senator Smith:	Mayor Harley:
Dear Senator Smith:	Dear Mayor Harley:

Follow the salutation with a colon in business letters and other types of formal correspondence, reverting to a comma only when writing to close friends and relatives.

Business letters	*Personal letters*
Dear Bill:	Dear James,
Hello, Sally:	Hi, Mom,

But what if we are writing just to a company, rather than to a person within a company? Until recently, we circumvented the problem by using the word *Gentlemen*. When we consider that women now constitute almost half the work force, and that the large majority of them are employed in office jobs, this masculine term is terribly inappropriate.

So what can we use as a substitute? Although there is no pat answer to this question, several people have offered suggestions— some of which appear practical, others less so.

Possible substitutes	*Impractical suggestions*
Hi:	Ladies and Gentlemen:
Hello:	Greetings:
Good morning:	Gentlepersons:
Dear Friends:	Dear People:
Dear Customer:	

If you feel comfortable using *Hi, Hello,* or *Good Morning,* then use them. After all, we do rely on these words to begin many of our conversations. Maybe you will find *Dear Friends* or *Dear Customer* to be appropriate in certain situations, but *Ladies and Gentlemen* seems more fitting for announcing some kind of act than for a business message. The salutation *Greetings* sounds too much like bad news from the government, and *Gentlepersons* and *Dear People* are a little too "far out." Maybe you can come up with a better idea.

But why should we go through this formality when we are writing about routine business transactions with people we don't even know? If you feel this way, you may omit the salutation altogether. Quite a few business people are doing so, and when they omit the salutation they also dispense with the traditional complimentary close. Either use both or neither.

Subject line

The subject line provides us with a practical replacement for the salutation. Rather than referring to the person's name a second time with a salutation, simply state the main topic of communication.

> *Example*
> Mr. Jon Smithe, Office Manager
> St. Regis Plating Company, Inc.
> 10 Davis Drive
> West Cambridge, NH 02138
> <u>Subject: Our Invoice 49566</u>

> *Example*
> Miss Cindy W. Wells, Office Manager
> PABCO Industries, Ltd.
> 1616 Ypres Road
> Indianapolis, Indiana 46204
> Subject: Your statement of June 15, 1979

The entire subject line is underscored only in the first example, and the complete name of the state is used only in the second example. Since both are correct, these are choices you must make when adopting your own particular letter format.

Attention line

Attention lines sometimes offer a way around the salutation dilemma. When we have no way of directing our letters to specific people within businesses, it is haphazard to route a letter just to the company. Rather than addressing a letter to the St. Louis headquarters of General Dynamics Corporation, which employs tens of thousands of people, we may use an attention line in place of a salutation.

> Example: General Dynamics Corporation
>   Pierre Laclede Center Building
>   St. Louis, Missouri 63105
>   Attention: Accounts Receivable Department
> Example: General Dynamics Corporation
>   Pierre Laclede Center Building
>   St. Louis, MO 63105
>   <u>Accounts Receivable Department</u>

The word *Attention* is included in the first example (with or without the colon), but not in the second one; whereas the entire attention line is underscored only in the second example. As with the subject line, these are choices you must make.

Textbook authors and other people may instruct you to use attention lines when writing directly to individuals, and they may suggest that you use salutations with attention and subject lines. Don't believe them, because it just isn't done that way in modern business communications.

Modern	*Outdated*
Mr. Joe March	JRB Appliances, Inc.
JRB Appliances, Inc.	2514 Seaway Lane
2514 Seaway Lane	Beaumont, Texas 77704
Beaumont, TX 77704	Attention Mr. Joe Marsh
Dear Mr. Marsh:	Gentlemen:

If the communication is for Mr. Marsh, why not address the letter directly to him?

Modern

TLM Computer Systems, Inc.
1600 Broadway
New York, NY 10019
Attention Sales Department

Outdated

TLM Computer Systems, Inc.
1600 Broadway
New York, NY 10019
Attention: Sales Department
Gentlemen:

The attention line helps to minimize the clutter by providing us with an excellent replacement for *Gentlemen,* a cumbersome and outdated salutation.

Body of letter

Single-space all business letters, and double-space (leave one blank line) between paragraphs. Do *not* indent the first line of each paragraph. The only purpose of indentions is to tell the reader when we are beginning new paragraphs, but we convey this message by double-spacing between single-spaced paragraphs. Such indentions are time consuming for typists and give the letters a jagged appearance.

If at all practical to do so, confine the first paragraph in letters to two or three lines—usually just one sentence. The same advice applies to the ending paragraph. Try to hold the middle paragraphs to a maximum length of from 12 to 14 lines—depending, of course, on the nature of the topics discussed.

Complimentary close

If we use a salutation, we definitely include a complimentary close. The most widely used close is just one word: *Sincerely.* The most commonly used closes are listed in descending order, with those used most frequently at the top and those used least frequently at the bottom; the column at right lists some interesting but infrequently used closes.

Popular closes	*Interesting closes*
Sincerely,	Hasta leugo, (until later)
Very truly yours,	Hurriedly,
Sincerely yours,	Regards,
Cordially,	Thank you,
Best regards,	With warmest regards,
Yours truly,	Best wishes,
Yours very truly,	

Would we even consider ending a business conversation on the telephone by saying, "I'm yours very truly?" Of course not, which is the reason that most business people opt for the least offensive, *Sincerely.* Why include such an ending at all? That is a question some people are beginning to ask themselves, as they break with tradition by omitting such trivia from their letters. If, on the other hand, you wish to show a high degree of respect for a business person or government official, use the word *Respectfully* as the complimentary close.

The *Dartnell Management Report* advises that some people tailor complimentary closes to express their true feelings. If Margaret Simes is unhappy with the person she is writing to, for example, she may end the letter "Angrily, Margaret Simes." Similarly, a firm in Sweden sells stationery with a choice of the sender's facial expressions printed near the signature line: a happy face, a look of concentration, an irritated expression, and one of rage—enabling the sender to use the stationery with the picture that best fits the mood of the message.

Signature, name, and title

Type your name directly below the complimentary close, allowing anywhere from three to five blank lines between the two for your signature, and show your position within the company or the department where you work on the following line.

Example
Sincerely,

Susan L. Snodgrass

Susan L. Snodgrass
Marketing Department

Example
Very truly yours,

R. Dennis Meeks

R. Dennis Meeks, Manager
Product Distribution
Department

Ms. Snodgrass lists her department, rather than a title; and Mr. Meeks lists part of his title on the same line as his name, separating the two with a comma and carrying the remainder of the title to the following line. The form that you select depends on (1) whether or not you have a title and (2) the length of the title or department name. Some letters still reflect the company name on the line immediately following the complimentary close (all in upper case), but most business people now consider the practice to be redundant and unnecessary.

Modern
Very truly yours,

R. Dennis Meeks

R. Dennis Meeks, Manager
Product Distribution Dept.

Outdated
Very truly yours
JRB APPLIANCES, INC.

Susan L. Snodgrass

Susan L. Snodgrass
Marketing Department

Why show the person's name twice, once in the signature and also typed? The typed name avoids the frustration that readers experience when they must rely on illegible signatures for identifying writers. Why, then, don't letter writers take enough time and effort to write their names more clearly? Some business people must sign their names dozens of times each day, which often makes speed seem more important than clarity; and others seek to make their signatures unique by making them fancy. What about your signature? Can you write it quickly? Does it have character?

ICE lines

ICE is an easy acronym to remember for the words *initials, copies,* and *enclosures.* When a letter is typed by someone other than the writer, the typist's initials should be placed at the left margin, two lines below the name and title (or department) of the writer. Some typists persist in showing the initials of the writer in addition to their own, but most people now consider this practice redundant and unnecessary.

Modern	*Outdated*
bt	SLS:bt
ems	RDM/ems

If you wish to send copies of letters to others in addition to sending the original to the addressee, list the name or names of the people below the typist's initials, leaving one blank line in between.

Example	*Example*
bt	ems
cc: Ms. Margaret Carlson	dd: Mr. William Bell
Miss Jennifer S. James	Field Representative

If you judge it necessary for the addressee to be told who the person is who is receiving the copy, show the person's title or department as in the example at right.

Circumstances sometimes make it necessary to send *blind copies* of our correspondence to certain people—usually to someone within our own company. If we are writing a letter that has potential importance to a manager in another section of our company, for example, we would remove the completed letter from the typewriter, reinsert the copies, and make a notation similar to the following example:

bc: Mr. T. A. Jones
Division Counsel

The notation that we are sending a copy to a member of our legal staff appears on the blind copy being mailed and also on the copy being retained for our files, with the addressee having no way of knowing from the original that a copy was sent to someone else.

When you include documents with letters, such as a price list or an invoice, place the word *Enclosure* or its abbreviation below the typist's initials. Also specify the number of documents enclosed, if there are more than one; and it is sometimes advisable to identify the enclosures.

Example	*Example*
Enc.	Enclosures: Current price list
Enclosure	Certified invoice
Enclosures (2)	

Postscripts

If you forget to mention something important, can you just tack on a P.S.? No, the letter should be retyped. When business people use postscripts in today's letters, they usually do so for emphasis. They begin one double-space (that is, leaving one blank line) after the last line of the letter, often omitting the letters *P.S.*

Example: P.S. Don't overlook our Summer Sale that begins this Thursday. It will be a long time before you see another one quite like it.

Example: Don't overlook our Summer Sale that begins this Thursday. It will be a long time before you see another one quite like it.

The identifying P.S. is included only in the first example, and the message is underscored in the second example for added emphasis. Which form do you prefer?

PLACEMENT ON PAGE

Now that you are familiar with all the possible parts of business letters, the challenge becomes one of bringing them together attractively. The first consideration, of course, is the quality of the paper and the typewriter ribbon. Make certain that the paper is of good quality (not the erasable kind), that the type is clean, and that the ribbon is sufficiently dark. Then you may decide on a letter style.

Full or modified block

Examples of the two most popular letter styles are shown in Figures 7-3 and 7-4. If you use full block, as in Figure 7-3, begin all writing at the left margin. If you use modified block, as shown in Figure 7-4, place the date, the complimentary close, the signature, and the writer's name and title at the right side of the page.

So which form should you use? Again, the choice is yours.

parfab
DIET SYSTEMS

P.O. Box 5000
Detroit, Michigan 48202
Telephone 313/993-6200

July 12, 1982

Ms. Virginia Kranz
200 North Atlantic Avenue
Monterey Park, CA 91754

Dear Ms. Kranz:

Thank you for taking the time to inform us of your reaction
to the can of peaches that you recently purchased.

If you still have the can, we would very much appreciate
your using the enclosed envelope to mail the lid to us--the
one with the code number recorded on it. This information
will help our laboratory technicians identify the batch of
product from which this particular can was shipped, so that
they can recheck the consistency and sweetness of the syrup.

In appreciation of this courtesy, Ms. Kranz, we are sending
to you via United Parcel Service three complimentary cans of
our DIET RITE peaches.

Very sincerely,

DuWayne Collins
Customer Relations

dba

Figure 7-3 Full-block format.

Springer Automotive Co.

Springerville, California 92077
Full Service Auto Supplies and Accessories

June 15, 1982

Mr. Charles L. Richards
United Petro Company, Inc.
1621 West 48th Street
Pittsburgh, PA   15219

Dear Mr. Richards:

We are interested in purchasing 500 cases of 6/12 oz. SURE STOP brake fluid,
as advertised in your special bulletin of June 10 at $15.90 per case, F.O.B.
delivered. Our offer to make the purchase is contingent upon the product
meeting our established specifications, and we will require a minimum of
10 sample cans.

Do you anticipate any specials on your antifreeze-coolant? We are projecting
sales of 3,000 cases of 6/1 gallon premium fluid, and plan to make a purchase
decision no later than July 15.

Sincerely,

Clara M. Cooke
Purchasing Manager

rle

cc: Mr. William Fields
     District Manager

Figure 7-4 Modified-block format.

Although the modified block requires more work (the typist must strike the tab key four extra times for each letter), many people believe that this form appears better balanced and therefore more attractive. Notice that the first lines of the paragraphs are *not* indented. Indenting single-spaced paragraphs takes extra time and serves no useful purpose.

Consider the letterhead

All companies have their individualized letterhead, and you should place letters on the page in a way that will complement this information. In Figure 7-4, for example, the left margin is aligned with the beginning (left side) of the boxed letterhead, and the date is aligned with the city of origin. Notice also that the complimentary close is in line with the date.

But isn't all of this a little picky? Yes, but it only involves setting the margin and tab stops—something the typist must do anyway—and the resulting letters are much more attractive than when elements of a letter are placed on the page helter-skelter. Remember, if you use full block (Figure 7-3), you need only be concerned with setting margin stops—not tab stops.

Set the margin stops

Although placement of the margin stops on your typewriter depends to a great extent on the design of the letterhead you are using, the usual left-hand margin is 1½ inches. If you are using pica (large) type, as in Figure 7-3, allow 15 spaces from the left edge of the paper. If you are using elite (small) type, as in Figure 7-4, allow 18 spaces. Leave a margin at the right of the page of from 1 to 1½ inches. This spacing is appropriate for letters, memos, and reports.

If you don't know whether your typewriter is elite or pica, type the following sentence and compare it with the examples:

```
Pica:   Type this sentence to check the size of your type.
```

```
Elite:  Type this sentence to check the size of your type.
```

Balance the letter vertically

You wouldn't want your letters to appear scrunched at the top or bottom of the page, so you must plan your vertical spacing before you start writing. Vary your spacing (blank lines) to accommodate the length of your letter, as illustrated in Figures 7-5 and 7-6. Notice that the typist leaves many more blank lines for the four-line letter than for the longer one.

```
            Letterhead            ------------------------
                                  ------------------------
                                  ------------------------
                                  ------------------------


       ⎧
4 lines⎨
       ⎩

          Date

       ⎧
4 lines⎨
       ⎩

          Title, name, position
          Company name
          Street address
          City, state, zip
1 line ⎨
          Salutation:  (if any)
1 line ⎨
          Xxxxxxxxxxxxxxxxxxxxxxxxxxxxxxxxxxxxxxxxxxxxxxxxxx.
          Xxxxxxxxxxxxxxxxxxxxxxxxxxxxxxxxxxxxxxxxxxxxxxxx. Xxx
          xxxxxxxxxxxxxxxxxxxxxxxxxxxxxxxxxxxxxxxxxxxxx.  Xxxxxxxx
          xxxxxxxxxxxxxxxxxxxxxxxxxxxxxxxxxxx.
1 line ⎨
          Xxxxxxxxxxxxxxxxxxxxxxxxxxxxxxxxxxxxx.  Xxxxxxxxxxxxxxx
          xxxxxxxxxxxxxxxxxxxxxxxxxxxxxxxxxxxxxxxxxxx.  Xxxxxxxxxxx
          xxxxxxxxxxxxxxxxxxxxxxxxx.  Xxxxxxxxxxxxxxxxxxxxxxx.
1 line ⎨
          Xxxxxxxxxxxxxxxxxxxxxxxxxxxxxxxxxxx.  Xxxxxxxxxxxxxxxxxxx
          xxxxxxxxxxxxxxxxxxxxxxxxxxxxxxxxxxxxxxxxxxxxxx.  Xxxxxxxxx
          xxxxxxxxxxxxxxxxxxxxxxxxxxxx.
1 line ⎨
          Complimentary close  (if any)
       ⎧
4 lines⎨  (Signature)
       ⎩
          Typed name
          Title or department
1 line ⎨
          Typist's initials
1 line ⎨
          Carbon copies (if any)
1 line ⎨
          Enclosures (if any)
```

Figure 7-5 Vertical spacing for a business letter of average length.

```
                              LETTERHEAD        ----------------------
                                                ----------------------
                                                ----------------------
                                                ----------------------


    4 lines

            Date line



    7 lines        ◄——— Extra 3 lines ————————————————————————




            Title, name, position
            Company name
            Street address
            City, state, zip



    5 lines        ◄——— Extra 4 lines ————————————————————————

            Salutation:

    2 lines        ◄——— One extra line ————————————————————————

            Xxxxxxxxxxxxxxxxxxxxxxxxxxxxxxxxxxxxxxxxxxxxxxxxxxx.   Xxxxxxxxx
            xxxxxxxxxxxxxxxxxxxxxxxxxxxxxxxxxxxxxxxxxxxxxxxxxxx.
    1 line
            Xxxxxxxxxxxxxxxxxxxxxxxxxxxxxxxxxxxxxxxxxxxxxxxxxxxxxxxxxxxx
            xxxxxxxxxxxxxxxxxxxxxxxxxxxxxxxxxxxxx.   Xxxxxxxxxxxx.

    2 lines        ◄——— One extra line ————————————————————————

            Complimentary close,


    4 lines            (Signature)


            Typed name
            Title or department
    1 line
            Typist's initials
    1 line
            Copies
    1 line
            Enclosures
```

Figure 7-6 Vertical spacing for a relatively short letter.

MIDWEST GRAINING INC.

104 West Van Buren Street Chicago, Illinois 60605

April 2, 1982

Ms. Denise Patrick, Director
Marketing Information Services
CROWN ROYAL INDUSTRIES, INC.
323 West 45th Street
Kansas City, Missouri 64112

Dear Ms. Patrick:

Mr. McIntosh, Director of Corporate Public Relations, has asked me
to provide you with the enclosed photographs of our L-1010 Customizer,
which may be useful to you in the preparation of advertisements for
your spring promotion.

Please let us know if you need any additional materials.

Very truly yours,

(Miss) Leslie L. Patrick
Managerial Assistant

encl - 2

Figure 7-7 Sample of a short letter.

A relatively short letter is illustrated in Figure 7-7, with the typist having left blank lines between the date line and the inside address, between the inside address and the salutation, between the salutation and the body of the letter, between the last line in the body and the complimentary close, and between the complimentary close and the typed name of the sender. Notice also that the typist used total capitalization for the name of the receiving company, a common practice when the inside address consists of more than four lines. Also notice that the word *Miss* precedes the typed signature of the writer. This method is used when the person wishes to be addressed in replies as *Miss* or *Mrs.,* rather than *Ms.*

For a simpler approach, especially if the name of an individual addressee is unknown, you may replace the salutation with a subject line and omit the complimentary close. This *simplified format* is illustrated in Figure 7-8, where the subject line is underscored for emphasis and a matching underscore is placed above the sender's typed name as a signature line. Notice also in Figure 7-8 that full-block format is used, and the left margin is aligned with the letterhead at the top of the page.

Multipage letters

Most companies stock a special form for use as additional pages to letters that are longer than one page. If such a form is not available, use blank stationery of the same quality as the letterhead paper. Leave at least a 1-inch margin (6 blank lines) at the bottom of the previous page, and show the addressee's name at the top of the new page—along with the date and page number—beginning about 1 inch (6 blank lines) from the top edge of the paper.

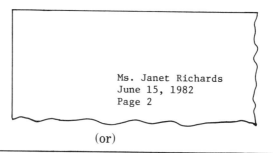

```
                                    Ms. Janet Richards
                                    June 15, 1982
                                    Page 2
```

(or)

```
        Ms. Janet Richards                -2-                June 15, 1982
```

Quality Food Corporation

772 Bonita Street San Pedro, CA 90053
(203) 916-1211

October 31, 1982

J. C. Spencer Wholesaling Co.
210 South Michigan Avenue
Chicago, Illinois 60604

Subject: Unearned discounts

Our credit terms are 2/10, n/30, as specified in our sales-order
confirmations and as printed on our invoice forms. When paying our
Invoice 13205 of August 31, 1979, therefore, the cash discount
of $73.12 should not have been deducted. The discount period ended
September 10, but your check did not arrive in our office until
October 15.

A similar situation exists with respect to our Invoice 14229 dated
September 10. Although payment was not received until September 30,
ten days past the discount period, you deducted the 2-percent discount
of $63.15.

We are prohibited by federal law from offering preferential treatment
to individual customers; therefore, we are enclosing copies of these
two invoices and asking that you respect our established terms of
sale by sending payment of the two unearned discounts in the amount
of $136.27.

James M. Cummings

James M. Cummings, Manager
Accounts Receivable Department

pvm

Enclosures

Figure 7-8 Simplified format.

PREPARATION OF ENVELOPES

Preparing the envelope is just as important as preparing the letter, because the letter is of no value if it doesn't reach the proper address within a reasonable time. Although you need to place only the receiver's address on most envelopes (because the name of your company is already printed in the upper left corner), there is a right way to do this; and you must know how to handle attention lines and mailing instructions.

Return address

Business envelopes have the sender's return address, including the company name, printed at the top left of the envelope. If you are writing a personal letter using a blank envelope, you must enter this information yourself.

Example:

```
Elizabeth M. McElviney
300 North Avenue
Atlanta, GA   30313
```

Receiver's address

The standard business envelope measures 9½ inches across and 4¼ inches vertically.* Begin the receiver's address 4 inches from the left edge (40 spaces pica and 48 spaces elite) and 2 inches (about 12 blank lines) from the top edge of the envelope. Although many people continue to type addresses on envelopes in the same form as inside addresses, the Postal Service is requesting that we use the form shown in Figure 7-9, which involves the following guidelines:

1. Capitalize all letters.
2. Eliminate all punctuation.
3. Single-space all lines.
4. Leave two blank spaces between the state abbreviation and zip code.

---

*Be sure to check with the Postal Service before buying odd-shaped envelopes, because they now return to the senders all pieces of mail smaller than 3½ by 5 inches. Odd-shaped letters larger than that but weighing one ounce or less are accepted, but a surcharge is assessed on each such mailing.

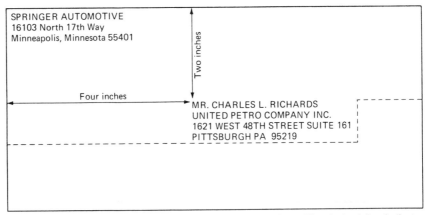

Figure 7-9 Spacing for standard-sized business envelope. The dashed line indicates that nothing should be written or typed below or to the right of the receiver's address.

5. Leave blank space to the right of and below the address (below the dotted line in Figure 7-9).
6. For letters being mailed to multiunit buildings, type the room or suite number at the end of the street address (on the same line).

This format is easier to use once you become accustomed to the change, and it enables the post office to automate sorting processes more fully.

Attention lines

When we are writing to specific individuals within companies, we address our letters to them. When we don't know a specific individual, we resort to attention lines. Place attention lines on envelopes immediately after the name of the company.

> Example: J C SPENCER WHOLESALING CO
> ATTENTION ACCOUNTS PAYABLE ⟵
> 210 SOUTH MICHIGAN AVENUE
> CHICAGO IL 60604

Mailing instructions

If you want the U.S. Post Office to give a letter special handling, place the instructions in the upper right corner of the envelope, allowing room for postage (about nine lines from the top edge of the envelope).

Example:

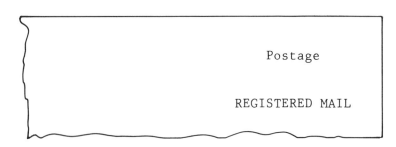

Inserting the letter

Let's not make a big deal out of folding and inserting letters, as people used to do. Simply fold the page into thirds as illustrated in Figure 7-10. Whether the letter is placed into the envelope one way or another has no importance. Virtually no one pays any attention to such trivia, and employees other than the reader generally open the mail.

MAILING THE LETTER

Comedians on radio and television poke a lot of fun at the U.S. Postal Service, and business people often blame many of their own mistakes and delays on this government service. In actuality, more than 99.9 percent of the mail is delivered on time and in good condition. To benefit fully, however, you must be aware of the different levels of service and the various postal systems available for processing mail.

Figure 7-10 Folding a business letter.

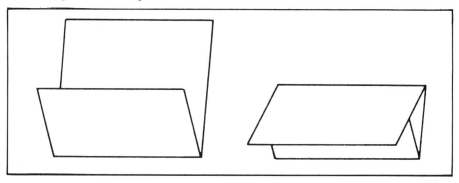

Postal services

Business letters, except for mass mailings of advertisements, are sent *first class*. The first ounce costs whatever the price of a regular postage stamp might be at the time you are reading this book, with each additional ounce costing slightly less than the first one.

Do not waste money by sending letters within the United States via *air mail*, because the post office now moves all first-class mail to distant places by air. If you are mailing publications, newspapers, or bulk mail, be sure to check with the post office beforehand for information about second-, third-, and fourth-class rates and regulations.

The post office offers several types of special handling. When you send a letter *special delivery,* a mail carrier at the destination post office makes a special trip to deliver the letter. If your letter or other documents are of special value, *registered mail* guarantees separate handling, and the postal employees must personally sign for the envelope at each exchange point. If you seal the envelope with any kind of supportive tape, make certain that it is *not* cellophane or masking tape. Sealed areas all around the envelope must be suitable for stamping with an inked stamper by postal employees.

Certified mail also provides an official record of the mailing, and at a much lower cost than for registered mail, but your envelope is not handled separately from regular mail. For an additional charge, you may request a *return receipt* for both registered and certified mail, and the postal department will return a card to you showing the date of delivery and the signature of the addressee.

You may use *express mail* within the continental United States for anything from a letter to a 70-pound package. If you deliver your item to one of the designated post offices (ask the post office for a list) before 5:00 p.m., delivery to the addressee's home or business sometime the next day is guaranteed. The cost of this service is high, but the post office refunds the full price to the sender if delivery is made later than promised.

If any of your mailings is destined for other countries, ask the post office for specific information concerning rules and rates. You may also check any almanac for a limited amount of postal information, including data relating to international mail service.

Also be sure to check with postal employees when dealing in large volumes of mail. They will advise you of the benefits of presorting your mail and presenting it to them in mailing trays or mail sacks. Such handling is necessary in some instances to secure lower mailing rates, and presorted mail is sent on its way faster than mail which must be sorted at the post office. You may even discover that your business is entitled to special pickups of mail by postal employees.

Postage equipment

No matter how small or large the mailing operation, private companies offer many devices to speed the process. Even a business that mails no more than ten letters a day may benefit from the purchase of a hand-cranked postage meter. At the other extreme, large businesses may buy electrically powered meters (see Figure 7-11) that automatically feed, seal, postmark, meter-stamp, count, and stack up to 200 pieces of mail per minute. No, postage meters do *not* actually manufacture stamps. To buy $1,000 worth of postage, for example, you take the sealed meter box to the local post office. They take your $1,000, set the meter to reflect an additional $1,000 postage, and reseal the box.

Metered mail, like that illustrated in Figure 7-12, has a more businesslike appearance, since practically all businesses now use postage meters. Also notice in Figure 7-12 that you may include an advertisement with your metered mail. Postage meters provide more control over postage because all mailings are recorded; and, since the post office doesn't have to cancel stamps on metered mail, it moves through the post office and on its way faster than stamped mail.

Figure 7-11 Pitney Bowes Model 5511 postage meter mailing machine. (Photo courtesy Pitney Bowes.)

C Company
89 Broad Street
Princeton, NJ. 08540

MR. JONATHAN P. BRADLEY
4482 WALNUT STREET
STAMFORD CO 06904

Figure 7-12 Sample of metered mail. (Courtesy Pitney Bowes.)

Businesses that have a high volume of mail each day may also find it economically feasible to buy machines that fold letters and place them in envelopes automatically. Machines that open incoming mail are also available.

CHECKLIST: LETTER STYLES

Top of letter
- If not using company letterhead, did you include your return address above the date line?
- Did you avoid abbreviations in the date line?
- If writing to an individual, did you use the person's title (Mr., Ms., Dr.) before the name?
- Did you double-check the spelling of the name?
- Did you show the person's position in the company, immediately following the name?
- If you are writing to a business employee, did you follow the person's name with the company name?
- Did you show either a post office box or a street address, but not both?
- If you used the two-letter state code, did you avoid the use of periods after each letter?
- Did you include a zip code? The correct zip code?
- Did you include an acceptable salutation (see recommended list on page 97), an attention line, or a subject line—but not more than one of these?

Body of letter

- Did you single-space the body of the letter?
- Did you begin each line at the left margin, rather than indenting the first line in each paragraph?
- Are the first and last paragraphs relatively short?
- Did you confine the middle paragraphs to from 12 to 14 lines?

Bottom of letter

- Did you use a popular close (see lists on page 100)?
- If you omitted the salutation, did you also omit a complimentary close, and vice versa?
- Did you allow enough space to accommodate your signature?
- Did you follow the space for your signature with your typed name?
- Did you follow your typed name with your title or the name of your department?

Bottom of page

- If someone other than you typed the letter, are the typist's initials shown?
- If you are including other documents with your letter, did you show the word *Enclosure* and the number or identity of documents enclosed?
- If you are sending copies of the letter to people other than the addressee, did you show their names and titles at the bottom?
- Do you have a comment to emphasize that would make the desired impact in a postscript?

Placement on page

- If you used modified block, did you align the complimentary close with the date line?
- If you used full block, do all lines begin at the left margin?
- Does the placement of your letter complement the letterhead?
- Did you leave approximately 1½ inches at the left and 1 inch at the right and bottom?
- If your letter is more than one page in length, did you show the addressee's name, the date, and the page number at the top of the additional pages—leaving a 1-inch margin at the top?

Envelope preparation

- If you are not using a business envelope, did you include your return address in the upper left corner—including your zip code?
- Did you place the receiver's address about 4 inches from the left and 2 inches from the top?

- Did you include the complete address: receiver's title (MR, MISS, MRS, MS, DR) and name; the company name; the street address, with no abbreviations; and the city, two-letter state code, and zip code?
- If not writing to an individual, did you include an attention line following the company name?
- Did you place any special mailing instructions below the stamp area?
- Did you fold the paper in thirds before putting it into the envelope?
- Did you use the correct amount of postage?

8

MINIMIZING LETTER WRITING

Before writing a letter, ask yourself these two questions: Is this letter necessary? Is there a better way to communicate the message? You should have a good reason for writing a letter, because letters cost money, sometimes a lot of money. You should also consider the practicality of using substitutes for letters.

REASONS FOR WRITING LETTERS

Business managers devote much time budgeting company funds for such expenses as wages, rent, electricity, telephone, and postage. Every expenditure is subject to careful analysis. Before spending money that has been budgeted for written communications, we should exercise similar constraint by making certain that a letter is the best medium for our message.

Doesn't interrupt

A letter doesn't interrupt the receiver the way a phone call does. Unless a person has a secretary to screen incoming calls, a ringing telephone usually intrudes on the receiver's work processes, thought patterns, and conversations; everything is stopped to answer the telephone.

Okay, so maybe you prefer to capture the other person's attention immediately with a phone call. But if the interruption happens to catch the person at an inconvenient moment, you may have blown the chance of conveying your message successfully. Conversely, the receiver of your letter may lay it aside until time permits reading it at a more leisurely pace—at a time when the person might be more receptive to your message.

Provides a reminder

When a phone call is ended, that's it; it's all over; and, as the old saying goes, "out of sight, out of mind." Sure, the other person *might* make a note of your comments while talking with you on the phone, and the person *might* give you the desired response. A letter, on the other hand, enables you to present your complete thoughts in a logical sequence—to tell the whole story without fear of interruption by the recipient. Also, unlike a telephone conversation, the letter remains in the other person's possession as a reminder of your request for action.

Establishes a record

After discussing complex business transactions with others, in person or over the telephone, we usually follow up with a letter of confirmation. We want to "put it in writing." Unlike the fleeting telephone conversation, the letter provides the receiver and the sender (who keeps a file copy) with a permanent record of the exchange. There is a proliferation of letter writing in business today, despite increasing reliance on telephones, largely because of the need to record business transactions.

But wouldn't a recorded telephone conversation serve the same purpose? Maybe, but how would you decide in advance which calls to record? Recording all calls would be expensive, and it would be much more difficult to locate a particular conversation on a tape than to retrieve a letter from a filing cabinet.

We must also consider the legal implications of recording telephone conversations. First, federal law requires that the person doing the recording notify the other person that their conversation is being recorded. Second, the person doing the recording must purchase and use an audible beep pump, an electronic device that emits a tone over the telephone line every ten seconds to remind whoever is talking that their words are being recorded.

Sometimes saves money

Does it cost less to write a letter than to pay for a telephone call? The answer to that question depends on the distance involved and the length of the telephone conversation, as compared with the cost of a letter. When employees routinely use the telephone for long-distance calls, the bill at the end of the month can be staggering. Correspondingly, many business leaders frequently admonish their employees to rely less on the telephone and more on letters.

REASONS
FOR *NOT* WRITING LETTERS

Sometimes a letter is just not the appropriate vehicle for a particular communication. The time element is the most important consideration, but the cost of letter writing is also a major factor when deciding whether to write letters or use the telephone.

Can't wait for the mail

If you want to buy 50,000 bushels of wheat at the current market price, you had better *not* submit your bid in a letter, because the price of wheat may change several times before you consummate the deal. Similarly, if you know that your competitor is about to close an important sale, the transaction may be finalized before you can get a letter to the customer. We rely on the telephone for urgent messages such as these, often confirming our conversations with follow-up letters.

Receiver might not answer

Letters often leave us hanging. Even under the most favorable of circumstances, we cannot expect an answer for a week to ten days; and the wait may be extended several more days if the other person doesn't respond promptly. When a reply is not forthcoming, our imaginations come into play: Maybe the other person is on vacation. Maybe the letter was lost in the mails. Maybe the person isn't interested in what we had to say. Maybe this and maybe that.

A telephone call is more definite. Not only do we hear the person's verbal response to our questions, we may detect the degree of enthusiasm and interest (or the lack of it) by listening closely to voice tone and methods of expression. If the other person is away from the office, we receive information about his or her return. By using the telephone, therefore, we often avoid days or weeks of delay and uncertainty.

Cost may be too high

What does one business letter cost? $1.00? $2.50? $5.00? Estimates range from as low as a few cents to as high as $25.00 per letter, but the cost varies widely with the situation. To illustrate, let's consider some of the costs involved in letter writing.

Dictation is usually the most costly element in letter writing, because the person who composes the letter is the highest-paid employee involved in the process. But consider the disparity here. When the president of International Harvester spends 15 minutes dictating a letter, the cost is about $140, because he is paid more than $1 million each year. For a middle manager receiving a more modest salary of $50,000, the cost of 15 minutes of dictation time is $6.51.

Secretarial time is usually the second highest cost, and this cost depends on the secretary's income, the amount of time devoted to letter writing, and the number of letters typed. If two secretaries each earn $50 per day and both spend half their time typing letters, the secretary who turns out 10 letters per day costs the company $2.50 per letter, compared to $1.25 per letter for the secretary who types 20 letters. We must also consider equipment and supplies required by the secretary: a typewriter (initial investment of from $1,500 to $6,000), ribbons, correction tape, dictation equipment, stationery, carbon paper, and a host of other items.

But what about space requirements? The person who dictates the letter and the person who types it occupy many cubic feet of space, space which must be built, maintained, and air conditioned. There are also mailing and filing costs to consider. When we assign a portion of these overall costs to each letter, we can see that a cost estimate of even $25 per letter might be on the low side.

Some business people say that it is more realistic to consider incremental costs. Instead of worrying about the total cost of writing each letter, we view the services of the dictator and secretary, the building, the typewriter, and air conditioning as bought and paid for. Since they are already in place, we consider only the additional costs involved in writing additional letters: the cost of stationery, typewriter ribbons, and postage. Using the incremental approach, the cost of each additional letter may be 50 cents or less.

Legal record needed

We may need a legal record of our communication, a document that will "hold up in court." But does the carbon copy of a letter meet this criterion? Isn't it possible for the writer to fabricate a letter by writing it after the fact, entering an earlier date, placing a copy in the files, and throwing away the original? Of course it is possible, except for mail that is either registered or certified, and it is for this reason that business people have difficulty convincing judges and juries that letters have actually been sent when adversaries testify under oath that the letters were never received.

So if a letter won't suffice, how can we establish a legal record? We may do so by sending a Western Union Telegram. The several levels of Western Union services, services that are extremely important in contemporary business, are discussed at length in the following chapter.

SUBSTITUTES
FOR LETTER WRITING

We can overcome some of the disadvantages of letter writing by using substitutes. We may use carbonized memos, form letters, canned letters, and postcards.

Carbonized memo forms

In the distribution department of a medium-sized food processing company, several clerks dictated letters each time an order was shipped from their warehouse to a customer, and stenographers typed the letters on company letterhead. When management consultants learned that these letters were being addressed to brokers—that is, people who were effectively working for the company—they quickly put a stop to the time-consuming and costly practice.

They instructed the clerks to write their messages on carbonized memo forms similar to the one illustrated in Figure 6-3 on page 88. And rather than dictating their memos for reproduction by stenographers, the clerks were directed to write or type their own messages on these forms. The formalities of salutations and complimentary closes were no longer necessary, and, unlike letter writing, the clerks could cross out any errors on the memos and just keep writing. The memo forms were an excellent substitute for letters.

Form letters

Form letters serve a very useful purpose in business communications. They are impersonal, but many of our business transactions with other companies are routine and impersonal. When we find ourselves writing the same type of letter many times, therefore, we should compose a form letter and have it duplicated. Such a letter is illustrated in Figure 8-1. Rather than dictating a letter every time they notice an error on a vendor's invoice, the people in this company simply type in the date and inside address at the top, and check or fill in the appropriate blanks below, making certain to keep a copy for their own file. Form letters ease the letter-writing burden for the sender, and the receivers of form letters soon accept the procedure as a natural and very acceptable part of their business transactions.

People who receive form letters like the one in Figure 8-1 immediately recognize them as such. But modern technology enables us to personalize form letters to a significant degree. With the use of word-processing equipment, as discussed in Chapter 10, we can enter the person's name in the address and at strategic places in the body of the letter—along with information that relates specifically

ROHRE
ASSOCIATES INC.
215 California Street
San Francisco, Callifornia 94111

Invoice No._____dated_____

When processing the above document, we found the following exceptions:

____Incorrect pricing

    Cases   Item Description   Priced at   Should be

_____

_____

_____

    ____Label allowance not shown.

    ____Swell allowance not shown.

    ____Marine insurance charged in error.

    ____Incorrect terms. Should be_____

    ____Corrected invoice requested. Mail two copies to ROHRE--SF.

    ____Check requested. Write to member buyer, but mail to ROHRE-SF.

                                     _____

Figure 8-1 Sample form letter.

to the reader—making the communication appear to have been written for the individual reader.

Canned letters

If you are saying to yourself that form letters are too impersonal in some situations, you are absolutely correct. But we still should avoid writing the same types of letters over and over. If there is a feature about your company's product or service that requires frequent explanations to customers, for instance, write the best letter that you can in responding to the customer. Then use the same letter as a guide when responding to similar demands in the future.

Some companies carry this idea to the extreme, developing entire books of canned letters (letters prepared in advance). For example, a credit manager might instruct an assistant to write a Form 213 letter to a particular customer using paragraphs A, B, and D. If we use such a system, we should do so with extreme caution, to make certain that our letters make sense. Although canned letters are usually grammatically correct, they are sometimes a little off target, leaving the recipient perplexed.

Postcards

Many people use postcards to reduce the volume of letter writing. Paul Dean, Staff Writer for a leading newspaper, uses the postcard illustrated in Figure 8-2 to replace as many as 50 letters a day. He says that the cards force him to write tightly by restricting his replies to a maximum of two paragraphs (short ones, obviously), while at the same time enabling him to acknowledge information and to answer inquiries in a personal way. Consider the time and money he conserves as opposed to writing formal letters, and he saves a few cents postage every time he mails a card in place of a letter.

Postcards can also be used for lengthier messages. After writing to a publisher concerning an adjustment in the subscription price for their magazine, the author received a card with the following message:

> We have received your recent communication concerning your subscription.
>
> Please be assured the matter will be handled promptly. If additional information is needed or a detailed reply is required, we will write again.
>
> Thank you for your interest.

About ten days later a follow-up card arrived:

> Your communication regarding your subscription will have our immediate attention. There may be a short delay before the correction becomes effective, but you have our assurance that adjustment will be made with the earliest possible issue.
>
> If you do not hear from us again, you can be certain your wishes are being followed.

```
Dear Maggie Eitzen:

Terrific.

Thanks for following
through.

Sincerely,
```

THE ARIZONA REPUBLIC

Figure 8-2 Postcard substitute for letters. (Courtesy Paul Dean, Staff Writer for the *Los Angeles Times*.)

The cards were preprinted, with only the author's address having to be typed. Were they effective? The author believes so. They corresponded promptly upon receipt of his letter; they told him what he wanted to hear (that they were complying with his wishes); and they did it in the most efficient and least expensive way. Many businesses computerize messages such as these, further lowering the cost of each communication.

Businesses sometimes use cartoon cards effectively. Cards (with accompanying envelopes) similar to those depicted in Figure 8-3 are available in quantities of at least 100 in black and white or color, and the vendor prints the company name and address on each card for an extra charge. Cartoon messages are less costly than letter writing, certainly; and in many situations they can be much

FRANKLY, YOUR BUSINESS MEANS **NOTHING** To Us...

NOTHING BUT **FOOD, CLOTHING** AND **SHELTER!** MANY THANKS!

THANKS...

FOR THROWING YOUR BUSINESS MY WAY!

Don't forget us!

We're still in business at the same old stand!

Figure 8-3 Cartoon cards as substitutes for letters. (Courtesy Harrison Publishing Co., Asheville, NC.)

more effective than letters. What would your reaction be to this type of communication?

Memo forms, form letters, canned letters, and postcards are not the only substitutes for conventional letter writing. We can also send teletype messages throughout the United States and to foreign countries, and we can use regular business telephones to transmit pictures of business documents to distant offices. The various types of electronic communications are discussed in Chapter 9, and modern techniques for lowering the cost of letter writing are presented in Chapter 10.

9

COMMUNICATING ELECTRONICALLY

Electronic devices have long provided several alternatives to letter writing; the telephone has been in existence many years, and the telegraph has been around even longer. Businesses began using teletype machines extensively in the 1950s, and centralized data banks were introduced in the 1960s. This chapter provides an overview of the complex and efficient communication networks that have resulted from these developments.

WESTERN UNION TELEGRAMS

If you were to ask the next several people you meet about the status of Western Union, they would probably connect the name with the era of a wild and woolly West. People tend to link Western Union with early railroading, when telegrams were handled at nearly every railroad station. While it is true that Western Union did begin service in the mid-1800s and did displace the Pony Express service, the company has since evolved into a modern corporation that does business in excess of $200 million annually.

Business orientation

Western Union still offers service to individuals. You can phone a toll-free number (see your telephone directory) to send a telegram, for example, and the charge will be placed on your next telephone bill. You may also send up to $1,000 to another person through Western Union—if you have a MasterCard and if the person to whom you are sending the money has access to a Western Union office.

But who wants to send a telegram, when they can phone someone for a comparable charge? Most individuals send money (checks or money orders, not cash) in the mail rather than wiring it. Second-day mail delivery is commonplace, and, you will recall from Chapter 7, express mail guarantees next-day delivery.

As more and more people replaced telegraph services with telephone and mail service, the managers of Western Union directed more of their services toward the business community. Telegrams have been replaced as the mainstay of their business by teletypewriter services, leased systems, commercial money orders, mailgrams, and datagrams—all of which are discussed in this chapter.

Straight telegrams

Exactly what is a telegram? A telegram is a message, usually a brief one, that is sent over Western Union wires with teletypewriters. To send a birthday greeting to someone right now, for instance, you call the toll-free number and give the destination address, message, and your name to an operator who, as you talk, types the information on a memory keyboard. Viewing the typed message on a cathode-ray tube, which is like a television screen, the operator corrects any errors without having to retype the entire message. When the message appears perfect, and after reading it back to you as a doublecheck, the operator simply presses a button to send the message on its way to the designated Western Union office.

Messenger delivery is available in large cities for an extra charge, but messages to suburban areas and small cities and towns are phoned from the nearest Western Union office. Confirmation copies of phoned telegrams are mailed upon request.

Western Union charges a flat rate for the first 15 words, the rate depending on the distance, plus an extra charge for each additional word. To minimize costs, therefore, the sender must condense the message. Consider the following communication:

Original message
I'll be arriving at the Los Angeles International Airport on Wednesday at 9:15 a.m. on American Airlines Flight 316. Please arrange for me to see Mr. Cantrell at Alpha Beta Company sometime in the morning, so that I can catch a return flight at 2:30 p.m. See you then, Margaret.

Condensed version for telegram
Arriving LAX Wednesday 9:15 American 316. Must see Cantrell Alpha Beta before noon.

The essential elements of the original message appear in the condensed version, and the word count is reduced from 49 to 13, meaning that the sender will pay the minimum charge for a telegram to Los Angeles.

Up to five combined letters, numbers, and symbols such as LAX (airline abbreviation for Los Angeles International airport) are counted as one word, as long as there is no spacing between the letters, numbers, or symbols. Correspondingly, if the sender specified 9:15 a.m., as in the original message, Western Union would count it as two words, even if the space between the numbers and letters were removed. Keep the receiver in mind, however, making certain to include sufficient information for complete understanding.

Overnight telegrams

Day letter service is no longer available, and night letters are now called *overnight telegrams*. Rates for overnight telegrams are significantly lower than for straight telegrams and you may include up to 100 words before extra-word charges are assessed. An overnight telegram sent today will be delivered tomorrow morning.

TWO-WAY TELETYPES

Two-way communications between customers represent the greatest volume of Western Union's business. Practically all medium-sized and large companies rent or own Telex or TWX units.

Telex service

Businesses may rent or buy Telex (and TWX) units from Western Union, the company that originated the service, or from any of several competing vendors. When a unit is connected to Western Union's Telex network, the business that is subscribing to the service may communicate directly with any of 75,000 other subscribing companies in the United States, Canada, Mexico, and Alaska—and with any of 250,000 companies on other continents.

A Telex unit is essentially a typewriter. The keyboard differs from a typewriter keyboard only slightly in having no separate row of numbers. Instead, the top row of letters (Q, W, E, R, etc.) becomes numbers after you press a numeric key, and the top row converts back to letters after you press a letter key. Anyone who can type can quickly learn to operate a Telex.

Upon dialing another company (just as in making a telephone call), users may either communicate directly on teletypewriter keyboards or by running previously prepared tapes. It is common, for example, for employees of two companies to carry on a discussion with each other using the teletypewriter keyboards, and each has a printed copy as a record of the two-way communication.

But when specific messages or detailed information is to be transmitted, operators usually record the communications on five-place paper tape as they are typing. Operators check the printed copies for accuracy, and after making any necessary corrections in the tapes, they direct dial the other companies and run the tapes at a speed of 66 words per minute. An automatic identification feature of the equipment ensures that the correct terminal has been reached, and Telex equipment provides an automatic acknowledgment of each message successfully transmitted. In this way messages can be sent to unattended teletypewriters in other offices, even at night when those offices are not open for regular business.

Telex service provides two-way communications and permanent records of the communications. The main advantage of the service compared to other communication media is the price. A Telex message costs anywhere from one fifth to one half the price of a telephone call; and if the other company doesn't answer your Telex call because the line is busy or out of order, you simply send the message to Western Union Teleprinter Computer services and a Western Union computer accepts and forwards the message when a connection can be made.

TWX service

Bell System developed the TWX network—a system of 50,000 teletypewriters throughout the United States and Canada that, like Telex, connects with 250,000 machines overseas—and later sold it to Western Union. TWX machines (see Figure 9-1) are similar to Telex units except that they have four rows of keys, almost identical to typewriters. They transmit messages at a faster 100 words per minute, and they utilize seven-place paper tape on both incoming and outgoing messages that is compatible with most computer systems. The TWX system also allows for conference calls, where people in several locations use teletypewriter keyboards to communicate with one another at the same time.

Compatible systems

So which service is better, Telex or TWX? The choice depends in large part on the type of industry involved. Businesses in some industries depend on Telex, and businesses in other industries use TWX. Western Union issues directories for each service, listing all subscribing companies in both alphabetical and Yellow Page format. Telex provides lower-cost service for some companies, depending on the particular price zone that applies to their location. Businesses that send relatively long messages, on the other hand, may

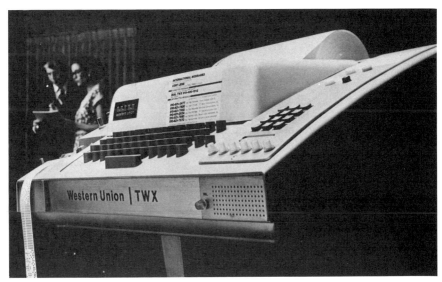

Figure 9-1 A Western Union TWX teletypewriter. (Courtesy The Western Union Telegraph Company.)

reduce communication costs by using the faster TWX service (100 wpm versus 66 wpm).

Subscribing to one service does not preclude access to the other system, however. By using a Western Union service called Infomaster, you may use a Telex to reach any TWX subscriber, and a TWX subscriber can reach you through the same service. There is no need to subscribe to both services.

ONE-WAY GRAMS

You may also use Telex and TWX machines to send telegrams—a service that we have already discussed—as well as mailgrams, datagrams, and cablegrams. Telex and TWX rates are significantly lower, in fact, than if you phoned Western Union for either of these other services.

Mailgrams

Mailgram service is provided through the joint efforts of Western Union and the United States Postal Service. Western Union directs mailgrams to teletypewriters at major post offices located nearest the destination addresses. Messages are removed from the teletypewriters and stuffed into window envelopes automatically and sent by mail carrier on the next scheduled delivery. Mailgrams are slower than telephone calls or telegrams but faster than mailed letters; and they provide a legal record of communications.

The Western Union insignia and the official emblem of the U.S. Postal Service are printed at the top of the mailgram form and envelopes, along with the word "Mailgram" in large letters, conveying a sense of importance and urgency; and the receiver must open the envelope and observe the contents to determine its source. Mailgrams are considerably less costly than long-distance telephone calls or telegrams; and if the same message is sent to more than one address, the cost of each mailgram declines to less than half the single-message rate.

Mailgrams provide an ideal medium for priority communications, and you may speed the transmission process by storing frequently used messages or parts of messages in a Western Union computer. You can provide a list of addresses later, or the addresses may also be stored at Western Union. Then, upon your command, the Western Union computer matches the addresses with the stored message, adds personal data to the message if desired, and transmits the resulting mailgrams electronically to the appropriate post offices.

Datagrams

But let's say that you are in another city and want to send some important information to your home office. Assume further that it is after 5:00 p.m. at the home office and no one is there to answer the telephone. Under such conditions, you may turn to Western Union's 24-hour datagram service.

If your company has added datagrams to its Telex or TWX service and has provided you with a Western Union datagram card, you may call a toll-free number (see the telephone directory) and give the information to a Western Union operator. The operator uses a magnetic keyboard and cathode-ray tube to record the information as you dictate, and transmits the datagram directly to your company's teletypewriter. The message will be at your home office when employees begin work the following morning, and its transmittal will have cost less than a long-distance telephone call.

Cablegrams

For communications to locations overseas, businesses may send cablegrams. The name is becoming a misnomer, however, since most international communications are now transmitted via satellites, not over cables. In fact, Western Union now operates Westar, its own satellite; and more than 9,000 miles of terrestrial microwave is integrated with the satellite system.

OTHER
WESTERN UNION SERVICES

As mentioned earlier in this chapter, individuals may send up to $1,000 by using a Western Union charge card money order. Similarly, when a business has established a commercial money order account with Western Union, employees may send money to one another—24 hours a day, seven days a week.

Businesses that have Telex or TWX machines may subscribe to a News Alert service, whereby Western Union transmits major United Press International bulletins directly to business offices. Telex and TWX customers may also dial Western Union for specific stock reports, or they may have reports of their choice sent automatically and at specific times of the day or week.

DATA BANKS

Many businesses rely on computers to such a great extent for their communications that they would be hard pressed to function without them. When you reserve a seat on an airplane, for example, the reservation clerk doesn't have to telephone or teletype a reservation center; the computer is the reservation center. The computer keeps track of the number of seats available, reducing the count each time another one is reserved.

Similarly, we no longer write letters to reserve motel rooms weeks in advance of a trip. We simply call a toll-free number and a reservation clerk queries a computer in the same way that airline clerks do, but for rooms rather than airplane seats. If no accommodations are available, the computer reveals the nearest locations where vacancies do exist—and lists the prevailing prices. How did motel companies handle all of this detail before the invention and development of computers? A few people made reservations by mail, but the large majority of travelers just pointed their vehicles toward their destinations and hoped that motel space would be available when needed.

Data banks are not used just for reservation purposes, of course. Many companies store all pertinent information in centralized computers, where employees may draw on and add to the information bank in the performance of their duties; and business people depend on computers for the generation of virtually all business reports.

ELECTRONIC MAIL

So far, we have discussed the electronic transmittal of words, words that operators must key into teletypewriters or computers. But what if we want to send a facsimile—not a retyped version, but an exact copy of the original document? If we have a facsimile machine like the one shown in Figure 9-2, the process is simple.

Facsimile units are used for transmitting exact copies of such documents as letters, contracts, legal briefs, newspaper clippings, photographs, sketches, and drawings. Upon reaching destination offices by telephone, senders place their telephone receivers into couples (cradle-like devices) and begin feeding materials into the facsimile units. Documents are transmitted at a rate of 2, 3, 4, or 6 minutes per page, depending on the type of units being used on each

Figure 9-2 Facsimile unit in use. (Courtesy Qwip Systems, a Division of Exxon Enterprises, Inc.)

end of the telephone connection, with the more advanced models being faster and capable of adjusting their speed to match the particular speed of the receiving units. Facsimile units can be set to answer incoming calls, receive the messages, terminate telephone connections, and eject the copies received—without any operator involvement.

Facsimile units transmit in black and white only, and copies must be made on a special type of paper measuring no more than 8½ by 11 inches. Despite these drawbacks, this method of communication represents a significant step toward the eventual displacement of most regular mail service. The U.S. Postal Service is already experimenting with electronic mail service—using satellites for transmittal, along with coding devices that prevent unauthorized persons from reading intercepted communications.

They are sorting and sending messages from one post office to another electronically, with mail carriers delivering the communications to homes and businesses. Eventually—say, in ten to fifteen years—computers will route all regular mail directly into our homes and businesses electronically—with no need for trucks, trains, buses, or airplanes to haul the mail and no need for carriers to deliver it; and the service will be instantaneous, reliable, and relatively economical.

10

WORD PROCESSING METHODS

Electronic computers are changing the way we live. Checkout clerks at grocery stores are turning their main duties over to computers. Computers keep track of airplanes, buses, trucks, and railcars; and they are used to operate fully automated assembly lines in modern factories. Many small businesses rely on computers at least to some extent, and computers are essential to the operations of most large businesses.

Computer technology is equally applicable to the modern office. Magnetic keyboards, visual display screens, optical scanning devices, "intelligent" copiers, and other types of electronic equipment are being used to convert traditional offices into highly productive word-processing centers.

WORD-PROCESSING CENTERS

Although employees at many small businesses continue to rely on traditional office procedures, many firms are equipping their offices with word-processing (WP) equipment. They generally place the equipment in centralized areas and refer to the operations as word-processing centers.

Source documents

Rather than having secretaries come to them for dictation, the people doing the writing are responsible for getting the messages to their WP centers. Depending on the system, employees may write messages longhand, dictate them to a recording device in their offices, or use their telephone to dictate directly to recording devices located in word-processing centers.

Magnetic keyboards

Operators in WP centers use standard typewriter keyboards to type messages onto magnetic disks, and, if the units have a CRT (cathode-ray tube) like the one pictured in Figure 10-1, messages appear on screens as they type. Operators may type fast without fear of mistakes, because mistakes can be easily corrected. When operators are aware of mistakes as they type, the need only backspace and type over incorrect words or numbers, and the correct words or numbers appear on the screen—no apparent strikeovers, no manual erasures.

Operators do not strike the carriage return key as they reach the ends of lines, because most WP units end lines and begin new ones automatically. And operators need not worry about format, because WP units handle the spacing. When writers desire the modified block format, for instance, WP units arrange the correct spacing automatically.

When operators have finished keying the information, they check the screens for errors. If they find misspelled words, they just type over them. If they notice that words have been omitted, they enter them. If they want to add words, they add them. But, you may ask, won't additions make the lines too long and deletions make

Figure 10-1 Word-processing operator using display system. The keyboarded data appear on the CRT screen and, once the operator has made any necessary corrections, the printer in the background types the document. (Courtesy Xerox Corporation.)

them too short? No, they won't, because most WP units automatically adjust the length of altered lines and all following lines to keep
the right margins straight.

Business forms

Frequently used forms may be stored magnetically and called forth
to CRT screens for typing purposes. With WP units making all tab-
ulations automatically, operators just enter the data. After checking
the displayed documents for accuracy, operators instruct printers to
type the information onto preprinted carbonized forms. With some
models, operators simply type the data on continuous lines rather
than in specific areas of the forms, and WP machines automatically
place the words and numbers in the correct format during printing
operations.

Repetitive materials

Operators do not need to type the same address or the same message
repeatedly. They store such information on magnetic disks instead,
and call it forward when needed. In the same manner, operators
may send the same message to several (even thousands) of addressees without having to retype it even once; and they may personalize each message by including the names of addressees and
other relevant data.

Statistical data

When operators enter statistical data with totals into some WP
models, the units automatically run continuous totals as the figures
are entered. When the entries are complete, operators may check
the machine totals with the totals shown on the source documents.
When the totals disagree, operators check their own entries for accuracy before returning the original document to its source for
checking. Some WP units also enable operators to compare statistics
for the current period (day, week, month, year) with stored figures
for earlier periods, with the WP unit automatically printing the
percentage increase or decrease.

High-speed printers

Having made any necessary corrections in the displayed image of
documents, and after having placed paper in a separate unit (a
printer), operators instruct the WP machines (by pressing a certain
key) to type the documents. Many printers type in both directions,
as the typing element moves from left to right and as it returns to

the left, at speeds of from 300 to 3,000 words per minute. Some printers have round typing elements (spheres), and others have faster spiderlike devices (daisy wheels), both of which will make from six to ten carbon copies.

Easy revisions

Employees in WP centers return typed documents to the originators. When originators are satisfied with the product, they add their signatures and place them in outbaskets for mailing. If they decide instead to make changes, they simply note the changes on the printed documents and return them to their WP centers.

Since the documents are stored magnetically on recordlike disks until operators are certain that the documents have been approved, any alterations can be done without having to rekey entire documents. When writers notice that a word has been misspelled, for example, operators may instruct their WP units to correct the word in the text and to search the entire text to see if the same word has been misspelled elsewhere. Corrections of any additional misspelled words are then automatic.

When writers decide to underscore certain words or phrases, operators may instruct their WP units to search out the particular words or phrases and underscore them. But what if writers decide to rearrange the paragraphs? No problem—WP units quickly rearrange the ordering of paragraphs without the necessity of retyping. Additionally, operators may instruct WP units to type communications in either one or two columns and to right justify all lines (make right margins perfectly even).

High-speed copiers

Xerox Corporation was the first to mass market copy machines, with IBM and other large companies eventually following. The recently developed copier-duplicator pictured in Figure 10-2 makes 4,500 copies per hour, or 1¼ copies every second. The unit copies on one or both sides of the paper, and collates (sorts) the resulting pages.

New developments in copiers may represent the next major breakthrough in word-processing technology. Using an ink-jet printing device, the copier pictured in Figure 10-3 accepts magnetic data and ink-sprays it on paper at the rate of 900 words per minute. This copier also prints addresses on envelopes and matches the envelopes with appropriate copies of the letters as they are produced. It should not be very long, therefore, before word-processing operators will simply press a button to convert screened images directly to printed documents—without the rat-a-tat-tat of conventional

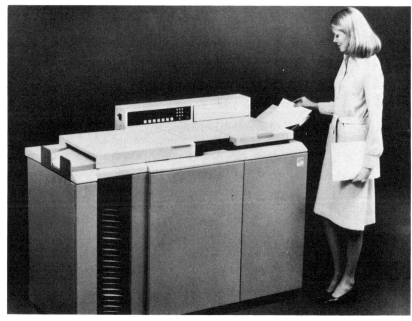

Figure 10-2 IBM Series 111 Copier/Duplicator, Model 20. (Courtesy International Business Machines Corporation.)

Figure 10-3 Ink-jet printer that operates at speeds of up to 900 words per minute. It automatically addresses envelopes and matches them with letters being printed. (Courtesy International Business Machines Corporation.)

printers. Eventually, the photo mechanism that produces the final documents will fold and insert them into envelopes, attach the correct postage, and sort them for mailing.

Micrographics

Micrographics provide a welcome solution to the filing problems outlined earlier in the chapter. Instead of stuffing filing cabinets and boxes with new and old records, some that will be used again and many that will not, more and more companies record their files on microfilm. The present state of the art enables them to film letters, reports, pictures, tables, graphs, and many other types of documents, in either black and white or color.

Businesses can now record thousands of documents on very small areas of film, and, with the assistance of minicomputers, can retrieve specific documents instantaneously and automatically. Existing equipment also makes it possible for employees to update filmed documents. If the company charged too high a price on the sale of a particular item, for example, the employee making the refund can observe the related invoice on a screen. And, if the company's micrographic equipment is sufficiently modern and sophisticated, the employee may use a keyboard to update the filmed invoice—noting on the film the amount refunded, the reason, and the date. Existing equipment also makes it possible for employees to reproduce on paper any of the microfilmed documents—instantaneously. Can anyone doubt that we are well on our way toward development of the much-heralded "paperless office"?

Cost factor

How much does all of this equipment cost? If you were to buy a keyboarded CRT and high-speed printer today, at the time this book is being written, you would pay anywhere from $10,000 to $20,000. By the time you read the book, however, prices may be significantly lower. Just as the prices of hand calculators entered a rapid decline, so too will the prices of WP equipment decline, as a greater number of companies expand production and compete more fiercely for this relatively new market.

But who can afford to pay $10,000 or more for a typewriter, even if it is a super typing system? A more appropriate question might be, "What business can afford *not* to buy one?" Assuming that the new typing system enables two people to do the work that previously kept three people occupied (a reasonable estimate), the savings will pay for the equipment in about one year. Moreover, the units will continue saving money for many years thereafter; the only part of the system that suffers any wear is the printer, and it has only a dozen or so moving parts.

One of the most frequently voiced complaints about word-processing centers is that the turnaround time is too long. Employees complain that by the time communications are prepared and returned for signing, they have forgotten the details involved. Optical scanning readers (OCRs) help to overcome this problem. Rather than having typists use expensive WP units to type original documents, which for even a medium-sized company might require two or three expensive units, companies may buy fewer word processors and use them only for editing previously typed materials. With an OCR, every typewriter in an office may be used as an input mechanism.

Secretaries type letters, reports, and other documents as usual on relatively inexpensive typewriters. Documents typed correctly the first time don't need editing on word processors. When a major alteration is required, one that would involve extensive retyping, the secretary goes to a nearby WP area and runs the document through an OCR unit, displaying the document on a CRT screen. The secretary then uses the WP keyboard to make the necessary alterations—using the expensive WP equipment only to circumvent the chore of retyping lengthy or difficult materials.

PLAN OF ACTION

The implementation of a word-processing system is not an easy task. When people have spent years preparing for and using traditional office methods, they tend to resist new ideas or procedures that materially alter the status quo. Recognizing this potential problem, management should plan the WP system carefully and undertake programs designed to gain employee acceptance and cooperation.

Outline the system

Word-processing systems should be tailored to the particular company, to accommodate varying conditions. One company might need five keyboarded-CRT units and just one printer for example, while another company might need three CRTs, two printers, and an OCR. The managers of one company may want to link the WP equipment with a computer, while others may not.

The most difficult choice in the planning stages, of course, is the selection of a particular make of WP equipment. Representatives of those employees who will use the service and those people who are going to operate the equipment should be identified as early as possible, so that they can help with the selection process.

To avoid the costly mistake of buying or leasing the wrong equipment, management should consider a wide variety of models, seeking demonstrations and feasibility studies from vendors and visiting word-processing centers that are already operational. They should keep in mind, however, that a system which works well for one company might be inappropriate for another.

An important issue is whether or not word-processing activities should be centralized. Centralization enables a company to gain maximum utilization from relatively few units but necessitates frequent mail service between the center and the offices it serves. Decentralization, on the other hand, places WP units near the offices (the same floor, at least) so that secretaries may use the equipment themselves in conjunction with their regular typewriters.

Potential obsolescence is a major concern with selecting word processors. Purchasers should be certain that the equipment is programmable, so that the memory units will receive new programs as they are developed by vendors. The state of the art is changing so rapidly that it would be impractical to change equipment each time a new feature is introduced to the market. Changing vendors, moreover, is complicated by the fact that their units are not compatible. To take advantage of a recent development by another vendor usually requires a complete change of equipment.

Sell the concept

So how do we overcome the built-in resistance to word processing mentioned earlier? The best way to gain acceptance, cooperation, and even enthusiasm from employees is to involve them in the planning stages of the system. Create dissatisfaction with traditional methods by identifying all existing problems and inefficiencies, and challenge employees to help the company maintain pace with the changing times.

Don't overestimate the willingness of business managers to adopt the new system. Case studies show that top managers often display formidable resistance to procedural change. Maybe they have dictated letters to the same secretary for many years. Maybe they had unpleasant experiences with cumbersome dictation equipment during an earlier period. Even more likely, maybe they fear the loss of an important status symbol—their secretaries.

Since managers generally respond to arguments based on sound economic concepts, they should be presented with the projected savings (in $$$ and ¢¢¢) with the new system. They also might be more receptive when they realize that their secretaries will have more time to assist them with administrative duties. Selling management on the merits of word-processing systems is important, because their support is essential to successful implementation.

Secretaries have even more to lose than their bosses do. Far from being enthusiastic about the new word-processing equipment, they generally imagine the obsolescence of long-nurtured typing and shorthand skills. But dictation and typing usually constitute only a portion of secretarial duties. Other responsibilities remain, such as handling telephones, making appointments, arranging itineraries, and preparing agenda for meetings. With the right attitude, and freedom from dictation and typing chores, secretaries may often assume a greater portion of the workload from their principals.

When word processors are introduced at some companies, secretaries receive the new title "administrative secretary"; and, to offset removal of dictation and typing duties, they are assigned to more than one principal. Greater responsibility? Yes! More interesting work? Certainly! Better opportunity for promotion? Definitely!

Once a vendor has been chosen, ask the sales representatives to conduct several demonstrations. Show the people who will be using the system how it will benefit them and the company, and make certain that those who will actually be operating the system have an opportunity to try it out. When word processors are demonstrated properly, most observers are amazed at their potential.

Set realistic goals

Don't promise more than the system can deliver. Don't promise employees that their documents will be prepared and returned (turnaround time) within two hours when it will be closer to four. Don't promise error-free documents, because people will still make mistakes—even when using word processors. If top management demands cost projections at the beginning of the program, don't be overly optimistic. Expected savings generally aren't realized until the second or third year of operation, after employees learn how to use the system properly; and many of the benefits are in quality of production rather than cost reductions.

Introduce in stages

Managers of some companies have taken a "big bang" approach to implementation, removing all typewriters and requiring all employees to rely totally on word-processing centers. In all reported incidents this approach has been traumatic for the people who operate the centers. They were bombarded with a barrage of source documents the operators had never seen before. The resulting delays in production produced a great deal of criticism and the need for new rounds of pep talks.

A more successful approach is to introduce new WP services in stages. Instead of serving all comers, begin handling the correspondence for just one department. The first stage enables dictators to become acquainted with the equipment, and the person coordinating the system to learn just what can be accomplished in a given time period. As each stage is perfected, include additional departments until the entire company is being served efficiently.

Maintain control

The quickest way to turn people off on a word-processing center is to lose some of their materials. Therefore, the WP supervisor or a special controller should be responsible for controlling the flow of paper to, from, and within the center. Records should be kept (called *logging*) of all materials entering the center, whether by messenger (a magnetic tape, a hand-written original, or a typed document returned for revision) or through a centrally located dictation mechanism. The center should be able to account for the receipt and delivery of all documents and the current status of those being processed.

WP operators take dictation either from cassette tapes received in the company mail or from centralized tape units. Following dictation into the centralized units, or even while materials are being dictated, operators transcribe directly to word processors. The tape drives show the amount of dictation remaining on any one tape, and transfer devices enable WP supervisors to equalize the typing load among the operators.

DICTATION GUIDELINES

If a word-processing center is to prove economical, employees must be persuaded to dictate their communications into some type of magnetic device. And, for optimal results, the people doing the dictating must follow prescribed guidelines.

Try dictation

Many people are reluctant to dictate their correspondence. They feel pressured when a secretary is waiting to record a steady stream of words, and some people are under the impression that they cannot organize their ideas well when talking to a dictation machine. So what do they do? Many authors write their communications in longhand before dictating or handing them to secretaries for typing.

Such a practice should be discouraged, because those employees who hold positions important enough to involve much writing are usually being paid too much money to spend their time pushing pencils. For maximum efficiency, they must be persuaded to dictate their communications, preferably to a recording device rather than a secretary.

When dictating to secretaries, most people accumulate materials until they have several items to dictate at once. This approach forces dictators to rethink the situation surrounding each letter while dictating, and improper preparation just prior to dictating wastes the time of secretaries unnecessarily.

Machine dictation methods are much more convenient. If you wish to respond to a letter you have just read while the response is fresh on your mind, you simply reach for a hand-held microphone, press a "Record" button with your thumb, and start talking. If you are interrupted during machine dictation, you may press a button for an instant replay of the last few words dictated. If you make a mistake in your dictation, press another button to alert the typist to watch for a correction. The machines do not represent any type of pressure on dictators because they do not start squirming or looking askance no matter how long it takes to formulate ideas.

Individual dictation units are portable, fitting nicely on desk tops, as shown in Figure 10-4. Pocket-sized units, also pictured in Figure 10-4, are widely used in business. Whether desk-top or pocket-sized, these dictation machines utilize reusable cassette tapes that are easily handled in interoffice mail and through U.S. mail. Some centralized systems also use regular telephones as part of their dictation systems. By picking up a push-button telephone at

Figure 10-4 Desktop recorder being used at left, with a portable unit pictured at right. (Photos courtesy of Dictaphone Corporation.)

the office or at home, employees may dictate directly to word-processing centers—day or night, 24 hours a day.

But what if employees make mistakes while dictating letters from home? After dialing the WP center, they press the 1 key on their telephones to start a magnetic tape. They press the 2 for corrections, the 3 for reply, and so on. Employees may dictate rush communications to special tapes for priority service, and they may close dictating sessions by either pressing the 4 key or hanging up the receiver. Convenient? Yes, and very economical when the volume of written correspondence is sufficiently large.

Provide
complete information

Employees who dictate directly to secretaries typically hand the files to secretaries at the end of dictating sessions. This procedure enables the secretaries to look at correspondence from other companies to copy the addresses, to proofread the spelling of names, and to check any unfamiliar terms that may have been used during dictation.

When dictation is to a tape in a word-processing center or to a cassette tape that is to be mailed to the center, the WP operator does not have the advantage of these files. Therefore, the dictator must provide complete information: the name of the addressee, the company name, the address (even the zip code), and the spelling of names and terms in the text of the communication.

Communicate thoroughly

Don't mumble when you dictate, especially during machine dictation. Secretaries taking shorthand can ask dictators to repeat something they miss, but magnetic tapes cannot. If any part of your communication is unclear to the transcribing operator, completion of the document is delayed. Begin by specifying the kind of communication it is—a long or short letter, a memo, a personal note. Also indicate the number of copies required, if more than the usual file copy. Then, when dictating the communication, clearly pronounce and spell all words that might be confusing; for example, the italicized words in the following paragraph should be spelled during dictation:

> We received a bid from *Matheson* Electronics, but we question their credit standing. Before making a final decision on the contract, however, we will check their Dun & Bradstreet and the financial reports that accompanied their bid. In the meantime, will you please check with Robert W. *Smyth* at International Bankers to determine the status of the mortgage loan

that is shown on the Matheson balance sheet. Smyth is the chief credit officer of International's *Royston* Branch at 1612 West *Orlin* Way in Belmont, California, and the zip code is 94002.

The dictator would rightfully expect the typist to be able to spell such words as *electronics* and *international,* and would spell the name *Belmont* only if it were a distant city. Some knowledge of surrounding geographic areas is assumed, and an acquaintance with commonly used business terms (such as *balance sheet* and *Dun & Bradstreet*) is expected.

Edit the output

It is tempting sometimes to leave the signing of correspondence to others, especially when the turnaround time is several hours. But to do so is risky. If at all possible, check completed communications for accuracy and appearance and sign them yourself. If you cannot be available to edit correspondence, assign the task to someone who is familiar with the transactions being discussed and who can spot an error when one exists. When employees sign letters dictated by someone else, they should sign the dictator's name and follow the signature with their own initials. Keep in mind that *all* your correspondence is a reflection on both you and your company.

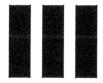

LETTER-WRITING TECHNIQUES

When you plan a communication, first determine if it falls within a specific category. Is it a routine communication? Are you conveying good news or bad news? Are you asking for money? Are you trying to sell someone a product, a service, or an idea? When a communication falls within an identifiable category, you may realize superior results by following the time-proven guidelines presented here.

11
RESPONDING TO
ROUTINE CORRESPONDENCE

Not all business correspondence relates to problem areas. Many people write to businesses to inquire about products, services, and prices; and businesses frequently receive letters of commendation from their customers. These routine communications are relatively easy to respond to, but we do not treat them casually. Prompt and courteous responses will almost certainly increase our business; whereas delayed and inappropriate responses tend to jeopardize future business opportunities.

FORMULATE
A MENTAL OUTLINE

Plan your communications, even when responding to routine inquiries. Having decided on the essential points of your communications, use the schematic in Figure 11-1 as a pattern for routine business communications

REFER TO THEIR
COMMUNICATION

Businesses do not operate in isolation from one another. Most businesses depend on other companies for raw materials, supplies, and services. Conversely, many businesses sell their finished goods to

Figure 11-1 Guide for routine communications.

Beginning paragraph	Middle paragraphs(s)	Ending paragraph
Refer to their communication	Provide complete information	Include goodwill close

153

other businesses. Each business is a customer of other businesses, and each business has other businesses as customers. The exchange of written and oral communications between two companies becomes extensive when they conduct transactions with each other on a regular basis. Rather than forcing the receivers of our many letters to match replies with copies of related letters they mailed to us to begin with, therefore, we start our correspondence with references to their specific communications.

> Example: In response to your letter of January 23 . . .
>
> Example: Here is the information that you requested in your letter of March 4.

Making reference to correspondence received is also a common and convenient way to begin our replies to individual customers and potential customers.

> Example: Thank you for your letter of the 23rd, in which you . . .
>
> Example: Your letter has been referred to Ms. Walker in our Customer Relations Department.

The initial correspondence is not always a letter, of course; many business letters are written in response to telephone and in-person conversations. We refer to these encounters at the beginning of our letters or conversations just as we do when responding to written communications.

> Example: After our talk during lunch on Friday, we decided to . . .
>
> Example: Your phone call this morning enabled us to . . .

When beginning a letter, a memo, or a conversation, ask yourself if there was a preceding communication (letter, memo, phone call, or face-to-face encounter) that should be referred to before starting the main part of your message. Provide other people with direction, rather than forcing them to undertake extensive search routines to learn what you are talking about.

PROVIDE
COMPLETE INFORMATION

You will usually satisfy the other person and avoid additional communications by providing complete information the first time. If a business customer requests price information relating to the purchase of 1,000 cases of your product, for example, be certain to specify whether the price does or does not include shipping costs. Failure to provide such vital information invariably results in additional communications.

When consumers request information about the availability of certain products, include extra information. After discussing availability, provide information on model choices, color options, delivery dates, and terms of payment. Make your communications complete by trying to answer those questions that might arise in the minds of customers as they contemplate purchases. We may consider our communications to be 100 percent successful only when they do not require further exchanges for reasons of clarification.

We can often minimize the detail in our letters by including bulletins and brochures. Instead of describing the various models of a product, for instance, we can allude to an accompanying brochure. Instead of detailing our terms of sale, we can mention an enclosed bulletin.

> Example: We are enclosing a brochure that describes the operation more completely.
>
> Example: This product is available in several models and colors, as illustrated in the enclosed pamphlet.

When writing to new customers, we may include promotional materials they would not have received during our regular mailings. As a matter of practice, however, we do *not* routinely include such items with all correspondence. To do so would require that all employees who write letters be provided with advertising materials on a regular basis. Enclosure of the materials with their regular communications would result in duplicate mailings and additional postage charges. Rather than sending promotional materials to the relatively few customers with whom we correspond individually, therefore, we rely on mass mailings of advertisements to *all* customers.

When several items are involved, we often send them separately—the letter in one envelope, promotional materials in a separate one. We mention in our letter that the materials are being mailed separately, but we avoid the worn expression "under separate cover."

> Example: You will also be receiving an operator's manual.
>
> Example: We are mailing these materials separately.
>
> Example: We will send a correct invoice right away.

INCLUDE GOODWILL CLOSE

We have begun our letter by referring to the other person's communication to us in a brief first paragraph. We then added one or two medium-length paragraphs to provide the necessary details. Now what?

Just as we avoid being terse when closing our telephone and in-person conversations, we avoid abruptness when ending our letters. Instead of just walking away from others at the end of conversations, we usually say something like "See you later," "Take care now," or "It's been nice talking with you." We ease out of our written communications in much the same way.

> Example: Thank you very much for providing us with this information.
>
> Example: We hope that you will be pleased with your new stereo.
>
> Example: Let us know if we have left any questions unanswered.

We refer to such closing statements as *goodwill closes,* because they tend to please people and cause them to think well of our companies and our products.

EXAMPLES OF ROUTINE CORRESPONDENCE

Now let's put the pieces together to form some complete communications. We have just received Purchase Order 36130 from a new customer, and we are shipping all the requested items, except one, from our Los Angeles plant on May 8 via Yellow Freight Lines. The remaining item, 500 cases of Product A-612, is being shipped from our New Jersey warehouse on May 7 via Brown Motor Freight. Following the schematic in Figure 11-1, we write the following message.

Routine letter	
Refer to their communication	Thank you for your initial order with our company, Purchase Order 36130.
Provide complete information	The 500 cases of Product A-612 will be shipped from our New Jersey warehouse on May 7 via Brown Motor Freight, and all other items will be shipped from our Los Angeles plant on May 8 via Yellow Freight Lines.
Add a goodwill close	We appreciate your business and will do our best to serve you well.

An investor has written directly to our company, Seymour Electronics, requesting a copy of our annual report for 1982. The letter is dated November 10, 1982, but our annual report for 1982 will not be available until February 5, 1983. Therefore, we must write a letter explaining that (1) we are sending a copy of last year's annual report at this time, and (2) we will send a copy of the new annual report as soon as it is published.

Routine letter

Refer to their communication	In response to your letter of November 10, we are enclosing a copy of our annual report for 1981.
Provide complete information	We will also send a copy of our 1982 annual report to you immediately upon its publication in early February. Please complete and return the enclosed card if you would like to receive copies of all future financial reports.
Add a goodwill close	Thank you for your interest in Seymour Electronics.

Before selling to our company on credit terms, a new supplier has written a letter (dated October 3) requesting copies of our most recent income statement and balance sheet. The request also includes a financial form that is to be completed and returned with the two financial statements. Our letter of transmittal (written on October 15) should follow the same pattern as the preceding communications.

Routine letter

Refer to their communication	We are returning the completed financial form that accompanied your letter of October 3.
Provide complete information	Enclosed also are copies of our most recent income statement and balance sheet, both dated December 31, 1982, and copies of our projected statements for the coming year. Both 1982 statements have been audited and approved by Smith, Finker, and Ralston Associates.
Add a goodwill close	Please let us know if additional information is required.

Working in the consumer relations section of an airline company, we have just received a very complimentary letter from a businessman concerning the services of Liza Herman, one of our Customer Service Agents. It seems that Liza's skill in the Portuguese language helped him locate a former business associate during a stopover in Portugal. Let's contribute further to the goodwill of this customer by responding promptly to his letter.

Routine letter

Refer to their communication	We were very pleased to receive your favorable comments about Liza Herman, and we know that Liza will also be pleased when she reads your letter.

Provide complete information	Although our language is the most widely used language throughout the world, many millions of people don't understand one word of English. It is for this reason that we recruit people who are skilled in several languages to work as Customer Service Agents on our international flights.
Add a goodwill close	Thank you for taking the time to tell us that you found this aspect of our service to be of special value.

The formula approach words very well, doesn't it? Once you recognize a particular communication as "routine," you write the prescribed segments for routine communications and presto, the letter is complete and highly readable. Use the following checklist when writing routine letters, and keep in mind the S*T*A*R approach (page 75), along with everything you have learned about mechanics and grammar in Part 1.

CHECKLIST:
ROUTINE CORRESPONDENCE

Beginning paragraph. Refer to their communication in one of the following ways:

- Acknowledge receipt of their written communication (letter, memo, purchase order, invoice, etc.).
- Thank them for the communication.
- Express your enjoyment of a previous conversation.
- Casually refer to their communication when outlining their requests.
- Tell them that their communication is being referred to another person for reply, when such is the case.
- Express appreciation for their business when their communication includes an order for products or services.

Middle paragraph(s). Provide complete information:

- Answer their specific questions.
- Include any extra detail that might prove helpful.
- Reinforce your statements and minimize verbiage by enclosing related brochures and pamphlets.
- Include promotional materials when appropriate, especially when corresponding with a new customer.
- Mention in the text of your letter any materials that are enclosed or mailed separately.

Ending paragraph. Add a goodwill close in one of the following ways:

- Thank them for their interest.
- Thank them for taking the time to communicate with you.
- Express an optimistic look toward the future.
- Offer additional information or assistance.
- Thank them for directing their business your way.
- Mention their continued enjoyment of your product or service.
- Express your desire to respond to their future needs.

Remember, these are just guidelines. Strive to use your own words and ideas when following the suggested format.

12

DELIVERING GOOD NEWS

Businesses receive many requests from suppliers, wholesalers, retailers, consumers, government agencies, and the general public—
requests for products, price adjustments, exchanges, refunds, employment, credit, and many types of information. When business
people respond to these requests in the affirmative, giving others
what they are seeking, we refer to their replies as good news communications. Although most people respond favorably to the receipt
of messages bearing good news, regardless of the word choice or
organization used, the following pages present several guidelines
for deriving the greatest amount of goodwill from such communications.

EMPHASIZE THE POSITIVE

Good news messages are relatively easy to communicate, but a good
plan makes the task even easier. The schematic in Figure 12-1
provides some guidelines for emphasizing the positive aspects of
good news communications. Psychologists contend that most people
remember the opening and closing remarks of letters and conversations more vividly than what is written or said in between these
remarks. We may benefit from this knowledge when conveying good
news.

BEGIN WITH THE GOOD NEWS

A main consideration with many messages is whether to use deductive or inductive reasoning. With the deductive approach, we begin
the communication with the main point of the message. With the
inductive approach, we preface the main part of our message with a

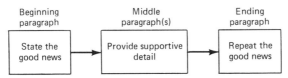

Beginning paragraph	Middle paragraph(s)	Ending paragraph
State the good news	Provide supportive detail	Repeat the good news

Figure 12-1 Guidelines for good news communications.

related explanation. When conveying good news, the more effective approach is clear; we follow the deductive method by placing the good news right up front. Consider the following opening remarks:

Example: We have just received approval for the issuance of full coverage on your 1979 Corvette.

Example: Although the warranty on the heating unit for your waterbed ended more than 60 days ago, we have decided to replace it free of charge.

Example: Closing costs on your new home totaled $946.50, or $45.20 less than originally estimated.

When the situation allows us to give people what they have requested, we don't keep them guessing about our answer. Instead, we remove the pressures of uncertainty by stating our positive response at the beginning of the communication.

PROVIDE SUPPORTIVE DETAIL

As the diagram in Figure 12-1 shows, the pattern for conveying good news begins and ends the communication by mentioning the good news. But to do this tactfully, we must separate both references to the good news with a middle paragraph or two.

A middle paragraph or two? About what? The content of the middle part of the communication depends on the situation. If you are providing automobile insurance, replacing a defective product, or refunding money, as in the preceding examples of opening remarks, you may provide some detail regarding the transactions.

Example: Your vehicle is insured against loss, except for the first $100, up to but not exceeding $6,000. Bodily injury liability insurance of $50,000 for each person is included, with a maximum payment of $100,000 for each accident. Property damage liability (damage that may be inflicted on the property of others) is covered up to $10,000 for each accident, and related medical payments will be paid to a maximum of $2,000.

Example: The L-1214 heating unit is guaranteed for one year, but we construct them to last much longer than that; and the overall performance of this particular model has resulted in an outstanding record of reliability. When a control unit malfunctions as yours has, therefore, we would rather replace it than have customers assume critical views of our fine products.

Example: Interest on the mortgage balance of $38,400 from July 13 to August 20 amounted to $256.00, instead of $296.00—a difference of $40,00; and the pro-rated taxes from July 13 to the purchase date were $61.50, instead of $67.00—an additional difference in your favor of $5.50.

The second example includes two attempts to resell the company's products, specifying that the heating units are made to last a long time and mentioning the company's "fine products." A certain amount of resell in good news letters can be very effective; we may alleviate any doubts that our customers may be having by restating the positive qualities of the products. The following sentences are additional examples of ways that we may resell our products in the middle sections of good news letters.

Example: You made a wise decision to buy your new home when you did, Mr. Burns, because we have had several people express interest in the property since you bought it.

Example: Despite this initial inconvenience, your new refrigerator will provide you with many years of satisfactory service. In fact, *Consumer Guide* judged this particular model to be the best designed and most energy-efficient refrigerator on the market.

Customers often experience what salespeople refer to as "after-purchase blues," especially when something goes wrong with the products they have just bought. When we correspond with them about repair, replacement, or some other type of adjustment, therefore, we should attempt to resell the items—to reassure customers that they have made wise purchase decisions in selecting our products.

Don't jeopardize the goodwill objective of good news communications by mentioning self-sacrifice. By telling customers about the trouble involved in accomplishing what they request, you may cause them to feel indebted to you, which in turn may make them reluctant to conduct further business transactions with your company, reasoning that if anything should go wrong with another of your products or services they would be embarrassed to bother you with a second request for assistance. Just convey the good news, and forget about any personal inconvenience you may have encountered.

REPEAT THE GOOD NEWS

As a way of generating as much goodwill as possible from good news messages, we again refer to the good news in our closing paragraphs. To illustrate, let's close the letters that we have written in the previous sections: (1) extending insurance coverage, (2) exchanging the waterbed heating unit, and (3) refunding an overcharge on the purchase of a home.

> Example: We are pleased to be able to provide this coverage, and the policy will be mailed directly to you from our home office within the next week to ten days. Please check it carefully and let us know if you have any questions.
>
> Example: You may take the enclosed card to any authorized dealer in your area, along with the used heating unit, for free replacement or for full credit toward the purchase of any other heating unit.
>
> Example: Our check for $45.50 is enclosed.

We opened these three communications with mention of the good news, provided some detail, and closed with a second reference to the good news. This pattern allows us to write well-balanced letters that leave readers with positive thoughts about our products and our company.

EXAMPLES OF GOOD NEWS COMMUNICATIONS

So we have a beginning, a middle, and an ending, just as with routine communications; we have changed only the content of those segments. To illustrate further, let's consider several business situations that call for good news communications. Having just received a letter from a customer concerning a mistake that we made in one of our billings, we find that the customer is correct and a refund is in order.

> *Good news letter—invoice adjustment*
>
> | State the good news | We agree with the figures cited in your letter of March 29, and we will refund the amount requested. |
> |---|---|
> | Provide supportive detail | Procedural errors such as this one, which resulted from a misplaced price tag, occasionally slip through—in spite of very stringent control measures. Thank you for setting us straight, and you may be sure that we will do |

everything within our power to see that all
future billings are 100 percent accurate.

| Repeat the good news | You will receive our check for $22.50 within the next few days. |

As an assistant to the personnel manager, let's inform a person of
acceptance for employment, having selected him from among several other applicants; and, as before, let's mention the good news at
both ends of the communication.

Good news letter—successful job applicant

State the good news	We are pleased to offer you the position of Assistant Production Manager at our Westgate Plant.
Provide supportive detail	Your background is ideal for the job, and your availability for work on July 1 is timed perfectly for this particular assignment. Ralph Snyder, to whom you will report directly, was especially impressed by your knowledge of assemblyline operations; excellent reports from your previous employers were also important in our decision to hire you from among several applicants for this position.
	Will you stop at my office for an hour or two before leaving for Westgate, to complete some tax and insurance forms? Please bring a copy of your birth certificate and any health or life insurance policies presently in effect.
Repeat the good news	Once again, Jeff, we are very happy to welcome you as a member of our Westgate production staff.

In responding to a customer's letter requesting that we apply a
quantity discount to previous purchases of our products, we find
that the discount does apply to three purchases. We use the first
paragraph to acknowledge our findings, the middle paragraph to
explain our reasoning, and the final paragraph to reiterate the good
news—the news that we are granting what the customer has
requested.

Good news letter—quantity discounts

| State the good news | Having checked the information in your letter of June 19, we find that you are entitled to the quantity discount of 5 percent on each of your last three purchases. |
| Provide supportive detail | Our computer did not identify these orders as being eligible for the discount because each was for fewer than 500 units. But since the |

cumulative total of the three orders exceeds the required 500 units, all received before the close of our May sales program, you are entitled to the requested discounts of $16.01, $26.35, and $32.50.

Repeat the good news

We are allowing the discount, therefore, and crediting your account in these amounts.

An educator has requested black-and-white glossy prints of our Model X-1212 and L-1010 duplicating machines for use in a textbook that she is writing. We are sending the requested pictures, but we have only a color print of the L-1010 machine. The color print is suitable for reproduction in black and white, however.

Good news letter—complimentary materials

State the good news

Here are the materials that you requested.

Provide supportive detail

The Model X-1212 duplicator is designed for relatively small business operations; the L-1010 is intended primarily for large volumes of information. The picture of Model X-1212 is in color, but our technicians assure us that the color contrasts are sufficiently distinct for satisfactory reproduction in black and white.

Repeat the good news

We hope that these materials prove useful to you, and we wish you the best success with your project.

Good news letters are easy to write, compared to many other types of communications, and this three-step formula makes writing them even easier. Use your own words and phrases when writing or conversing, however, rather than trying to adapt the words of other people to fit your communications.

CHECKLIST: GOOD NEWS COMMUNICATIONS

Beginning paragraph. Begin with the good news, referring to their communications when appropriate, in one of the following ways:

- Acknowledge that they are correct.
- Inform them that their request has been approved.
- Advise that you are giving them what they want, such as
    a refund
    a discount
    a replacement

an appointment
a job
materials and information
an adjustment
credit

Middle paragraph(s). Provide supportive detail, avoiding mention of self-sacrifice.

- Outline data related to the transaction, such as
  computational errors made
  technicalities overlooked
  wrong prices charged
- Reassure customers that they made wise purchase decisions by
  calling attention to the favorable attributes of products
  citing public and professional recognition of products
  comparing with competing products
  presenting testimony of satisfied customers
  mentioning scarcity (limited supply) when applicable
  outlining warranty provisions

Closing paragraph. Repeat the good news, adding goodwill comments where appropriate.

- Indicate that you are pleased to have taken the action.
- Provide instructions for any action that they must take.
- Tell them how and when the adjustments will be made.
- Include positive statements about future expectations.
- Express hope that materials will be helpful.
- Offer further assistance and best wishes.

Remember, these statements are not all-inclusive; they are only suggestions for ways that you may open, detail, and close good news communications. The exact words and phrases you use depend on your normal manner of speaking, since you will use your own words and phrases, and the particular business situation with which you are confronted.

Apply the S*T*A*R approach (page 75) to all business communications.

13

SOFTENING BAD NEWS

Businesses cannot always give people what they want; they must sometimes say "no." We refer to such messages as bad news communications, and we try to convey the bad news in the most acceptable way possible.

PLAN YOUR APPROACH

The primary objective in communicating bad news messages is the same as for routine and good news messages; we want to maintain or enhance the goodwill of those with whom we are communicating. We want them to think positive thoughts about our products and our services. But how, you may ask, can we deny people what they want and still retain their goodwill? We may do so by following the inductive approach outlined in Figure 13-1.

In the first paragraph, we briefly mention the situation that has served as the catalyst for our letter. We provide details, state the bad news, and present alternative courses of action in the middle section, which may consist of one or more paragraphs. We then close our letter with a short paragraph—a neutral statement or a positive comment about the future.

Figure 13-1 Guidelines for bad news communications (dotted lines indicate that the middle parts are sometimes combined into one or two paragraphs).

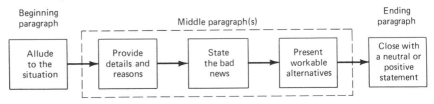

ALLUDE TO THE SITUATION

Bad news messages require the inductive pattern. Rather than going straight to the main point of the communication, as with good news messages, we assume an indirect approach. To illustrate, let's write negative responses to the three situations that were presented at the beginning of Chapter 12. We will decline the request for insurance on the Corvette; we will refuse to replace the waterbed heater; and, rather than refunding an overcharge of closing costs on the new home, we will ask the buyer to pay an undercharge.

> Example: When you applied for insurance coverage on your 1979 Corvette, we told you that we would submit the application to our home office for consideration, but that coverage would not begin until approval was received.
>
> Example: The heating unit that you returned has been checked in our laboratory.
>
> Example: The estimated closing costs on the property at 6210 North Euclid Avenue, which we originally estimated at around $790, can now be compared with actual costs.

When writing beginning paragraphs to bad news letters, we avoid statements which might lead the reader to believe that good news is to follow. To preface bad news with statements of thanks or agreement would only make the impact of the bad news more pronounced when encountered by the reader. Instead, we begin with a statement of fact: a neutral statement concerning the situation.

PROVIDE DETAILS AND REASONS

After alluding to the situation, we still are not ready to break the bad news. We must first explain some of the factors that influenced our decision.

> Example: You informed us at the time of your application that you had been cited for one moving violation and one chargeable accident. We find, however, that you have had three moving violations; although the state counts for licensing purposes only those moving violations during the past year, our company takes into consideration all such violations during the past three years.
>
> Example: The pad and connecting cord in all of our heating units are sealed to provide complete safety to the sleeper in the event of a leaking mattress, which makes it impossible for our technicians to repair

the heater or identify the exact cause of malfunction. They are fairly certain in this instance, however, that one or more of the wires within the pad have been broken, which (again as a safety feature) stops the flow of electricity through the pad. Broken wires may result from improper positioning during installation or from mistreatment of the pad once it is in place.

Example: Interest on the mortgage balance of $38,400 from July 13 to August 20 totaled $316.50 instead of $296.00—a difference of $20.50; and the prorated taxes from July 13 to the purchase date were $73.00, instead of $67.00—an additional difference of $6.00.

Rather than hitting readers right between the eyes with bad news, we have prepared them for it. If we word our message correctly, readers will anticipate the bad news part of the message as the logical course of action. Who could blame an insurance company for refusing coverage to a high-risk driver? How could anyone expect a company to replace a heating pad that is no longer under warranty, especially if there is a possibility that it received improper treatment? And who would argue about having to make an extra payment for closing costs that are based on factual evidence?

STATE THE BAD NEWS

We then present the bad news, not in separate paragraphs where it would be emphasized, but by adding a sentence or two to the preceding paragraphs, where the bad news will be deemphasized.

Example: Consequently, we cannot provide the requested coverage at this time.

Example: We must limit our warranty to one year, therefore, even though these units often last for many, many years; and since your heater is no longer under warranty, we cannot assume responsibility for its replacement.

Example: So that we may finalize the closing, will you please send a check to us for $26.50?

In the first example, we are leaving the door open for future business by adding the words "at this time." Maybe the applicant will represent an acceptable risk sometime in the future. We "buried" the bad news in the second example by placing it at the end of a long sentence. But in both instances (first and second examples), we made sure that we conveyed the bad news, even resorting to use of the word *cannot*. Don't be so subtle in communicating bad news that you fail to make your point. Don't leave the reader wondering whether the subject is still open for discussion. Our meaning in the third example is abundantly clear; we are asking for more money.

PRESENT
WORKABLE ALTERNATIVES

The receipt of bad news often leaves readers in the lurch; for example, the insurance applicant is left without coverage, and the waterbed owner is without a functional heating unit. If we have assumed a service attitude toward our business communications, we must help people solve their problems by suggesting alternative courses of action.

> Example: We hope that you will come to us for your insurance needs sometime in the future—after you have established an acceptable driving record. In the meantime, we suggest that you apply to a company that specializes in high-risk coverage such as Miles Insurance Group or TransGlobal Insurance Company.
>
> Example: You may recall that the M-13 heater is the lowest priced of the three models that we offer. Our T-120 heater carries United Laboratories certification, and our T-150 (a solid-state unit) carries a five-year warranty.

When we cannot satisfy the needs of customers, as with the first example, let's refer them to companies that can. When one of our products does not meet the precise needs of customers, as in the second example, let's suggest alternative products that we offer. Isn't this the type of treatment that most of us expect from business people? In the absence of such treatment, customers often experience a feeling of being stuck with inferior products or services from companies that have no concern for their welfare; and they seldom patronize or speak well of those companies again.

CLOSE WITH A NEUTRAL
OR POSITIVE STATEMENT

We opened our bad news letters by mentioning something about the topic of discussion. Then, in a middle paragraph or two, we provided an explanation of our position, stated the bad news, and suggested alternative action that might be taken. Now, let's end the letter with a neutral or positive statement.

> Example: Thank you for thinking of us concerning your insurance needs.

Example: Any of our four authorized dealers in your city will be happy to provide additional information and assist you with selection of the best unit for your particular uses.

Example: We thank you very much for the consideration that you have shown us during these transactions, and we hope that you experience many years of happiness in your new home.

Don't close your letter by asking them to contact you when and if you can help them in some other way. Since you didn't help them much to begin with, it is insulting to offer "additional help." Also avoid the common urge to include an apology in the final paragraph. If we have done all that is possible for the person, and if our decision is based on sound logic, there is no need to apologize. An apology unnecessarily reminds readers of the bad news and, when placed at the end of the letter, tends to leave them with unpleasant thoughts about our products and our company.

EXAMPLES
OF BAD NEWS COMMUNICATIONS

To illustrate further this suggested approach to communicating bad news messages, let's take four situations that were used in Chapter 12 as examples of good news messages. Rather than agreeing with the figures cited by the customer in the first situation, however, let's assume that she has erroneously shown a $42.50 item at the sale price of $20.00.

Bad news letter—price adjustment

Allude to the situation	We have checked the prices shown in your letter of March 29 with our master price list.
Provide details, reasons, and then the bad news	Your figures are correct, with one exception; you list a B&H Encyclopedic Dictionary at $20.00 when the actual price is $42.50. Another customer might have placed this publication among the sales items, or perhaps one of our salespeople inadvertently placed it on the wrong rack. In either event, the correct price of the item is $42.50, and the total amount of your purchase during February is $135.15, as billed.
Present a workable alternative	We realize that you may not have purchased the dictionary if you had known its true price and that you

	may wish to return it. If the item has not been marked and is returned promptly, therefore, we will gladly credit your account for the full purchase price.
Close with a neutral or positive statement	Please let us know if you have any further questions, Mrs. Smith, because we do value you as a regular customer.

In our second example, we have decided not to hire Jeff Rogers for the position of Assistant Production Manager at our Westgate plant. This decision comes after Rogers has invested considerable time in completing an application, taking tests, and being interviewed.

Bad news letter—unsuccessful job applicant

Allude to the situation	As we mentioned during our first meeting, several people applied for the same position that you were seeking.
Provide details, reasons, and then the bad news	Your background in manufacturing operations is impressive and your references favorable, but other applicants had experience that was more directly related to our Westgate operation.
	Realizing the importance of the selection decision to all applicants, and in consideration of the interests that they expressed, the final decision was a group effort of four officers of the company. We wish that we could report that you were the successful candidate, Jeff, but such is not the case.
Present alternatives	Your application will be kept on file, of course, because of the possibility of future openings. You also might consider applying with Jonathan Industries, Inc., a New York-based firm that is presently constructing new facilities in Colorado and Utah.
Close with a neutral or positive statement	We want you to know that we very much appreciate the time and effort that you afforded us during this selection process, and we wish you success in your search for a managerial position in production.

As our third example of a bad news communication, we will deny a customer's request that quantity discounts be allowed for three earlier purchases of our products. We offered a quantity discount of 5 percent only on individual orders of 500 or more units, but each of this customer's three orders was for less than that amount.

Bad news letter—quantity discounts disallowed

Allude to the situation	The discounts that you have requested in your letter of June 19 related to three individual orders.
Provide details, reasons, and then the bad news	If you will review our bulletin of May 1 (copy enclosed), you will see that the 5 percent discount applied to individual shipments of 500 or more units. We were able to offer this discount because of savings we experience with larger shipments. The cost of the paperwork and physical processing of one large order is about one third that of three smaller orders. Since your three orders were for 150, 250, and 200 units, even though the combined total exceeded the 500-unit minimum, they do not qualify for the quantity discount.
Present alternatives	Will it be possible for you to combine your smaller orders into one large order during future sales promotions? Maybe you and one or two other retailers will be able to submit your individual orders to us as one shipment, requesting that the trucker make split deliveries to your individual stores.
Close with a neutral or positive statement	Many of our customers operate relatively small retail outlets; therefore, we are always eager to help them benefit from all provisions of our sales promotions.

As a final example of a bad news communication, let's refuse an educator's request for pictures. We find that we are not the legal owners of the requested pictures, but we do have two other photos which might be appropriate.

Bad news letter—request for materials denied

Allude to the situation	We appreciate your offer to include in your upcoming publication a picture

	of one of our large steam shovels, because we value this type of publicity.
Provide reasons, the bad news, and alternatives	The pictures you have requested are the legal property of a professional photographer that we employ for all our publications; therefore, we cannot provide copies or authorization for their use. You may write to Professional Photographers at 1612 West 16th Street, Chicago, Illinois 60607, concerning use of the photos, but the fee involved for each print would be at least $50. As a possible alternative, we are enclosing black-and-white photographs of two of our Series 210 models. If you use either of these two pictures, please make the credit line read "Courtesy FMQ Corporation."
Close with a neutral or positive statement	Thank you for your interest in our products, and good luck with your publication.

CHECKLIST:
BAD NEWS COMMUNICATIONS

Beginning paragraph. Allude to the situation that gave rise to the communication in one of the following ways:

- Refer to their communication to you.
- Mention what they have requested.
- Advise that the communication has been given to you for reply or that you are handing it to someone else—if such is the case.
- Outline any action that has been taken, such as inspecting a product, calculating figures, and checking records.
- Inform them that you have been seeking authorization.
- Make a neutral comment about the situation at hand.
- Express appreciation.
- Do *not* make misleading statements that create false hope.
- Do *not* reveal the bad news before reasons have been given.

Middle paragraph(s). Provide details and reasons in one of the following ways:

- Tell them that their goods are no longer under warranty.
- Explain why it is necessary to limit such warranties.

- Suggest possible reasons for product failure, sometimes implying that part or all of the blame might rest with the user.
- Explain that the limitations you are imposing are the same for all customers.
- Provide facts and figures when available.
- Compare your products with competing products, when yours compare favorably.
- Compare their personal qualifications with the qualifications of competing applicants or employees, in decisions involving employment or promotion.
- Refer to official documents that contradict their claims.
- Tell them that their requests are unreasonable and explain why.

State the bad news by:

- Using positive language where possible.
- Being certain to make your point, using the words *cannot* and *deny* when essential to full understanding.
- Asking for money due your company.
- Deemphasizing it in long sentences and long paragraphs.

Present workable alternatives by:

- Suggesting substitute products.
- Referring them to another company.
- Suggesting corrective action that they might take.

Ending paragraph. Close with a neutral or positive statement by:

- Thanking them for taking the time to communicate with you.
- Thanking them for their help, if they have assisted you in any way.
- Expressing appreciation for their interest.
- Asking if they have any questions.
- Telling them you appreciate their business.
- Mentioning the possibility of future relationships.
- Wishing them luck in their future endeavors.
- Do *not* repeat the bad news.
- Do *not* apologize.

Remember, apply the S*T*A*R approach (page 75) to all types of business communications.

14

USING PERSUASION

American businesses spend billions of dollars each year trying to persuade people to buy their products and services, and most of their advertising appeals follow the pattern discussed in this chapter. The techniques of persuasion are not confined to sales messages; we may follow the same pattern, for example, when trying to sell an idea to colleagues and when trying to land a job. This is not to say that the composition of all persuasive messages is an easy task; as you have probably observed, much of today's advertising is clever, original, and a product of the combined talents of professional writers, artists, and photographers.

ORGANIZING
SALES MESSAGES

Before beginning their sales messages, most writers of advertisements identify key selling points and thoroughly analyze the product or service to be advertised—including all related aspects of a company's operation. Having taken this critical first step, they plan their communications according to the guidelines in Figure 14-1. After designing the first paragraph to capture the interest of readers, advertisers attempt to maintain interest by relating the product or service to the needs and wants of readers. The middle part of the message is devoted to maintaining reader interest by making product claims and presenting supportive evidence. Advertisers use the final paragraphs to invite readers, listeners, or viewers to take the desired buying action.

Advertisers do not always follow this format, of course; they sometimes rely on pictures of their products, using very little, if any, verbiage. When advertisers must rely on words to convey persuasive messages, however, they usually follow the steps outlined here.

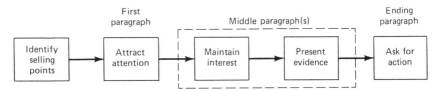

Figure 14-1 Guidelines for persuasive messages (dotted line indicates that the two middle steps are sometimes combined into a single paragraph).

IDENTIFYING
KEY SALES POINTS

A lot of planning goes into advertisements, and most advertisers take a systematic approach to the preparation of newspaper, magazine, billboard, radio, and television advertisements. Before even beginning work on advertising messages, they study the four P's of marketing: product, price, place, and promotion.

Beginning with the company's product (or service), they identify unique attributes of the product. Is it faster or more attractive than competing products? Is it more durable? Is the packaging distinctive? They compare price. When the price of the company's product is lower than that of competitors, price usually becomes a key selling point. When the price isn't competitive, advertisers usually avoid mentioning the subject. Advertisers also consider the availability of products, which they refer to as place. Is the product available at many stores? What types of stores?

The final consideration is promotion. Having identified the key selling points of a product—through analysis of product, price, and place—advertisers must decide on a method for communicating these points to consumers. Promotion includes personal selling, advertising, publicity, and all the appeals they may use to motivate consumers to sample their products.

ATTRACTING ATTENTION

Persuading people to do what we want them to do isn't always easy. As a defense mechanism, people screen out most of the sales messages that they are confronted with each day. If an advertisement is to penetrate this protective screen, its opening statement must strike consumers as relevant to their personal interests.

Some advertisers gain this effect by promoting their products as new and improved.

Example: Your **** dealer has something new and exciting for you on his showroom floor.

Example: The new **** reduces tar intake without sacrific-
ing flavor.

Urgency appeals are good attention getters.

Example: Wednesday and Thursday are RED HOT value
days at your **** stores.

Example: End-of-month clearance of ****! While they last!

Advertisers of such products and services as auto tires and insurance often attract attention by using fright appeals.

Example: Don't compromise the safety of your family by . . .

Example: How would your family cope without you and your
regular income?

When the price of a product or service is the main selling point,
advertisers may use thrift appeal to good advantage.

Example: Would you like to save money on your next purchase of ****?

Example: Prices will never be lower than they are right now
at ****.

Advertisers often use bandwagon appeal to impress consumers that
they should move with the crowd and be popular by using certain
products.

Example: Everybody's doing it, doing it, doing it. Doing
what? Switching to Diet-Free ****, naturally.

Example: What? You're still using ****? Haven't you heard
about ****?

Companies occasionally use snob appeal by implying that their
products are intended for a specific segment of the market.

Example: **** cigarettes are *not* for just everyone.

Example: The new **** is designed for discriminating people, people who value a touch of elegance in their
lives.

The most effective means of overcoming consumer resistance to advertisements is sex appeal, which usually involves the use of pictures. We might expect to see pictures of attractive men and women
in ads that promote health spas and certain diet foods and beverages, but advertisers often use sex appeal to attract attention to
products that have absolutely no relation to the human anatomy. A
scantily clad woman sitting on the hood of a new car is not relevant
to the appearance or operational features of the car, nor is a macho
male atop a large Arabian horse related to the flavor of a particular
brand of cigarette. But the presence of "beautiful people" in adver-

tisements does attract a lot of attention to the products being promoted.

MAINTAINING INTEREST

Medical doctors are concerned with the ability of the human body to keep all bodily functions in balance, a condition they call "homeostasis." Regardless of prevailing temperatures, our bodies make the adjustments necessary to maintain an almost constant 98.4 degrees. Similarly, psychologists speak of a mental imbalance called *cognitive dissonance,* theorizing that when people are discontent they take action to restore a mental balance. Advertisers strive to create cognitive dissonance among consumers by causing an imbalance that can be corrected only through the purchase of their products or services. Haven't you sometimes experienced discontent after being introduced to a particular product, wanting it so badly that you couldn't be perfectly happy until buying it?

Advertisers begin to create cognitive dissonance during the early stages of their advertisements by making enticing claims about their products and services.

Example: The new **** will outperform any car in its class.

Example: **** can help you lose 20 pounds in four weeks.

Example: The **** fleximatic will give you razor-close shaves, time after time.

Business people are seldom modest when it comes to praising the favorable attributes of their products and services. Consumers have come to expect a certain amount of trade puffery in advertising, in fact, especially when the product or service advertised has outstanding features.

PRESENTING EVIDENCE

Advertisers add to the cognitive dissonance of those consumers who get hooked on their advertisements by presenting evidence to support their product claims. One effective way to convince people that a product or service is worthy is to have a famous person make favorable comments about it.

Example: Bumper-to-bumper driving on a freeway can be hard on a car's engine, but I minimize engine wear and improve performance by using the same oil in my family car that I use on the race track, **** motor oil.

Example: Hi, I'm ****. Shooting a weekly TV series keeps all of us hopping here on the set, often making it necessary for us to eat on the run. **** crackers help me minimize calorie intake while maintaining a high level of energy, and they are *very* tasty.

The Federal Trade Commission, the agency that regulates advertisers, is trying to increase the authenticity of such testimonials by requiring those people to use the products or services before endorsing them.

Advertisers have found that they can convince many consumers of the accuracy of their product claims by having experts (or apparent experts) voice favorable opinions about their products or services.

Example: As a biochemist, I appreciate the high nutritional value that is present in ****, and I serve it to my family every day.

Example: Medical doctors recommend **** twice as often as any other pain killer.

Some advertisers resort to name-calling by directly comparing their products with competing brands. They no longer refer to an anonymous Brand X, and they don't bleep out the brand name of the competing product.

Example: In a comparison with Sealy, Simmons, and five other leading brands, *Consumer Reports* judged the King Koil Spinal Guard mattress to be the most durable.

The most convincing way to support advertising claims, perhaps, is with statistics.

Example: The **** has an automatic transmission that reduces the engine RPMs by 31 percent in overdrive and delivers smooth, quiet, powerful performance. These features are enhanced by a 2.6 liter, 6 cylinder overhead cam engine—a combination that is unique to the new ****.

Example: With the ****, a typist can format page sizes up to 254 characters wide and 99 lines long. The low-cost diskettes (4 inches by 4 inches) store up to 70,000 characters each, to satisfy the demands of most typing jobs.

The objective of these various appeals, you will recall, is to convince consumers that our initial claims are credible, to convince them that our products and services are more appropriate for their needs and wants than competing products might be.

ASKING FOR ACTION

Having established cognitive dissonance by creating a nagging desire for the product or service being promoted, advertisers usually end their persuasive messages with appeals for action. They show consumers how mental comfort can be restored by purchasing the advertised items.

> Example: Put yourself in the picture when you buy or lease a new **** at your **** dealer—today!
>
> Example: Why don't you begin your subscription to **** right now by calling (800) 866-4711, a toll-free number?

Advertisers sometimes follow a request for action by adding a statement such as "You'll be glad you did" and "Wouldn't you really rather own a ****?" But most advertising specialists contend that a greater impact is achieved when the persuasive message ends with a call for action, with no additional comments tacked on.

SAMPLE SALES MESSAGES

Let's apply this four-step approach to persuasive communications by composing a sales message for a certain brand of moped (motorized bicycle).

Persuasive message—advertisement for a moped

Attract attention	More than 100 miles per gallon?
Maintain interest	No, we're not kidding. And when you swing your Ronda Moped into a filling station and say "fill 'er up," you'll be talking about pennies—not dollars.
Present evidence	The Ronda's two-stroke engine will speed you along at 30 mph for 125 miles on each gallon of regular gasoline. Farther if you decide to pedal part of the way.
	The Ronda Moped is great for your trips to school, the store, the beach, almost anywhere. No clutching. No shifting. No parking problems. Just smooth, fun-filled riding.
Ask for action	See for yourself. Drop in at any Ronda dealership first chance for a free trial ride.

Notice that product and place are emphasized, and that price is not mentioned. Notice also that long sentences in advertisements are *out* and short sentences and sentence fragments are *in*.

The length of the advertising message depends on the medium. If this were to be a radio or television commercial, for example, we would plan the message to fit the allotted time. Whatever the medium, though, we should avoid the temptation to say all there is to say about a product. When too many words are crammed into a limited space, people are inclined to block out the entire message.

As a second example of persuasive messages, let's consider a home refrigerator. Although competitive, the price of the Alaskan refrigerator is not a main selling point. The unit has all the usual features, plus a new snap-out ice maker.

Persuasive message—advertisement for a refrigerator

Attract attention	No more yelling at the kids. No more wasted energy.
Maintain interest	Not with the Alaskan's new snap-out ice cubes.
	The Alaskan refrigerator has tempered glass shelves, patterned steel doors, cold water tap, humidrawer control, 10-day meat keeper, egg bin, slide-out freezer drawers—all the standard features.
Present evidence	But the Alaskan also has snap-out ice cubes. No more standing there with the freezer door wide open. Just press a button and out snaps a cube. The family-size bin holds up to 300 cubes. Use one cube at a time or remove the entire bin. A super convenience. And practical too.
Ask for action	See the new Alaskan refrigerator in an exciting array of rich colors. Today. At most appliance stores.

Now, let's consider a service—a weight-loss clinic which includes the usual exercise programs. The service is directed at both men and women, and a special price is being offered through June 1. As in the preceding examples, our attention-getting opener is brief, and we lure consumers into the verbal picture we are drawing with frequent use of the word *you*.

Persuasive message—advertisement for a weight-loss clinic

Attract attention	Last chance before going swimming.
Maintain interest	You'll look great this summer in al-

most any of the new slim-line bathing suits if you let Slim-N-Trim help you trim off that excess weight.

Present evidence	Under the individually programmed guidance of our professional staff of doctors and nurses, along with a sensible diet, you will see those unattractive layers of fat fade away—quickly, safely, beautifully.
	Both men and women may enjoy our 3-week introductory program for only $10.* Includes participation in aerobic exercise classes and full use of our jogging track, exercise equipment, whirlpool, and sauna.
Ask for action	Stay in the swim of things. Call 934-2611 for an appointment with one of our weight counselors. And bring along a chubby friend.
	*Offer expires June 1.

Persuasive techniques are not confined to sales messages. We also use memos, letters, and conversations as tools of persuasion. If we were trying to persuade the managers of the company where we work to take a certain type of action, for example, we could follow the same persuasive format.

Persuasive message—interoffice memorandum

Attract attention	We recommend that a second shift of workers be added beginning October 1, and that construction of the proposed factory be temporarily postponed.
Maintain interest	Although we will have to pay a penalty rate for approximately 125 hours of overtime worked each day, the cost will be more than offset by the greater utilization of existing facilities. Postponement of construction will reduce the risk of loss in the event of a recession, and we probably will not have to pay as high a rate of interest on funds borrowed at a later date.
Present evidence	We have ample capacity for our existing plants, by adding a second shift of workers, to satisfy projected sales until about December, 1985.
	Several workers are prepared to assume supervisory positions, and we can

hire additional supervisors from outside the company. Any shortages of managerial personnel will be filled by having our supervisors work anywhere from 10 to 20 hours overtime each week. The supply of unskilled labor is ample, but it will be necessary for us to assign from 10 to 20 hours of overtime to certain skilled employees. (Expanded report attached.)

Interest rates on building funds have never been higher than at present—from 15 to 20 percent per annum. By postponing new construction for at least two years, therefore, we should be able to secure a borrowing rate that is low enough to offset the continuing effects of inflation.

Ask for action   If you agree with these recommendations, will you please authorize the addition of a second shift and postponement of construction.

We know that the addressee will read this interoffice memo; therefore, we do not have to give much thought to attracting attention. But we are trying to persuade this person to approve our recommendations, and a persuasive approach will go a long way toward helping us achieve what we want.

CHECKLIST: PERSUASIVE COMMUNICATIONS

Product
- Is the product superior? Unique? New? Improved?
- Does the packaging have identifying characteristics?
- Is the product or service guaranteed?
- Has maintenance been simplified?

Price
- Is the product or service competitively priced?
- Is the prevailing price limited to a specific time period?
- Is this a sales item?
- Does the price include delivery? Installation? Servicing?
- Should price be deemphasized or avoided entirely?
- Should the item be promoted as worth a relatively high price?

Place

- Where can the product or service be purchased?
- Is the product or service presently available?
- Is the point of purchase more convenient than those of competitors?

Promotion

- Are there any promotional gimmicks that may be used? A chance to win something? A free gift for taking prompt buying action? A cash rebate?

Attract attention by:

- Calling attention to the "new and improved" status of the product or service.
- Stressing the importance of taking prompt buying action.
- Outlining possible adverse consequences of not owning the item.
- Showing consumers how they can save money by buying the product or service.
- Informing consumers that many other people are already benefiting from use of the product or service.
- Implying that the item is intended for only certain types of people—a select group.
- Suggesting that use of the product or service tends to make the user more attractive to the opposite sex.

Maintain interest by:

- Making enticing (but supportable) claims about the product (service), price, or place.

Present evidence by:

- Using the endorsement of a famous person.
- Conveying the opinion of an expert.
- Comparing with competing brands.
- Presenting supportive data.

Ask for action by urging consumers to:

- Request additional information.
- Take immediate buying action.
- Make similar comparisons for themselves.
- "Come in" for a demonstration.
- Sample the product or service.

15

ASKING FOR MONEY

Many businesses sell their products and services on credit, and the people in their accounts receivable departments are responsible for collecting these debts. But asking customers to pay their bills can be a sensitive task; business people want to collect money that is due their companies, but they do not want to lose valuable customers during the collection process.

What about people who don't pay their bills on time? Businesses that sell directly to consumers may charge their customers interest on unpaid balances; if no payments are forthcoming, they may discontinue further credit sales. But consider the dilemma of business people who sell their products and services to other businesses. What can be done when the late-paying customer is a giant corporation? If sellers become too demanding in their collection efforts, large corporations may cease doing business with them; and canceling the credit of a large business customer is almost unthinkable.

But don't big corporations generally pay their bills on time? A surprisingly large number do not. With high interest rates (the cost of borrowing money), many companies retain money as long as they can—urging people who owe money to them to pay promptly, while delaying payments that they owe to other companies. As you can see, therefore, the writing of credit letters requires good judgment and an effective plan of action.

THE GAME PLAN

We usually begin the collection process with a friendly reminder, gradually strengthening our approach to the point where we issue a final warning. We start out as "nice guys" and systematically

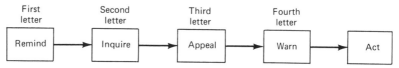

Figure 15-1 Steps in the collection process.

strengthen our appeals. This four-step procedure is outlined in Figure 15-1. Why, you might ask, can't we just telephone slow-paying customers? Since both the men and the women of most households now work, many telephone calls to residences during the daytime would go unanswered. Also, according to recently enacted consumer credit laws, telephone calls after normal business hours may be viewed as undue harassment of debtors.

It would be even more impractical to phone businesses regularly for information about past-due bills. People in the accounts payable departments of businesses cannot readily determine the status of the many bills they process for payment each day; and the cost of phone calls and the expenditure of employee time for making the calls would be prohibitive.

An additional drawback to the use of telephones for collection purposes is that telephones leave us without written records. The file copies of collection letters, on the other hand, can be used as evidence that we are treating all customers equally. The law requires that we be consistent in our treatment of customers, not pressing some customers for the prompt payment of bills while overlooking slow payment by others.

ROUTINE REMINDER

We don't want to wait many days after bills have become due before sending a reminder. If we let many of our customers pay late as a matter of practice, we would soon have thousands of additional dollars outstanding—money that is rightfully ours, money that we should be investing to increase our income. Within a day or so after bills become delinquent, therefore, we should send reminder letters, mailgrams, or telegrams.

Except for those customers who habitually pay late, we give our customers the benefit of the doubt. Maybe they have overlooked the bill. Maybe they have been on vacation. It is even possible that they have already paid the bills that we are writing about. We neither scold nor accuse; we simply remind customers that their payments are past due. Consider the following letter to a consumer and the other to a business customer.

Reminder letter—to a consumer
Did you forget about us?
The first of two $500 payments came due four days ago, but we still haven't received payment.
If you have not already done so, Ms. Smith, will you please send a check to us today?

Reminder letter—to a business customer
Our records show that we have not yet received payment for Invoice 10705 which, under the prevailing terms of sale, became past due September 12.
Will you please check to make certain that this invoice has been received and processed for payment.
Thank you.

Both letters outline the situation and provide friendly reminders. Some companies substitute humorous cards for reminder letters, as illustrated in Figure 15-2. Comments at the bottom actually appear on the inside of the cards, where there is ample space for the sender

Figure 15-2 Cartoon cards as substitutes for reminder credit letters. (Courtesy Harrison Publishing Co., Asheville, NC.)

to include brief messages. These cards are not inexpensive, even when purchased in large quantities, but you will recall from Chapter 8 that the cost of producing business letters is usually much higher.

LETTER OF INQUIRY

When customers do not respond to our reminders within a reasonable time, we follow up with a letter of inquiry. We assume a "What's wrong?" and "How can we help you?" attitude. The following examples are continuations of the preceding situations.

Letter of inquiry—to a consumer

Why haven't you responded to our letter of June 10?

The first payment of $500 is now 20 days past due, and the second payment of $500 becomes due just 10 days from today.

If unavoidable circumstances have prevented you from paying at the agreed times, please come in and talk the situation over with us. You will find us to be reasonable and cooperative; and we will do our best to arrange some terms that you can manage.

If nonpayment has merely been an oversight, on the other hand, will you please send a check to us at this time for the $1,000 balance.

Letter of inquiry—to a business customer

This letter is our second inquiry concerning our Invoice 16765, the payment of which is now 25 days past due.

Did you receive the invoice? Have you processed it for payment? Has a check been issued?

We are attaching a copy of the invoice, with the thought that the original might have been lost in the mail or otherwise misplaced.

May we have your payment of $1,212.50 right away, please.

Yes, we are pressing them a little. As already indicated, some people habitually use money that rightfully belongs to their creditors by paying their bills as late as possible. It is advisable to sound a note of urgency in these second letters, therefore, to convince customers that we expect to be paid on time.

We must be careful not to overstate our position during this second step in the collection process. Maybe there has been a tragedy within the consumer's family. Maybe the invoice actually was misplaced or lost. Or, as often happens, maybe the customer's check was misplaced or misapplied by employees in our own company.

APPEAL FOR ACTION

If and when our second communication is ignored, we make an urgent appeal for action. We want our money, and we want it now. We do so by appealing to the customer's sense of fair play. We also appeal to the customer's honor, pride, and self-interest. The following letters illustrate this approach.

Letter of appeal—to a consumer

When you purchased your new dining room furniture on April 15, you agreed to pay the balance of $1,000 in two monthly payments, $500 on June 1 and $500 on July 1.

We extended these interest-free terms to you as a matter of courtesy, Ms. Smith, on the basis of your credit standing within the community and your agreement to make payments on the designated dates.

Won't you honor that agreement and protect your credit reputation by making payment at this time? You may clear the account by paying $1,000 before July 15; otherwise, we shall begin assessing interest charges from that date at the rate of 1½ percent per month.

Letter of appeal—to a business customer

Although we recently reminded you that Invoice 16765 for $1,212.50 was seriously past due, our records show that as of October 20 the invoice remains unpaid.

We value your business, but we must receive payment within the next few days if we are to continue serving you on a credit basis. Will you please send a check to us today? If extenuating circumstances prevent your making payment at this time, please sign and return the enclosed interest-bearing note— along with an explanation.

Please help us continue our mutually beneficial business relationship by taking immediate action to correct this unfair and unfortunate situation.

We communicated our messages loud and clear, but we left the door open for corrective action. If customers act promptly on our suggestions, we may be able to salvage the business relationship. And, as most salespeople will attest, attracting and keeping customers are essential functions in any business.

AN ULTIMATUM

By the time we reach the fourth step in the collection process, we have waited for our money for a significant period and have undergone the expense of writing and mailing three communications. We must now issue an ultimatum, as illustrated in the following two letters.

Letter of ultimatum—to a consumer
Since our three previous letters have gone unanswered, Ms. Smith, we must demand your immediate payment of $1,000, plus $15 interest, a total of $1,015.
Payment by August 15 is your last opportunity to settle this account without jeopardizing your credit rating. We plan to file a breach-of-contract report at that time with Central Credit Agencies.
Also, if payment is not received by August 15, we will take immediate action to repossess the dining room furniture.
What are we to do, Ms. Smith? Our course of action depends entirely on you.

Letter of ultimatum—to a business customer
Because of your failure to respond to our previous inquiries concerning payment of Invoice 16765, we must suspend any further credit sales to your company.
Moreover, if payment in full (including interest at the rate of 15 percent annually from September 12 to the date of payment) is not received by November 30, we will be forced to assign the account to a collection agency.
Why don't you restore your credit standing with us and avoid future unpleasantries by making payment at this time.

We have issued ultimatums, certainly; but we have still allowed these customers to take positive action. We may be reluctant to sell to them on the same credit terms as before, but we probably haven't lost them forever as customers. By maintaining a firm but helpful attitude throughout the collection process, we may avoid adverse reactions from customers who would be offended by unduly harsh communications.

There is nothing sacred about this four-step approach to the collection process. The number of messages sent and their timing depends entirely on the situation. We may send telegrams to customers when large amounts of money are involved and write letters for all other delinquent accounts. We might write individual letters regarding large debts and send form letters for smaller ones.

Because it is impossible to present sample credit letters for every possible situation, the letters presented in this chapter are used only to illustrate one approach to the collection process, *not* as a guide for all collection communications. The tone and style of effective collection messages depend on several variables: the type of company you work for, its credit policy, industry patterns, and the customer's payment record.

CHECKLIST: COLLECTION COMMUNICATIONS

Routine reminder
- Act promptly to let customers know that we expect them to pay on time.
- Assume that the customer has merely overlooked payment.
- Maintain a friendly tone, frequently using the words *please* and *thank you*.
- Consider the use of cartoon cards.

Letter of inquiry
- Try to determine what is preventing payment.
- Maintain a helpful attitude.
- Consider the practicality of asking for payment in full at this time.
- Keep it friendly—no accusations, no insinuations.
- Enclose a copy of the invoice (bill) if practical.
- Use a tone of urgency, but continue giving the customer the benefit of any doubts you may have.
- Consider the possibility of extenuating circumstances.

Appeal for action
- Ask for immediate action.
- Appeal to the customer's sense of fair play.
- Refer to protection of the customer's honor.
- Appeal to the customer's self-interest, honor, and pride.
- Suggest that the customer protect his credit standing by paying now.
- Hedge your remarks with such qualifers as "Our records show that . . ." to avoid potentially embarrassing statements.
- Consider the imposition of penalty charges.
- Mention the possibility that credit sales may be discontinued.
- Provide alternative courses of action when possible.
- Maintain a positive attitude about future business relationships—if the customer pays now.
- Try to maintain the customer's goodwill.

Final warning

- Issue an ultimatum: discontinuation of credit sales, issuance of damaging credit statements, repossession of products, use of a collection agency.
- Maintain a businesslike approach.
- Leave the door open for positive action by the customer for restoration of a viable seller-buyer relationship.

Remember, credit letters should be designed specifically for each business situation, and these sample letters are intended only as illustrations of the four-step collection process.

Finally, don't overlook the potential benefits of using the S*T*A*R approach (page 75) when writing collection messages.

16

SPECIAL COMMUNICATIONS

Business people must occasionally write letters and memos that fall outside the scope of what might be labeled "typical business correspondence." Sometimes they congratulate their counterparts for promotions earned and subordinates for outstanding performance. Deaths and illnesses require thoughtful letters of consolation. Business people write letters or memos to welcome newly hired employees, and they frequently send written messages to simply say "thank you."

This chapter contains helpful guidelines for these types of communications, along with a set of sample letters for each type. Note also that Chapters 22 and 24 deal with a wide variety of employment communications, ranging from application letters to letters of resignation, and that Chapter 20 includes a transmittal memorandum.

COMMENDATION LETTERS

Letters and memos of commendation should be presented to subordinates who have demonstrated outstanding performance and to colleagues who have earned promotions.

	Commendation letters	
	To a subordinate	*To a colleague*
Begin with praise	I was very pleased to learn of your recent academic accomplishments.	Congratulations, Jack! And a great big handshake.
Add specifics	Attending night school while working full time during the day is quite a challenge for anyone, and pulling a high grade-point	Your educational background and experience made you the ideal candidate for the position. Everyone here seems to agree

	average and an honorable mention from the Dean requires both intelligence and perseverance.	with this assessment, and we all stand ready with any support that might be needed.
Close with a pleasant look toward the future	Keep up the good work, Carolyn, and let us know if there is any way that we can adjust the work schedule to accommodate your continued studies.	I could close by wishing you luck, but realize that your success in any job is based on a much more solid foundation.

CONSOLATION MESSAGES

Letters that offer consolation are sometimes necessary in business, most generally to incapacitated employees and to families of deceased employees.

Consolation messages

	Illness	*Death*
Allude to the situation	Just a brief note, Marla, to let you know that we are thinking of you.	May we offer our most sincere condolences on the passing of your beloved husband.
Emphasize the person's importance	Management should express its appreciation to dedicated employees more frequently perhaps, not just when forced to get along without them. And, as you can see from all of the signatures on the enclosed card, you <u>are</u> being missed.	Your loss was the greatest, of course, but Chuck had also become an important part of our lives. Not only did he play a pivotal role here in the marketing department, he had over the years become our unofficial mentor and counselor. He will be greatly missed by us all.
Offer best wishes (illness) or sympathy (death)	The progress reports that we have been receiving from your husband are very encouraging, and we all look forward to your full recovery.	Again, Mrs. Mitchell, I convey the heartfelt sympathy of every employee at this company.

THANK-YOU LETTERS

Letters of thanks may be written in appreciation for an order from a new or established customer, a courtesy shown a sales representative, or a host of other business situations. Such communications are good public relations because they let people know that we do not take their business or their contributions for granted.

Thank-you letters

	For a warm reception	*To a new account*
Thank them	I wish to thank you personally for the courtesies extended to Maria Sanchez when she called at your office last week.	Thank you for placing your highly valued account with our agency. Gil Swanson just phoned the good news, and all of us here at Dunn & Smythe are elated.
Allude to relevant details	Maria indicated that you are favorably impressed with our new packaging, and has requested that two additional samples be sent to you. We are sending them today via UPS.	Beginning with preliminary analysis of your current advertising schedule, with regard to both content and cost, we will develop a comprehensive proposal for the ensuing year. Alberta Redding, who is being assigned full time to your account, will coordinate the preliminary analysis and present you with a tentative timetable of events within the next week to ten days.
Restate your gratitude	Thanks again, Mr. Appleton, and please let me know if any additional information is required.	We appreciate your vote of confidence, Mr. Batastini, and look forward to a mutally profitable association with you and your firm.

WELCOME LETTERS

Welcome letters are used to secure the goodwill of such groups as customers, suppliers, and stockholders. Welcome messages also take the form of interoffice memos when greeting new employees.

Welcome letters

	To a new broker	*To a new employee*
Welcome them	We are very pleased to be the beneficiary of the extraordinary strength that your company adds to an already impressive list of brokers.	One of our favorite duties is that of welcoming employees like you to our organization. We are happy to have you with us.
Include relevant details	Three copies of our standard contract are enclosed. You will note that commis-	As a new employee, you are undoubtedly interested in learning more about the

sion checks are mailed on the 15th of every month, at a standard rate of 3 percent on the net sales of brand-label merchandise and 2 percent on all private-label sales. Please sign and return all three copies, one of which will be signed here and returned to you.

Also enclosed are warehouse differential schedules and instructions for completing our FC (from consignment) invoices. An initial supply of invoices is being mailed separately.

Add a positive look toward the future

This agreement should be the start of a mutually rewarding association, Doug, with your company spearheading our entry into the lucrative Denver market.

many employee benefits that our company provides. The enclosed brochures and accompanying application forms pertain to our health and life insurance coverage. Please return the completed forms to us at your first opportunity so that we may initiate coverage as soon as possible. Forms for our pension program will be made available upon completion of sixty days of employment.

We look forward to working with you, and are always available for any questions that you may have.

Add to the effectiveness of your memos and letters by typing them in an attractive and correct format. For details and samples, see Chapter 6 (Writing Interoffice Memos) and Chapter 7 (Adopting a Letter Style).

IV

BUSINESS REPORTS

Skills in report writing are essential in many areas of business, because reports are the most widely used form of upward communication within these organizations. Reports are used routinely to keep managers informed of progress within the areas of the company for which they are personally responsible, and business managers also have recurring needs for special information that is most effectively conveyed through written reports.

This section of the book deals with common elements in the planning, researching, and writing of reports—reports that will be well-received in business, government, academic, or any other organizational setting.

17

PLANNING THE STUDY

Do you respond negatively when someone asks you to write a report, as so many people do? Or do you view the preparation of reports as an opportunity to advance yourself in business? You will be more likely to adopt a positive attitude toward report writing after you have been introduced to the five steps in report preparation outlined in Figure 17-1. The first three steps involve subject matter, preliminary research, and outline preparation—all of which are dealt with in this chapter. Chapter 18 is devoted to Step 4, researching the topic; Chapter 19 shows you how to prepare graphic illustrations; and Chapter 20 deals with the essential elements of a semiformal report, Step 5.

SELECT A TOPIC

In some business situations, you will not have the privilege of selecting a topic on which to report; your superior will outline the area of study. But alert employees observe details in company operations that should be analyzed, and they request permission to conduct studies and submit written reports on their findings. Why would people of sound mind make such offers? Because they realize that well-conceived and well-written reports impress all who read them.

In either case, you would do well to base your choice of topics on as many of the following criteria as possible: First, make certain

Figure 17-1 Key steps in report preparation.

Step 1	Step 2	Step 3	Step 4	Step 5
Select a topic	Conduct preliminary investigation	Prepare an outline	Research the topic	Write the report

that the topic is directly related to a part of the business in which you have a legitimate interest. If you work in the production department, for example, a report in the marketing area would probably be unappreciated.

Second, select a timely topic. A subject that has current interest will be more relevant to whoever reads your report, and the availability of current newspaper and magazine articles will make a timely subject easier for you to research.

Third, choose a topic that isn't too broad. Rather than assimilating data on total transportation costs incurred by your company, for example, analyze the situation in only one segment of the overall operation. Rather than studying marketing trends throughout the country, consider the effects of a declining birth rate on a specific product. Keep the topic sufficiently narrow to where your reported findings will have a direct influence on managerial planning and company operations.

Fourth, pick a topic that you find interesting. If you have a genuine interest in the chosen subject, the research effort will become an enjoyable adventure. And as you broaden your knowledge of the subject, you may be able to expand the initial study into more comprehensive reports for future report-writing challenges.

CONDUCT
PRELIMINARY INVESTIGATION

Test the topic you have chosen before fully committing yourself to it. If you plan to study a morale problem in your company, sample the feelings of several employees throughout the company to make fairly certain that a problem actually exists. If you plan to report on the adverse effects of wage legislation, locate some newspaper and magazine articles that relate to the topic, to make sure that you will be able to find sufficient data supporting this view.

Maybe you have formulated some thoughts about a subject through observation. You may have noticed over the course of several weeks or months, for example, that the movement of a certain product through the factory and the warehouse is not as efficient as it could be, or you may have observed that the flow of paper through an office could be improved. Regardless of the method used, you should base your report on some prior knowledge of the subject to be studied.

Instructors in graduate schools and scientists often base their studies and the resulting reports on hypotheses (plural for hypothesis). A hypothesis is an informed guess, a guess that is based on a limited knowledge of the subject that is to be studied. In analyzing the effects of minimum-wage legislation, as previously mentioned, we might base our study on the following hypothesis: "The minimum wage requirement is detrimental to teenage employment within our firm." We would then conduct a study to prove or disprove the hypothesis. Note, however, that a hypothesis is not applicable to many business reports, because not all studies involve concrete statements that are to be proved or disproved.

Researchers often follow what is called the scientific method. Rather than approaching a study in a hit-or-miss fashion, they (1) make a clear and concise statement of the problem in writing, (2) gather and analyze all available data pertaining to the problem, (3) develop alternative courses of action on the basis of that information, and (4) choose and implement the best alternative. The scientific method of study provides the best approach for ensuring that your planning is sound, objective, and comprehensive.

PREPARE AN OUTLINE

How do you suppose authors write books? Do you imagine that the author of this book just started writing one day with the hope that the words, sentences, paragraphs, and chapters would fall into place as he went along? Of course not; when beginning a new book, he first outlines the main divisions and chapters. Then, after planning the main parts of each chapter, he decides which points are to be discussed in each part of each chapter. Sure, this procedure consumes a lot of time, but a complete outline provides organization and direction, prevents repetition, and allows him to divide a book into manageable parts.

An outline represents the same useful tool in report writing. Once you have organized your ideas on paper, you can begin researching the topic systematically and confidently. Begin your outline by dividing the study into three to five main parts, as shown below (these are main parts for two separate reports).

Advertising is surviving

    I. Problems in advertising

    II. Changing image of advertising

    III. Future role of advertising

    IV. Summary and conclusions

Investing in stocks and bonds

    I. Understanding securities exchanges

    II. Securing market information

    III. Selecting appropriate investments

IV. Making securities transactions

V. Summary

Organize the main divisions of your report into a logical sequence:

1. Time sequence—going from the past to the present to the future.
2. Cause and effect—identifying a problem, its cause and effects, and possibly offering a solution.
3. Level of importance—progressing from the most important item to the least important, or vice versa.
4. Routine procedures—following steps normally taken in a well-established function, such as beginning a new business, opening an account with a stockbroker, and hiring new employees.
5. Five Ws and an H—answering as many of the following questions about the topic as possible: What? Where? When? Why? Who? How?
6. Deductive approach—beginning with a statement of your findings and then providing explanations and supporting data.
7. Inductive approach—presenting explanations and supporting data, followed by a statement of your conclusions.

Then, to form complete outlines as illustrated below in two completed outlines, divide all but the closing parts of your main divisions into several subdivisions.

Advertising is surviving

    I. Problems in advertising

      A. Excessive claims

      B. Youthful impressions

      C. Credibility gap

    II. Changing image of advertising

      A. Industry self-regulation

      B. Consumer pressures

      C. Restrictive legislation

   III. Future role of advertising

      A. Ideas that aid consumers

      B. Advertising that adds value

      C. Truth in advertising

   IV. Summary and conclusions

Investing in stocks and bonds

    I. Understanding securities exchanges

      A. New York Stock Exchange

B. American Stock Exchange
C. Over-the-counter market
II. Securing market information
A. Regular publications
B. Television and radio reports
C. Financial services
D. Corporate publications
III. Selecting appropriate investments
A. High price or low price
B. Risk or certainty
C. Growth or income
D. Value or glamor
E. Bull or bear
IV. Making securities transactions
A. Opening an account
B. Making the purchase
C. Settling the transaction
D. Selling the security
V. Summary

Try to maintain parallelism in outlines, because each line becomes a heading in the report. Notice in the first outline that each of the main sections has a preposition (*in* and *of*), except for the terminal (final) section, which does not need to be parallel with the others. Each of the main headings in the second outline begins with an *ing* action word (*understanding, securing, selecting, making*), except for the terminal section. Only the main parts must be parallel with one another; they do not need to be parallel with the ABC sections.

In the same way, we consider the subsections separately from the main parts of the outline. The ABC headings in the first two sections of the first outline are parallel, and each consists of two words. Keeping the lines in each section about the same length is desirable but not mandatory. The *AB* lines in the third section contain the word *that*, while the *C* line contains the preposition *in;* we do not force parallelism in this instance because *truth in advertising* is a commonly used legal term. Each of the main parts of the second outline "Investing in Stocks and Bonds" begins with an *ing* action word, as already mentioned, but only the ABCD lines in the last section begin with action words.

Let's clarify these and other important points by analyzing the following incorrect outline. In checking parallelism, we first consider the main (Roman numeral) sections. Only the first one begins with an action word. Only the second one begins with an article. Only the third one is a complete sentence and a question.

*Establishing and operating
a health food store*

   I. Choosing the best location
      A. Strategic location
      B. Provisions of the lease
      C. Demographic patterns
      D. Traffic patterns
  II. The sources of financing
      A. Security deposit required
      B. Buying the necessary equipment
      C. The cost of beginning inventory
      D. Adequate working capital
      E. Securing a bank loan
 III. What are the legal obligations involved?
      A. Federal regulations
      B. State regulations
      C. County regulations
      D. City regulations
 IV. Sales and service considerations
      A. Buying practices
      B. Methods of pricing
      C. Credit sales
      D. Store hours
      E. Hiring employees
      F. Advertising in local newspapers
  V. Summary and conclusions

So what can we do? We can be consistent in our word choice, as illustrated by the two outlines of Roman numeral headings below. These are two examples of parallel construction:

I. Choosing the best location	I. Site selection
II. Locating favorable financing	II. Initial financing
III. Identifying legal obligations	III. Legal obligations
IV. Outlining sales strategy	IV. Sales and service
V. Summary and conclusions	V. Summary and conclusions

The outline to the left in the preceding list is parallel because each of the first four lines begins with *ing* action words. The last line in an outline usually consists of one or more of the following words: *summary, conclusions,* and *recommendations*—depending on what you plan to write in that section of the report. The outline to the right in the preceding list consists of two- and three-word lines. The fourth line contains a conjunction (and), while the first three lines do not, but this small breach in parallelism is acceptable. We don't force parallelism when the results would appear awkward.

    Both outlines are correct, because the lines in each outline are fairly consistent with one another; incomplete sentences are not mixed with complete sentences in either outline, nor are questions mixed with declarative sentences; and all the lines are about equal in length. These considerations are also reflected in the completed outline presented below.

Establishing and operating a health food store

 I. Site selection
   A. Strategic location
   B. Lease provisions
   C. Demographic patterns
   D. Traffic flow
 II. Initial financing
   A. Security deposit
   B. Equipment and fixtures
   C. Beginning inventory
   D. Working capital
   E. Bank loan
III. Legal obligations
   A. Federal taxes
   B. State regulations
   C. County requirements
   D. City regulations
 IV. Sales and service
   A. Buying practices
   B. Pricing policy
   C. Credit card sales
   D. Store hours and employment
   E. Newspaper advertising
  V. Summary and conclusions

Having already considered the Roman numeral (RN) lines, we turn our attention to the individual subsections, the ABC lines. We only need make the lines under RN-I parallel with one another, those under RN-II parallel with one another, and so on. In the original outline on page 206, the I-B line included the preposition *of*, which has been removed in the preceding outline. If one of the lines has a preposition, they all should include one, and vice versa; it is an all-or-nothing situation unless the resulting change proves awkward. Rather than repeating the word *patterns* as in the outline on page 206, we have changed the word in I-D of the corrected outline to *flow*. The action words *buying* and *securing* in II-B and II-E of this outline have been eliminated, rather than beginning all five lines with an *ing* word. Lines II-C and II-D in the improved outline begin with *ing* words, but they are not action words. These *ing* words may be used in this manner because *beginning inventory* and *working capital* are accounting terms that are commonly used in business.

These changes and others you will notice in comparing the two examples have been made to develop a tight and accurate outline that will help us (1) organize our data and (2) provide functional and attractive headings throughout the completed report. Although none of the outlines presented here reflects a special introductory section, each report would include an unlabeled introduction. This point is explained further in Chapter 20.

If six people were preparing an outline for the same study, we would probably end up with six very different outlines. Outlining can be done in a number of ways, all of which are correct so long as the main sections are parallel with one another and so long as each line within a subsection is parallel with other lines within the same subsection. Quite a lot of effort, yes, but once you have prepared a workable outline you have progressed at least halfway toward completing the final report.

18

RESEARCHING THE TOPIC

With a clear objective in mind and a tentative outline in hand, you are ready to begin researching the topic. Before beginning the research effort, however, you should secure permission to conduct the study. Once you have been given the go-ahead, assuming that your research proposal is approved, you must decide whether you are to rely on primary data, secondary data, or both; and you should develop a card system to record your findings.

RESEARCH PROPOSAL

Avoid the risk of wasted time and effort by submitting a research proposal and tentative outline to your superior. Make certain that you both agree on the type of study you have in mind, reasons the study is needed, methods for conducting the study, limitations of the study, sources of data, resources needed (if any), and estimated time of completion.

    The length of your proposal will depend on the extent and importance of the study, and it should be written in future tense with frequent use of the words *would* and *could.* You are requesting permission, so be persuasive rather than assuming. If you plan to study a problem, provide evidence that a problem exists, that a solution is needed, and that you can successfully conduct the study. If you plan to explore certain company expenditures, for example, provide evidence that the expenditures are disproportionately high and that you are prepared and qualified to make the needed analysis. Figure 18-1 shows a sample proposal. The proposal in Figure 18-1 is in memo format, but a letter would be more appropriate if it were being mailed to someone outside the company. The author of this proposal will be able to use it as the introductory section of her final report by changing the wording from the subjunctive mood

INTEROFFICE MEMORANDUM

DATE: February 21, 1982

TO: Mr. W. T. Miller, Executive Vice-President

FROM: Charlotte J. Purcell, Marketing Manager

SUBJECT: Feasibility study for retail outlets

In connection with our new policy of limited diversification, and in response
to James Mason's suggestion at yesterday's board meeting, I am requesting
authority for a study to explore the implications of a pilot project--the
establishment of a health-food outlet somewhere within the metropolitan
Phoenix area--to guage the feasibility of entering this segment of the
industry on a regional scale. Our interest in this particular project is
based on high returns being realized in the retailing of health foods, as
reported in the December, 1981 issue of Health Food Monthly:

> Inventory turnover in the retailing end of the health-food business
> is low, compared to most other types of food retailing, but a relatively
> high markup on cost (ranging from 25 to 75 percent) results in an
> average return on investment of approximately 17 percent.

We have also received favorable comments during discussions with several
individuals who presently own and operate their own (nonfranchised) health
food stores.

in conducting an exploratory study to learn more about establishing and
operating a health food store, we would secure primary data from in-depth
interviews with operators and owners of established health food stores,
from actually observing the procedures that employees follow at several
successful stores, and through direct contacts with real estate agents
and vendor representatives. Extensive secondary data are available in
the form of statistics developed by the City of Phoenix and outlying
municipalities, and from numerous publications relating to the sale,
distribution, and consumption of health foods.

The proposed study could be completed by the due data that has been established for the submission of 1984 projects, and the primary objective
would be to explore the details involved in establishing and operating
a health food store. More specifically, we plan to (1) find a suitable
location for the business, (2) secure adequate local financing, (3) establish guidelines for sales and services, (4) outline legal obligations
of the business, and (5) make a firm recommendation on whether to proceed
with the venture. The study would not include projections of profit
(loss) levels or cash flows; that information is being prepared separately
by Bill Miller.

May I have your permission to conduct this rather extensive study?

Attached: Tentative outline

Figure 18-1 Example of a research proposal.

(what she hopes to do) to past tense (what she has already accomplished).

PRIMARY DATA

Primary data consist of evidence that researchers develop themselves, usually through observations, interviews, experiments, and surveys.

Observations

Researchers may develop primary data through their personal observations of whatever it is they are studying. If researchers were analyzing the flow of baggage between airline passengers and airplanes, for example, they would be able to make definite statements about the existing system from having observed it in operation. Such evidence is usually very convincing to report readers, because most people attach high credibility to statements that are based on what researchers have personally witnessed.

Interviews

Most readers find data secured through interviews relevant and interesting, especially when interviewees are experts in their fields. If you are researching some aspect of the stock market, for example, an interview with a stockbroker may increase your knowledge on certain aspects of the subject, and information attributed to the stockbroker will add authenticity to your report. Try to arrange interviews in advance, so that the interviewees will allow sufficient time; and always have specific questions prepared for such occasions.

Experiments

When we hear the word *experiment,* most of us picture scientists in laboratories, but business people also conduct experiments regularly—both inside and outside laboratories. Before marketing new breakfast cereals, for instance, manufacturers conduct taste tests, in-home usage tests, and market tests. Subsequently, before spending hundreds of thousands of dollars to broadcast breakfast-cereal commercials, they normally conduct experiments to determine the potential effectiveness of their appeals. They show trial commercials to many children in different geographic areas, trying to learn through the children's responses whether these commercials would motivate children throughout the country to ask their parents for the advertised brands.

Companies also test the effects of advertising by making comparisons. Using two cities that are similar in such respects as size, population density, and per capita income, they run an advertisement in one city to see how much more of their product is sold compared to the other (control) city, where the advertisement is not run. They test one factor (such as an advertisement, price change, or packaging) at a time, holding all factors constant in the control city. Then, if they find that the one factor that is changed increases sales significantly in the test city, they can be fairly certain that it would be successful in other areas of the country.

Business managers sometimes conduct experiments within their own companies. By changing one factor at a time (such as an incentive system or some working condition) for the test group, while holding all factors constant for a similar (control) group, they may compare the productivity of the test group with that of the control group to see if a significant difference occurs as a result of the change.

Surveys

Surveys represent a fourth way to develop primary data. Researchers may learn how people react or might react to certain products or services simply by asking them. They may survey purchasing managers to see how they view a certain product, for example, or they may survey a group of employees to determine their views on company policies.

Surveys are usually based on carefully worded questionnaires. Consider the following questions from a questionnaire administered for a large bakery. As shoppers selected loaves of white bread (any brand) from store shelves, researchers asked them the following questions:

1. What brand of bread do you think of when I mention packaged white bread?
2. Would you please tell me what brand of packaged white bread you usually buy?
3. Which of these brands do you buy most frequently? (A list of five breads was provided.)
4. Suppose you happened to overhear two housewives in a store talking about packaged bread. Which brand of white bread would you say the women were most likely talking about if you heard the following remark: "My husband's boss is coming to dinner tonight, so I am buying this brand of white bread."
5. What if you heard this remark: "I like white bread that's really fresh and stays fresh, so I'm buying this brand"?
6. At about this time last year, what brand of packaged white bread did you use most often?

Notice that all of these questions call for specific answers—the name of a particular brand of bread. Researchers can easily calculate the number of times consumers mention a particular brand or respond to questions with concrete answers, but answers to open-ended questions, ones that call for a wide variety of personal opinions, are usually difficult to interpret. Notice also that none of these questions are "leading" questions; no question prompts consumers to respond to a particular brand of bread, because no brand names are mentioned in the questions.

Researchers concluded from the results of this study that consumers were not reacting favorably to the brand being studied, and that a large percentage of consumers had switched to competing brands during the preceding year. Correspondingly, they advised the bakery managers to adopt programs for improving the quality or image of their bread, or both.

It is advisable to test questionnaires before using them by administering them to selected small groups, to make certain that the questions will be understood and will derive the required information. Questionnaires may be administered over the telephone, in person, or through the mail. Questions that may be considered personal, such as asking a person's age or income, should be placed near the end of questionnaires, because people are more likely to answer such questions once they have already invested some time by answering earlier questions. Finally, questionnaires should be kept fairly brief to avoid exhausting interviewees to the point where they answer carelessly or stop responding altogether.

Statistical analysis

If the population (number of people or things that we are studying) is small—say, 500 or fewer—we may conduct a census by studying each person or thing. If we are concerned with whether the morale of 250 employees of a company is high or low, for example, we can instruct each employee to complete a questionnaire. When the numbers are large, researchers sample the population. If the managers of International Telephone and Telegraph Corporation wished to survey the attitudes of their more than 400,000 employees, for example, they would administer questionnaires to relatively few employees (1,000 or so, depending on the results of a preliminary sample) and project the attitudes of all employees based on the answers received from those included in the sample. Rather than checking every machine part that is produced on an assembly line, quality control personnel may check a relatively small number of them and assume with almost complete certainty that if the samples are acceptable, all the machine parts are acceptable.

Whether the results of such samples are truly representative of entire populations (all employees or all machine parts) depends on statistical analysis. Researchers may use simple formulas to (1) determine the required size of samples, that is, the number of people or things to be studied; and (2) establish a specific level of confidence in the sample results, such as 95 percent or 99 percent certainty that the results are representative of total populations. Numerous books on business statistics include detailed formulas and explanations of their applications.

SECONDARY DATA

Secondary data include facts, figures, and information recorded in books, magazines, and other types of publications. Although the subject of primary data is discussed first in this chapter, research should actually begin with a review of secondary data. If someone else has already studied the subject that you are considering, you may avoid duplication of effort by learning of their findings before beginning your own study. You may use secondary data from books and magazines that you possess, or you may use those that are available in public and school libraries.

Card catalog

To locate books in libraries, you may consult a card catalog. A set of drawers may contain cards in alphabetical order according to the names of authors, subjects, or titles; or, if the library is large, separate sets of drawers may be provided for each of these three categories. Some libraries also record this information on microfiche, filmstrips that may be viewed on television-type screens.

Each listing (card) includes the author's name, the title of the book, and a call number, such as HF 5381 S275. To locate the book represented by this number, you check a map or list provided by the library that shows where the HF books are stacked (shelved). Upon locating HF, you look for HF 5381 books, among which you will find the specific S275 book. If the book is missing from the shelf, it probably has been checked out by someone else, in which case the people at the service counter might permit you to reserve it for your use when it is returned.

Reference books

Librarians keep many of the current reference books at centrally located reference desks, and they stack earlier copies of reference books on nearby shelves. Reference books include atlases, almanacs, encyclopedias, certain government publications, and manuals.

Atlases don't consist entirely of maps. They also include detailed information on population, minerals, energy, and food in different areas of the United States and throughout the world.

Almanacs are an extremely valuable source of secondary data. The *World Almanac & Book of Facts* consists of almost 1,000 pages of statistics and information about cities and states in the United States and most foreign countries, providing facts and figures on subjects ranging from automobiles to zip codes and cataloging details of historical and current events. The *Information Please Almanac Atlas and Yearbook* also deals with a large array of subjects, including facts about colleges, the economy, health, law enforcement, news, religion, science, transportation, and a host of other topics. Almanacs are published annually and sold at most bookstores for a nominal price.

Encyclopedias contain a wide variety of secondary data, including such areas of business as accounting, advertising, economics, insurance, investments, labor relations, management, marketing, quality control, public relations, real estate, retailing, salesmanship, statistics, transportation, and wholesaling. Among the leading encyclopedias that you will find in the reference sections of most libraries are *Encyclopedia Americana, Encyclopedia Britannica,* and *Collier's Encyclopedia.*

Some government publications are kept in the reference sections of libraries, such as the annual *Statistical Abstract of the United States,* which contains a wealth of facts and figures, and *Census of Business,* for retail trade, wholesale trade, and selected service areas, which are based on the national census every ten years. Many other government publications are available, with large libraries devoting entire floors to the maintenance of government documents.

A major financial service kept in the reference sections of most and city libraries is *Moody's Manual.* These manuals (which are actually large books) are published annually to cover separately the industrial, over-the-counter, public utility, bank and financial, and transportation markets. If you are interested in learning something about American Airlines, for instance, you may consult the transportation manual. If you need information on International Business Machines, you may check the industrial manual, and so on. *Moody's Manual* provides historical and current information, including a company's address, officers, operation, and financial condition; and they generally provide statistical detail for a range of several years.

Magazine and newspaper indexes are a vital part of most library reference sections, because they enable researchers to check categorized titles of articles that relate to specific topics without having to read through hundreds or even thousands of issues. The leading indexes and their uses are explained in the following paragraphs.

Magazines
and newspapers

Magazines and newspapers are an important source of secondary data, especially for timely reports, and most libraries subscribe to several of them. When you want to locate magazine articles on a particular subject, you shouldn't look through magazines randomly; instead, you should consult one or more indexes. Indexes are published annually, and supplements are issued throughout the year to index articles that have been published since the last annual edition was printed.

Readers' Guide to Periodical Literature, the most widely used index, categorizes articles according to subject area from more than 150 magazines. At the front of each index is a list of the periodicals and reports that are indexed, showing abbreviations used for each entry—such as "Bsns W" for *Business Week* and "Mo Labor R" for *Monthly Labor Review.* Consider the following typical listing, which would be found under the heading "Business Management":

> Insider's view of a board room, R. Ladeau
> Pop Sci 84:70-2 O 5 '82

This listing indicates that the article is about a board of directors in some corporation and that it was written by R. Ladeau and published in *Popular Science* magazine, volume 84, pages 70 to 72, October 5, 1982. Magazines are called periodicals because they are published periodically: weekly, monthly, quarterly, annually.

The *Business Periodicals Index* is of special value to business people, because it deals mainly with business-related articles published in about 270 magazines. A list of the magazines indexed appears at the front of each issue, along with a list of abbreviations. Consider the following typical listing:

> Making money in high-growth stocks. W. H.
> Rentz. Bests R 82:21-2 Jl 15 '82

This listing indicates that the article relates to profits to be made by dealing in common stocks, and that it was written by W. H. Rentz and published in *Best's Review,* volume 82, pages 21 and 22, July 15, 1982.

The *New York Times Index* categorizes according to subject area all articles that have appeared in the *New York Times,* the country's leading newspaper, since the year 1913. This index, quite properly called the "master key to the news," is an invaluable tool for tracing historical events as they were reported in headlines.

Similarly, the *Wall Street Journal Index* categorizes all articles that appear in the *Wall Street Journal,* a weekday newspaper. The *Journal,* which contains many articles on business and some on

216

nonbusiness subjects, is the most widely read publication among business people. The *Index to the Christian Science Monitor* provides a similar service for researchers.

If you don't find the types of articles you are seeking listed under one category in an index, try others. If you are trying to locate articles about salesmanship but can't find what you want under that heading, also check under such headings as Marketing and Retailing. The people who prepare these indexes have lightened our research task immeasurably, but we still must use our imaginations occasionally to find correct categories. Also consult librarians for assistance in locating elusive articles.

Having used one or more of these indexes to identify articles of interest, you must then locate the publications that carry the articles. Librarians usually keep current and recent newspapers in special areas of libraries, where you may ask for a particular paper by name and date. They keep all copies of the *New York Times* and other selected newspapers on microfilm, but they destroy the actual newspapers as limited storage space dictates.

All but the smallest libraries maintain alphabetical lists of periodicals (magazines) that they carry, and in large libraries these lists consist of several books of computer printouts. One book might list the names of periodicals that begin with the letters A, B, and C; a second book might list those beginning with D through F; and so on. To locate a copy of *Industry Week* magazine, for instance, you would look under the I's and find that the call number is TS3001-745. Then, looking at a map or directory of the library, you would see that TS publications are located in a particular area of the third floor. Going to that section of the library, you find your issue of *Industry Week* bound in a large book—in date order—along with several other issues of the same magazine.

If the issue of *Industry Week* is recent, on the other hand, you would go to a section of the library called Current Periodicals, where a librarian, with knowledge of the call number that you provide, would locate the magazine and check it out to you for an hour or so—depending on the rules of the library. How recent must a magazine be to still be a current periodical? Magazines may be considered current anywhere from six months to several years, depending on library policy, before they are bound and placed in open-access stacks.

CARD SYSTEM

If you begin recording magazine references and call numbers on one piece of paper, you will soon be going around in circles. Even when dealing with as few as ten articles, you will benefit from the use of a card system.

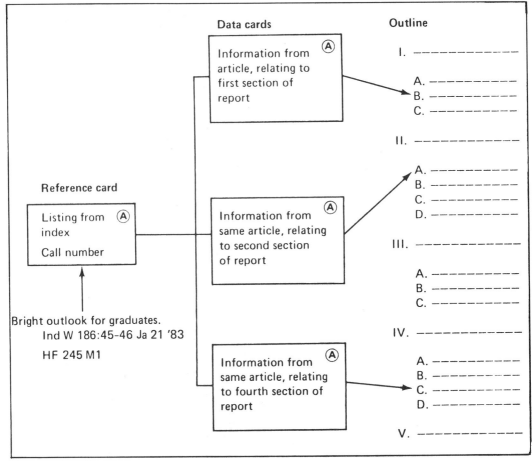

Figure 18-2 Card system for researching a report topic.

To begin with, therefore, record the magazine references that interest you, as you find them, directly from the indexes onto small reference cards. Be certain to record the references exactly as they appear in the indexes so that you won't have to retrace your steps later in search of information you overlooked.

Later, as you locate and read articles, record on large data cards all information that appears relevant to your study and report. Place different bits of information on separate data cards so that you can easily relate the cards to separate sections of your report; and cross-reference the data and reference cards as illustrated in Figure 18-2.

Notice in Figure 18-2 that all three data cards contain information from one magazine, *Industry Week*, that is listed on the one reference card, and that the data cards and reference cards are cross-referenced with the letter A. Three data cards are necessary in this instance because all three bits of information relate to different parts of the report. You should follow this same procedure throughout your library research. The size of the cards is unimportant so long as the data cards are larger than the reference cards. And whether you cross-reference with letters or numbers is immaterial so long as you relate data cards to the appropriate reference cards. A note of caution: List the related page numbers from books and periodicals on all data cards, along with the information recorded.

You may use photocopies of articles in place of data cards, which can be made for as low as 2½ to 5 cents per page, depending on whether you can fit one or two pages on a single copy. Cut the copies into several parts, if different parts of an article relate to different sections of your outline and report, but be sure to cross-reference each part of the photocopy with the corresponding reference card.

Using this system, you will end up with a small stack of reference cards and a relatively large stack of data cards and photocopies. You may then arrange and rearrange the data cards and copies to fit the outline and begin writing the report. When it is necessary to give credit to someone for information you are using, you know from the cross-reference letter (or number) which reference card to use for a footnote. The following chapter contains information about footnotes, alternatives to footnotes, and other information that is essential to good report writing.

TIME SCHEDULE

Don't wait until the last possible day to begin your study. When your boss sets a deadline for completion of a report, prepare a schedule for (1) conducting the preliminary research, (2) developing an outline, (3) completing the research, and (4) writing the report. Allow yourself sufficient time to have a rough draft on hand for at least a couple of days before finalizing the report, because when you leave a report for a while and then return to it, you will invariably see possibilities for improvement.

Another worthwhile suggestion is to read the rough draft of your report aloud. Your reading will tend to falter on sentence fragments, improper grammar, mispunctuation, and illogical statements. And that is the right time to improve the report—before it is typed in final form.

19

PREPARING GRAPHIC ILLUSTRATIONS

When business people begin writing or talking in numbers, they soon lose the interest of their audiences—unless they accompany their remarks with graphic illustrations. It is important, therefore, for you to learn to construct and use various types of tables and graphs.

TABLES

People in business commonly use tables to place numerical data in columns and rows, where readers can see more readily the relationships and meaning of numbers. Rather than trying to convey product sales information in paragraph form, for example, we may construct the following table:

TABLE 19-1. Annual Sales of Products A, B, and C for Years 1975 through 1982

Year	Product A	Product B	Product C
1975	$40,000	$25,000	$ 5,000
1976	45,000	27,500	7,500
1977	37,500	25,000	10,000
1978	40,000	28,000	15,000
1979	32,000	22,500	15,000
1980	35,000	29,000	17,000
1981	30,000	23,000	18,000
1982	28,500	24,750	21,750

Tables must be properly labeled so that they tell the reader exactly what the data represent. Table 19-1 tells the reader that the data are for sales of three separate products for an eight-year period and that (1) sales of Product A have declined to a significant degree, (2) sales of Product B have fluctuated from year to year but with no

significant increase or decrease for the eight-year period, and (3)
sales of Product C have increased continuously.

LINE GRAPHS

We may present a still clearer picture of the sales data given in
Table 19-1 with a line graph. Although line graphs may consist of as
many as four sections (quadrants), most line graphs in business
contain only one quadrant, with the bottom line as the horizontal
axis and the side line as the vertical axis.

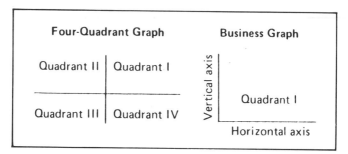

Let's begin a line graph by plotting the sales data from Table
19-1 for Product A. Normally, time is shown on the horizontal axis
and dollar amounts on the vertical axis; to avoid the use of lengthy
numbers, we often list money in thousands, millions, or even billions of dollars. To plot the sales for Product A in 1975, we place a
dot directly above the year 1975 at the 40 ($40,000) level. We place
dots above each of the years in the same manner, as shown in Figure
19-1, and we connect the dots with a continuous line, as shown in
Figure 19-2.

Figure 19-1.

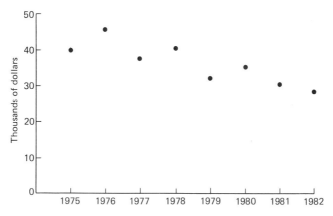

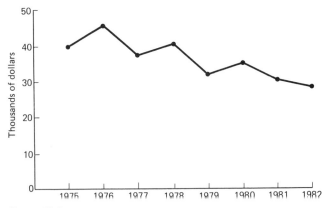

Figure 19-2.

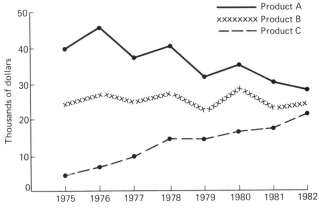

Figure 19-3 Annual sales of Products A, B, and C.

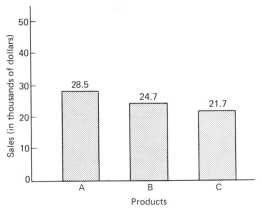

Figure 19-4 Product sales for 1982.

We then complete the graph by plotting the sales for Products B and C and by adding a description (labeling) of the information contained in the graph. The complete graph in Figure 19-3 presents readers with a vivid illustration of sales trends for these three products.

Notice in Figure 19-3 that Product A is represented by a continuous line, Product B by a series of small crosses, and Product C by dashes so that the reader can distinguish one product from another. Such distinctions are especially important when the lines cross one another, as these three product lines seem destined to do. We may also distinguish one line from the other on graphs by using a different-colored pen or pencil for each line.

BAR GRAPHS

We sometimes use bar graphs for the presentation of business data. Although a single bar graph cannot be used to illustrate sales data given in Table 19-1 for the three products for each of the eight years, we can plot the sales on a bar graph for a single time period—either a one-year period or the total of two or more years. Figure 19-4 shows a vertical bar graph for 1982 sales, and Figure 19-5 presents the same data in a horizontal bar graph.

Figure 19-5 Product sales for 1982.

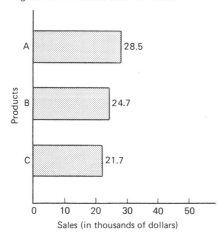

Figure 19-6 Compass.

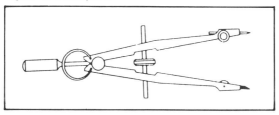

CIRCLE GRAPHS

Circle graphs, sometimes called "pie graphs," provide us with another method of presenting business data. Again using the data given in Table 19-1 for 1982 sales (one time period only), we follow six steps to construct a circle graph.

Step 1: Compute the total amount of whatever it is that you are plotting. Since we are concerned with sales for 1982, we total the sales for the three products:
28,500 + 24,750 + 21,750 = $75,000.

Step 2: Calculate the percentage that each segment is of the total by dividing each segment by the total.
28,500 ÷ 75,000 = 0.38
24,750 ÷ 75,000 = 0.33
21,750 ÷ 75,000 = $\underline{0.29}$
1.00

Step 3: Multiply the percentages by 360 (the number of degrees in a circle).
0.38 × 360 = 136.8
0.33 × 360 = 118.8
0.29 × 360 = $\underline{104.4}$
360.0
(Sum of degrees should always be 360 degrees.)

Step 4: Draw a circle with a compass (Figure 19-6), marking the place where the steel point is placed on the paper. The size of the circle depends on your needs, and the same steps are taken for a very small circle as for a very large one.

Step 5: Use a protractor (Figure 19-7) to mark the degrees. Place the center of the flat part of the protractor at the center of the circle, as shown in the accompanying drawing, and draw a straight line from the center to the right edge of the circle. Follow the scale from the

Figure 19-7 Protractor.

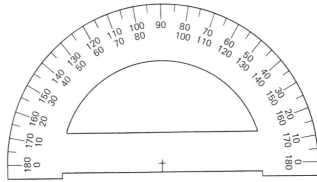

224

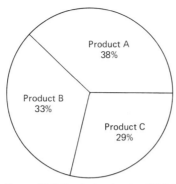

Figure 19-8 Product sales for 1980 (percentage of total sales).

lower right of the protractor to the 136.8 (137 is close enough) and draw a straight line from that point to the center of the circle. Then place the flat part of the protractor on the newly drawn line, with the center mark placed at the center of the circle, and mark 119 degrees for Product B. The area of the circle remaining is the 29 percent for Product C.

The completed circle graph of Figure 19-8 is shown after the segments and the graph itself have been properly labeled.

COMPONENT GRAPHS

We can also use line graphs and bar graphs to show the various components that, together, comprise a whole, as illustrated in Figures 19-9 and 19-10. Figure 19-9 provides us with information not just of total company income (as specified by the top line), but also a clear picture of the relationships between costs, expenses, and net income (profit). Costs for 1978 were $240,000, the three zeros at the top left indicating that the dollar amounts are being stated in thousands. Costs were $280,000 in 1979, $300,000 in 1980, and so on.

Expenses for 1978 were $60,000. Rather than plotting (placing a dot for) that amount above 1978, however, we add the $60,000 to the $240,000 in costs, totaling $300,000. Similarly, we plot our $40,000 in expenses for 1978 at $340,000 (an accumulation of the $240,000 in costs, $60,000 in expenses, and a $40,000 net income).

After plotting company data in this manner for the remaining years, we can easily see that costs have increased steadily each year, that a leveling off of expenses in 1980 resulted in a widening (increasing) of net income (profits), and that a subsequent acceleration in costs and expenses resulted in a narrowing (decreasing) of net income. This graphic illustration has enabled us to identify relationships that would be very difficult to interpret from lists of figures.

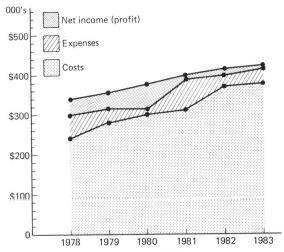

Figure 19-9 Income data, 1978–1983.

Figure 19-10 is a graphic illustration of the relationship between the earnings of a company and the dividends paid to stockholders. Notice that the amounts of money on the left are shown in units ($1, $2, etc.), not in thousands of dollars as in Figure 19-9, and that the amounts shown are "per share." From the $4.80 earnings per share in 1983, for instance, owners of the company received dividends (share of company earnings) of $1.75 for each share owned. The main information that we glean from this graph is that, except for a relatively small dividend paid in 1978, the payout (portion of earnings paid to owners as dividends) has remained fairly

Figure 19-10 Earnings and dividends—per share 1978–1983

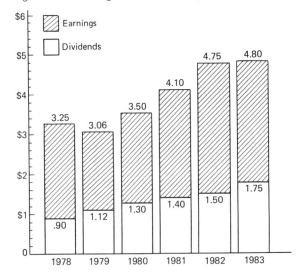

constant, with increases in earnings being closely matched with increases in dividends.

VISUAL AIDS

The table and graphs we have just discussed are suitable for inclusion in business reports as supplements to your verbal descriptions and explanations. They may also be modified for presentation on chalk boards, charts, overhead projectors, and movie projectors. But remember one important point: Visual aids must be kept relatively simple. If you burden the audience with too much detail, you will lose their interest.

Chalkboards

If your data are not extensive and if the room is not large, you may print large enough on a chalkboard so that everyone will be able to read your table or graph. Place your information on the board before your presentation, if at all possible, because too much time taken for this purpose during a presentation will lessen the impact of your materials.

Having placed tables or graphs on a board ahead of time, cover them in some way until you are ready to use the data so that the

Figure 19-11 The speaker pictured here is facing his audience directly while referring to a simple illustration on the chalkboard; notice the overhead projector and screen at the right. (Courtesy Raytheon Company.)

audience will listen to what you are saying rather than reading what you have written. Direct your voice toward the audience rather than the board; and if you must turn your head away from the audience to write or explain something on the board, be sure to raise your voice so that everyone can still hear what you are saying.

And what about that squeaking chalk? If you will take a few minutes beforehand to practice writing on a chalkboard, you will find that you can prevent this nerve-shattering noise by applying less pressure on the chalk. A practice session will also give you a good idea of the spacing and time required for illustrations that you plan to develop during the presentation.

Charts

You may decide to use charts, rather than a chalkboard, because charts can be prepared ahead of time and kept out of sight of the audience until you are ready to discuss them; and they can be used more than once. The most common-sized chart measures about 30 by 40 inches, large enough to permit everyone in the audience to read the illustration. Charts that cannot be read at the back of the room are absolutely useless to those people who happen to be sitting there, so make your drawings and letters sufficiently large and use bold colors. Dark colors can be seen from quite a distance; light colors such as pink and yellow cannot.

Face your audience when discussing a chart, permitting yourself an occasional glance at the chart; avoid standing between the chart and the people you are addressing. Some speakers avoid blocking the audience's view by using a long stick to point to the parts of the charts they are discussing.

Rooms regularly used for lecturing generally have some device for displaying charts. Check beforehand to determine whether charts may be hung from overhanging clips, tacked to a bulletin board, or taped to a wall. Many speakers use flip charts mounted on stands; when they finish with one chart, they flip it up and over to expose the chart that follows. When you use flip charts, it is a good idea to index them in some way so that you can refer to a specific chart without going through a lengthy search routine as your audience watches.

Overhead projectors

Transparencies for display with overhead projectors may be made from most documents by simply running each document (along with a blank transparency) through a multilith machine. If any part of a document is in color, however, the transparency must be made from a photocopy of the document. You may use felt-tip pens to add color to your transparencies.

Most overhead projectors may be operated from the front of the room, allowing the speaker to confront the audience directly while handling and discussing transparencies. If the projector is the type that must be placed at the back of the room, try to arrange for someone else to project the transparencies on signals given by you from the front of the room.

Transparencies are generally superior to materials displayed on chalkboards or flip charts because the materials can be magnified on the screen to a significant degree, depending on your positioning of the projector in relation to the screen. They are also easy to handle and to store. The main disadvantage of transparencies is that they must be displayed in dark or semidark rooms, which often interferes with the rapport the speaker has established with the audience; so restrict your use of them. Do not torture your audience by continually turning the lights off and on as you discuss various transparencies; once you have closed or dimmed the lights, leave them that way until you have finished showing transparencies.

You may direct the audience's attention to different parts of an illustration by pointing with a long instrument to images on the screen or by using a pen or pencil to point to different parts of the transparencies. Some speakers use their pens and pencils as arrows, laying them right on the transparencies pointed toward the appropriate part of the illustration. As with most visual illustrations used in group presentations, transparencies should not have a cluttered appearance. Although the idea that you are illustrating may be complex, the illustration should be relatively simple.

A final note: Don't wait until the moment of your presentation to experiment with the overhead projector; set up the screen and test your transparencies beforehand so that the actual presentation will run smoothly. Don't unplug an overhead projector until the cooling fan has stopped running, because doing so will probably ruin the bulb. Learn how to replace a burnt-out bulb, and always have a replacement available.

Movie projectors

Many businesses have their own film libraries, and some lend their films to groups outside their companies. If you expect to talk before groups regularly, therefore, you should take a few minutes to learn to operate a movie projector. Always preview a movie before showing it to a group, to help you introduce the film properly and to note key points for discussion following the film. A preview is also necessary to make certain that the film supports the main points of your presentation. Even projectors with automatic feeders sometimes malfunction, so avoid any last-minute panic by mounting the film well in advance of your presentation.

20
WRITING THE REPORT

Pictures, no matter how skillfully painted, have a much greater impact when placed in attractive frames. Reports also have greater impact when properly packaged, and the procedures set forth in this chapter will help you write reports that will be well received in business, government, and academic environments.

Reports consist of several parts, the number depending on the length of the report, the degree of formality involved, and the nature of the contents. When organizing the parts of your reports, place them in the following order:

> Transmittal
> Title page
> *Contents
> *Summary
> Body of report
> *Bibliography
> *Appendix

Those parts preceded with asterisks are required in some reports but not in others. Tables of contents are used when reports consist of more than ten pages. Summaries are sometimes placed near the beginning of reports that consist of more than 15 pages. Bibliographies are used when report writers must credit the contributions of others, and appendixes are useful when maps, charts, pictures, statistics, and other types of data are too voluminous to fit neatly within the related chapters.

Having established the ordering of report parts, let's discuss them in the order of preparation. The completed sample report that begins on page 244 helps to illustrate each of these parts.

TITLE PAGE

You can begin with preparation of a title page, if you have decided on a title for your report and if you know the date that you are to submit it. As illustrated in the sample report (Figure 20-2), all letters in the title are capitalized and all lines on the title page are centered. The vertical spacing of title pages for formal theses and dissertations must follow precise specifications, but there are no established guidelines for less formal academic or business reports. In the sample report, the title begins on the 10th line, and the "Presented to" begins on the 17th line after the words "Los Angeles, California." You may follow these guidelines or simply use your judgment in preparing attractive title pages, so long as you include five bits of information: (1) a title, (2) the name and identification of the recipient or recipients, (3) the location, (4) your name, and (5) the date of submission.

Titles of reports should be descriptive rather than clever, to provide others with some indication of what the reports contain; and they should be brief. Titles consisting of more than 14 words are considered too long, with those of from five to ten words considered most appropriate.

BIBLIOGRAPHY PAGE

Although the bibliography is often the last page of a report, you may find it most convenient to prepare it before beginning the actual writing. Rather than placing footnotes at the bottom of report pages or on separate footnote pages, many report writers are using numbered bibliographies. A numbered bibliography like the one in the sample report (page 256) is identical to a regular bibliography except for numbers added at the left. Sequential numbering enables you to use entries on the bibliography page as footnote references. You will notice on the first page of the sample report that the first footnote is (7:13), which refers to page 13 of the 7th entry in the bibliography, a magazine article written by Harold R. Simon. Isn't this system easy and practical? And no more *Ibid; loc. cit.,* or *op. cit.* to deal with.

In preparing a bibliography, organize your reference cards according to whether they represent books, government documents, periodicals, newspapers, pamphlets, speeches, or interviews; then arrange each group alphabetically by the last name of the first author shown. If the author's name is not given, alphabetize according to the first significant word in the title of the article. You may use the illustration in the sample report (Figure 20-2) as a guide, numbering the entries at the left only if you are preparing a numbered bibliography. Notice in the illustration that the centered heading at the top is placed on the 10th line, and that each of the following centered headings is preceded and followed by two blank lines (triple-spaced).

You may include in the bibliography any references you have consulted even when you have not used any of the information for your report. Bibliographic entries 1, 2, 5, and 6 (page 256) are included even though the writer did not make specific reference to these publications in the body of the report. She consulted them during her research effort, however, so they may have contributed to the report indirectly. Although she wasn't required to include these four references, since they were not noted in the report, she did so because they made the bibliography appear more comprehensive and impressive.

We should consider the differences between footnotes and bibliographic entries because you may sometime be required to use traditional footnotes. In the following comparisons, the letters FN stand for "footnote" and the letters BIB for a bibliography entry. Notice that the first letters are capitalized in the main words of titles of articles and publications, but not articles (*a, an, the*), conjunctions (*and, but, or, nor, for*), or prepositions (*at, because, before, between, by, in, on, through, to, until, with*).

Books with one author

FN   [1]John W. Mercer, <u>How to Retail Dietetic Foods Successfully</u> (San Francisco: Winston Press, Inc., 1980), pp. 217–18.

BIB Mercer, John W. <u>How to Retail Dietetic Foods Successfully</u>. San Francisco: Winston Press, Inc., 1980.

The FN is numbered (elevated half a line), the first line is indented five spaces, and page numbers are specified. The BIB is numbered sequentially only when it is part of a numbered bibliography; and the second line, rather than the first, is indented four spaces. Notice also that the punctuation uses periods, rather than commas, following the author's name and the title.

Books with two authors

FN   [14]Sarah P. Moore and Benjamin Stewart, <u>Health Guide for Life</u> (New York: Javitts Publishing Company, Inc., 1981), p. 315.

BIB Moore, Sarah P. and Benjamin Stewart. <u>Health Guide for Life</u>. New York: Javitts Publishing Company, Inc., 1981.

Books with more than two authors

FN   [7]Rosie S. Stein and others, <u>Marketing in the 80's</u> (Boston: Business Publishers, Inc., 1980), pp. 95–99.

BIB Stein, Rosie S. and others. <u>Marketing in the 80's</u>. Boston: Business Publishers, Inc., 1980.

Or, if you wish, you may list the names of all authors.

Broadcasts

FN   [11]"The Current Housing Dilemma," <u>CBS News Reports,</u> Columbia Broadcasting Station, January 27, 1983.

BIB "The Current Housing Dilemma." <u>CBS News Reports,</u> Columbia Broadcasting Station, January 27, 1983.

Encyclopedias

FN   [5]<u>Encyclopedia Americana</u> (1980), XLI, 541–45.

BIB <u>Encyclopedia Americana</u>. 1980. XLI, 541–45.

The year is used to locate encyclopedias, because they are revised continuously.

Government publications

FN   [8]Interstate Commerce Commission, <u>96th Annual Report</u> (Washington: Government Printing Office, 1982), p. 82.

BIB Interstate Commerce Commission. <u>96th Annual Report</u>. Washington: Government Printing Office, 1982.

Interviews

If you are using a numbered bibliography, include references to interviews; otherwise, list them only in footnotes and endnotes. Show the name of the interviewee, the person's title, the organization with which the person is affiliated, the location, and the date.

FN   [12]Interview with Lydia Gonzales, Commercial Agent, Milt Jackson and Associates, Phoenix, Arizona, March 12, 1983.

BIB Gonzales, Lydia, Commercial Agent, Milt Jackson and Associates, Phoenix, Arizona, March 12, 1983.

The BIB does not show that this was an interview, because the entry would appear under the heading INTERVIEWS in the bibliography.

Newspapers

FN ¹²"Glendale in Rapid Growth Area," <u>Glendale Star</u>, December 4, 1982, p. 5.

BIB "Glendale in Rapid Growth Area." <u>Glendale Star</u>, December 4, 1982, p. 5.

Since the date is not placed within parentheses, as in footnotes for magazine articles, the only difference between the FN and BIB for newspaper articles is the footnote number in the FN, the period after the article title in the BIB, and, of course, the different indentations.

Pamphlets

If you use data from one or more pamphlets, show as much of the following information as the pamphlets provide—in both footnote and bibliographic format—in this order: title of pamphlet, issuing organization, city of publication, and date of publication.

FN ³<u>A Comparison of Economic Systems</u>, National Federation of Business, San Rafael, California, 1983.

BIB <u>A Comparison of Economic Systems</u>. National Federation of Business, San Rafael, California, 1983.

Periodicals
with names of authors

FN ⁵Leon T. Flood, "You Aren't What You Don't Eat," <u>The Health Food Store</u>, 181 (April 4, 1982), 23.

BIB Flood, Leon T. "You Aren't What You Don't Eat." <u>The Health Food Store</u>, 181 (April 4, 1982), 23.

The number following the underscored title of the magazine is the volume number, which, despite its lack of meaning to report writers or readers, is still in general use.

The number following the date is the page number. When a reference includes both a volume and page number, the abbreviations "vol," and "p." need not be used. When a magazine such as *Business Week* has no volume number, the page number or numbers should be preceded with the abbreviation "p." (for one page) or "pp." (for more than one page). Notice that both the FN and the BIB show page numbers. When some volume numbers in your references appear in Roman numerals and some in Arabic numbers, be consistent; convert all of them to Roman numerals or all to Arabic (Arabic is preferred).

Periodicals
with author's name omitted

FN   [12]"Location Is the Name of the Game in Retailing," National Health Guide, 47 (December 1981), 10–11.

BIB "Location Is the Name of the Game in Retailing." National Health Guide, 47 (December 1981), 10–11.

Speeches

FN   [5]From a speech by Gloria P. Graham, President, Graham Fashions, University of Chicago, December 15, 1982.

BIB Graham, Gloria P., President, Graham Fashions, University of Chicago, December 15, 1982.

The BIB does not show that it was a speech, because the entry would appear under the heading SPEECHES in the bibliography.

Take a moment to study these relationships in the numbered bibliography of the sample report (page 256).

BODY OF THE REPORT

You have already gathered and sorted the data to fit your outline, so writing the body of the report should be relatively easy. This section contains several helpful guidelines, which, after you have applied them two or three times, will become routine procedure in writing attractive reports.

Placement on page

Telling employees to write attractive reports is not enough; invariably, they want specifics. Accordingly, the following measurements have become standard for most types of reports:

Top of page: Begin all writing (except page numbers) on 10th line.

Left side: Allow 1½ inches (18 spaces elite, 15 pica), so that you can attach the left side of reports to folders and notebooks.

Right side: Leave a margin of approximately 1 inch (12 spaces elite, 10 pica).

At bottom: Leave a margin of approximately 1 inch (6 blank lines).

The body of the report should be double-spaced, except for indented quotations (see page 246) and some short reports (see page 258).

These margins are also appropriate for most letters. If you use the same typewriter regularly, make a mental note of the proper margin settings, so that you won't have to be concerned with such detail every time you type a report or letter.

Page numbers

We assign a number to every page of a report, but do not place numbers on the title page or the first page of the contents, the first page of the report, the first page of the bibliography, or the first page of the appendix. We number sequentially with Roman numerals all pages preceding the body of the report, so that a report with two contents pages and a three-page summary would be numbered as follows:

  i   Title page (not shown)
 ii   1st page of Contents (not shown)
iii   2nd page of Contents
 iv   1st page of Summary (not shown)
  v   2nd page of Summary
 vi   3rd page of Summary
  1   1st page of body (not shown)
  2   2nd page of body
  .
  .
  .
 12   Bibliography (not shown)
 13   2nd page of Bibliography

The bibliography in the sample report (page 256) is actually page 12 (page number not shown); and a second page of the bibliography, if there were one, would bear the number 13. Small Roman numerals, when they are used in the front pages of reports, are placed in the center of pages, 1 inch from the bottom; and Arabic numbers in the body of the report and subsequent pages are placed on the eighth line from the top of each page, just inside the right margin.

Introductory section

Very formal and lengthy reports usually have special sections at the beginning under the heading INTRODUCTION. Most business reports also have introductory sections, but they are not labeled as such. The authors simply begin writing about the chosen topic, as shown in the sample report (page 246)—telling readers what the study is about and how the report is organized. Notice that the introductory section of the sample report is an almost exact copy of the research proposal on page 210, having been reworded to express past tense.

Indentations

The first lines in paragraphs are indented five spaces in informal reports and from six to eight spaces in formal reports. Lists such as those shown on page 7 of the sample report (page 252) are indented the same number of spaces as the first lines of paragraphs. Notice in item 2 of the second list that when more than one line is required for an individual listing, the additional lines are begun immediately beneath the first word in the listing.

Levels of headings

Imagine trying to read this book if it had no headings. The headings used here, which were taken directly from chapter outlines, help you understand the organization of the book; and they enable you to locate specific materials. Similarly, the Roman numeral sections of the initial outline (page 207) become the main headings in the sample report (pages 244 to 256), and the ABC subsections become subheadings. The following lists provide details of both levels of headings:

Main headings:	Preceded by two blank lines (triple-spaced)
	Placed flush with left margin
	First letters of main words capitalized
	Stands alone on the line
	Followed by punctuation only if a question
	Underscored
Subheadings:	Preceded by one blank line (normal double-spacing)
	Indented the same number of spaces as first line of paragraphs (five spaces in the sample report)
	First letter of main words capitalized
	Followed by punctuation
	Underscored
	Writing begins on same line

As guidelines to report writing, however, outlines should be flexible. Having decided on Lucky Center as the best location for opening a health food store, for example, the employee wrote the entire first section of the sample report about this one shopping center. Correspondingly, she used "Lucky Center" as the first main heading in the sample report, rather than "Site Location" as shown in the original outline.

The sample report actually contains three levels of headings: centered headings for the title page, contents, and bibliography, and two levels of headings in the body of the report. This number of headings is sufficient for the large majority of formal and informal reports you may encounter in business. In short reports, ranging anywhere from one to ten pages, you may find just one level of headings adequate, in which case you may choose any one of the three types of headings illustrated here.

Transition statements

Notice on pages 1 and 2 of the sample report (pages 246 and 247), that the writer includes a transition statement at the end of the introductory section, just before reaching the first main heading, telling readers what they may expect to find in the body of the report. Notice also on pages 2, 5, 7, and 8 that the writer follows each main heading with a transition statement, telling readers something about the materials that follow in the subsections. Transition statements in these areas of reports enable writers to tie their thoughts together for good reading, and the statements have the added benefit of separating main headings from subheadings. Transition statements are *not* required or recommended when moving from one subsection to another.

Documentation

When we include in our reports ideas or statements by other people, we usually document the materials by referring to the sources. If we cite statistics from a textbook, for example, we use a footnote, endnote, or numbered bibliography to inform readers of the source of the data.

If you must use footnotes (which appear at the bottom of the respective pages) or endnotes (which are placed on a separate page or pages at the end of reports), rather than a numbered bibliography, refer to pages 231–235 for illustrations of the different types of footnotes. Footnotes and endnotes also require the use of three Latin terms, as illustrated in the following series of footnotes:

[1]John W. Mercer, How to Retail Dietetic Foods Successfully (San Francisco: Winston Press, Inc., 1980), pp. 217–18.

[2]Ibid.

[3]Rosie S. Stein and others, <u>Marketing in the 80's</u> (Boston: Business Publishers, Inc., 1980), 95–99.

[4]Ibid., p. 47.

[5]Mercer, <u>loc. cit.</u>

[6]Stein, <u>op. cit.</u>, pp. 105–6.

Footnote (FN) 2 indicates that the materials are from the same source as those referenced by FN 1, the preceding footnote—the same book and the same pages. FN 4 refers to FN 3, the preceding footnote, but to a different page number. FN 5 tells readers that the materials referenced are from the Mercer book, *loc. cit.* indicating that other footnotes intervene between FN 5 and the Mercer reference, and that the materials are from the same pages shown in the original reference. FN 6 tells readers that the materials referenced are from the Stein book, *op. cit.*, p. 105–6 indicating that other footnotes intervene between this footnote and the Stein reference and that the materials are from *different pages* than those shown in the original footnote. Many authors now list the entire footnote in each instance, rather than burden readers with Latin terms. Entire footnotes should be listed even in very formal reports, rather than using Latin terms to refer to footnotes several pages away from the materials being referenced.

If you choose to use footnotes, you should double-space following the last typewritten line, strike the underscore key 15 times, double-space again, and enter the footnote. Footnote numbers should be elevated one-half line, in the body of the report and in the footnotes, as shown in the following example (assuming that this is the last typewritten line on a page).

---

[3]Leon T. Flood, "You Aren't What You Don't Eat," <u>The Health Food Store,</u> 181 (April 1982), 23.

[4]"Location Is the Name of the Game in Retailing," <u>National Health Guide,</u> 47 (December 1981), 10–11.

[5]Ibid.

We would have to stop typing soon enough to allow five lines at the bottom of the page for the first footnote, an additional three lines for the next footnote, and an additional two lines for the last one—ten lines altogether. A guide sheet, prepared with a sheet of paper that is slightly wider than the standard 8½-inch page, can be used to indicate the number of typing lines remaining on a page, so that you

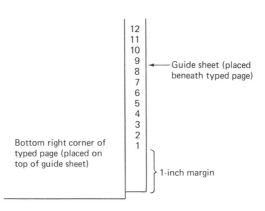

Guide sheet (placed beneath typed page)

Bottom right corner of typed page (placed on top of guide sheet)

1-inch margin

can reserve enough space for the number and length of footnotes to be listed. When spacing makes it difficult or impossible to complete a long footnote, you may carry forward the extra lines to the bottom of the next page, following the required 15-space underscore.

We must document all direct quotations, of course. On page 5 of the sample report, at the end of the first paragraph (page 250), the writer credits a real estate agent for having used the term "strong client" by enclosing the agent's exact words within quotation marks. The footnote that follows refers not only to the term, but also to other data within the same paragraph.

When a direct quotation or part of a written document consists of more than three lines, as in the first paragraph of the sample report, the lines are set off from the regular paragraph, single-spaced, and footnoted. Notice that the quotation is indented on the left only, the first line an extra three spaces, and it is without quotation marks. Lead readers into quotations as the writer does here by providing them with some indication of the source.

Example: As the president of our company once commented, ". . .

Example: In a recent interview with the press, Frank Borman stated, ". . .

Because quotation marks are used only with direct quotations by individuals and with materials copied verbatim, many reports are written without the use of even one set of quotation marks. Instead of using the exact words of others, we paraphrase what they have said or written by stating the same information in our own words. On pages 2 and 3 of the sample report (pages 247 and 248), under the heading "Demographic Patterns," data in three separate sentences are footnoted. No quotation marks are used, because the writer stated information from the referenced articles in her own words.

She followed each sentence with a footnote, however, to credit authors of the original articles for the information used.

Not all information needs to be documented. As you research a topic, you will notice that some of the information is discussed by more than one author in different books and articles. Such knowledge is general information which does not require documentation. Similarly, any knowledge of the topic that you possessed to begin with may be used without documentation.

Writing style

Although the trend in business writing is toward an informal style, in which authors write as they would talk, many people prefer a more formal approach. When writing formal reports, you must avoid the use of personal pronouns such as *I, me, we, us,* and *you.*

> Informal: *I found* that working people do much of their shopping during trips home from work.
>
> Formal: *Studies show* that working people do much of their shopping during trips home from work.
>
> Informal: Having decided on a location for the business and the amount of rent to be paid, *I estimated* the total required investment.
>
> Formal: Having decided on a location for the business and the amount of rent to be paid, *the writer estimated* the total required investment.

Informal writing sometimes adds life to reports, but formal writing often spares readers the tedious repetition of personal pronouns. Also, many business managers avoid personalizing research efforts and report writing as a way of stressing teamwork over individualism.

TERMINAL SECTION

The final section of the report (which may be considered part of the body of the report) may consist of a summary, conclusions, recommendations—or any combination of the three. If the material presented has been quite varied or extensive, a summary might prove helpful to readers. You will want to add separate sections or paragraphs to outline any conclusions you have derived or any recommendations that you wish to make. All relevant data and information should be presented earlier, so that when reading the terminal section readers will not be confronted with any new information (or any footnotes).

SUMMARIES AT THE BEGINNING

After writing long reports (more than 15 pages), authors often replace summaries in the terminal section with summaries (more formally referred to as *synopses,* which is plural for *synopsis*) at the beginning of their reports. Such summaries allow readers to grasp major details and important findings without having to read entire reports. This feature is an important consideration for busy people, especially when they have only a minor interest in the report topic. They may scan the summaries and then refer to specific sections of the report when detailed information is desired. Many business reports consist of hundreds of pages, which makes beginning summaries (one to five pages) essential.

APPENDIX

Report writers (and the authors of books) often refer readers to supplementary materials placed near the end of their reports in sections labeled APPENDIX. In fact, some reports contain more than one appendix, separating such materials as maps, charts, tables, questionnaires, letters, and legal documents—materials that are supportive but too lengthy to include in the main parts of reports or books. If you have a need to include an appendix (or appendixes), place it following the bibliography, and, when appropriate, refer readers to those materials.

CONTENTS PAGE

A contents page like the one in the sample report (page 245) is useful when a report consists of more than ten pages, because it allows readers to grasp the organization of reports and helps them locate specific segments.

The contents page shown here is simply a copy of the outline on page 207, with the Roman numerals and subsection letters deleted and page numbers added. In lengthier reports, you may elect to show page numbers for each subsection as well as for each main part of the report.

FILE COPY

As with letters, memos, or any other written communication, keep file copies of your reports. If it is impractical for you to make copies or to have your reports photocopied, at least hang on to the rough drafts, so that if something should happen to a paper, all of your effort will not be lost.

TRANSMITTAL

When you have completed all parts of the report and have combined the pieces to form an attractive package, take a moment to write an accompanying letter or memo. When business people submit reports, they invariably have some comments to make about the report—interesting findings, difficulties encountered, incomplete information, and so forth. You will be wise to put such comments in writing as a permanent record for all who may read the report. Keep the transmittal brief, telling readers that you are including the report that was previously authorized; add some comment about the research effort or the report itself, and offer any required clarification of key points. Place the letter (memo) and the report (stapled in the top-left corner) in a suitable envelope or folder so that it will not be folded or soiled. Before actually releasing the report, however, review the sample transmittal (Figure 20-1) and sample report (Figure 20-2) and compare your report with the checklist on pages 257—261.

Figure 20-1 Sample letter of transmittal.

```
                        INTEROFFICE MEMORANDUM

    DATE:   April 14, 1983

      TO:   Mr. W. T. Miller, Executive Vice President

    FROM:   Charlotte W. Purcell, Marketing Specialist

 SUBJECT:   Pilot program for retailing health foods


The accompanying report outlines details of the study that you requested
on February 25.

Our findings, coupled with favorable projections by Bill Miller in a
separate financial statement, are supportive of tentative plans for taking
an initial step into the retailing segment of the health-food market.
A suitable location has been identified in an area with favorable demographics
and traffic flows, and tentative arrangements have been made for equipment
purchases, beginning inventory, local financing, and details of operation.

May we have your response, please?
```

ESTABLISHING AND OPERATING
A HEALTH FOOD STORE
IN METROPOLITAN PHOENIX

Presented to:
Mr. W. T. Miller
Executive Vice President
Western Division
Los Angeles, California

Presented by
Charlotte J. Purcell
Marketing Specialist
April 14, 1983

Figure 20-2 Sample report.

CONTENTS

LUCKY CENTER   2

    Strategic Location
    Demographic Patterns
    Traffic Flow
    Lease Provisions

INITIAL FINANCING   5

    Security Deposit
    Equipment and Fixtures
    Beginning Inventory
    Working Capital
    Bank Loan

LEGAL OBLIGATIONS   7

    Federal Taxes
    State Regulations
    County Requirements
    City Regulations

SALES AND SERVICE   8

    Buying Practices
    Pricing Policy
    Credit Card Sales
    Store Hours and Employment
    Newspaper Advertising

SUMMARY AND CONCLUSIONS 10

NUMBERED BIBLIOGRAPHY 12

In exploring the feasibility of establishing a retail outlet in metropolitan Phoenix, as a pilot program for further diversification, our initial interest in this particular project was based on knowledge of high returns in the retailing segment of the health food industry-- as reported in a leading trade journal:

> Inventory turnover in the retailing end of the health-food business is low, compared to most other types of food retailing, but a relatively high markup on cost (ranging from 25 to 75 percent) results in an average return on investment of approximately 17 percent.(7:13)

We also received favorable comments during discussions with several individuals who presently own and operate their own (nonfranchised) health food stores.

In conducting an exploratory study to learn more about establishing and operating a health food store, we secured primary data from in-dept interviews with operators and owners of established health food stores, from actually observing the procedures that employees follow at several successful stores, and through direct contacts with real estate agents and vendor representatives. Extensive secondary data were available in the form of statistics developed by the City of Glendale, where we would locate the business, and from numerous publications relating to the sale, distribution, and consumption of health foods.

The objective of this expanded study was to explore the detail involved in establishing an operating a health food store in Glendale, Arizona. More specifically, we (1) found a suitable location for the business, (2) secured adequate financing, (3) established guidelines for sales and service, (4) outlined legal obligations of the business, and (5) made a firm recommendation to proceed with the project. Not included in this study are projections of profit (loss) levels and cash flows; that information, which is favorable, is being compiled by the accounting department in a separate report.

Lucky Center

Lucky Center is a neighborhood shopping center that is dominated by a Lucky Stores supermarket, and our choice of this particular location is based on the types of businesses that are present occupants of the center, demographic patterns within the surrounding community, traffic flows, and lease provisions.

Strategic Location. Lucky Center is located on the northwest corner of 51st and Northern Avenues in the City of Glendale—just eight blocks west of 43rd Avenue which divides the cities of Glendale and Phoenix. As shown by the diagram in Figure 1, the mix of stores in Lucky Center is complementary to a health food store, and the nearest competitors are General Nutrition Centers (a retail chain) at Valley West Shopping Center (five miles to the west) and at Metrocenter (six miles to the northeast). Although customers of the beauty salon, sewing center, and health spa may occupy parking spaces for relatively long period of time, many of these people are also regular consumers of health foods.

Demographic Patterns. According to a recent survey, 65 percent of all health food sales are made to working women between the ages of 25 and 45 years of age—women whose family income is significantly above the national median.(4:30) Correspondingly, the population of Northwest Phoenix (Metropolitan area, which includes Glendale) is young

247

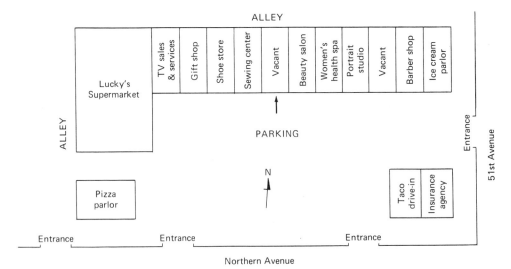

Figure 1

Diagram of Lucky Center
Glendale, Arizona

(median age 28), prosperous (median family income $31,150), and well-educated (65 percent of adults have had some college education).(8:22) Also, Northwest Phoenix is the fastest-growing area in Arizona and one of the fastest-growing communities in the country.(9:5)

Traffic Flow. Studies show that working people do much of their shopping during trips home from work and that they tend to patronize businesses that are located at the right of streets, where they need not make left turns.(3:231-32) As the diagram in Figure 2 illustrates, Lucky Center is ideally situated to receive the heaviest flows of "going home" traffic from Phoenix. Of the night (P.M.) traffic in all directions, which totals 26,090 vehicles, 18,922 (70 percent) may turn into Lucky Center without having to make left-hand turns.

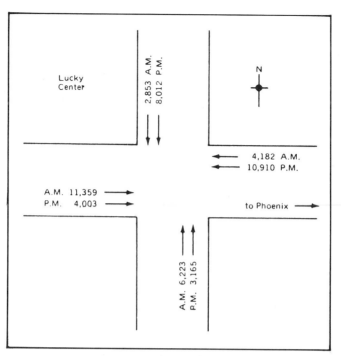

Figure 2

Traffic flow at intersection of
51st and Northern Avenues
Week of August 13, 1981

Source: City of Glendale, Department of Engineering

Lease Provisions. The property to be leased (see arrow inFigure 1)

is 15 feet wide and 50 feet deep, a total of 750 square feet. Monthly

rent under a five-year lease is $812.50, plus a common-area maintenance

fee of approximately $40.00 per month. The maintenance fee is subject to

adjustments each year, with any underassessments charged to occupants

at the end of the year and any overassessments refunded. The lessor

requires a security deposit of $1,625.00, the equivalent of two months'

rent, on which no interest is paid. The lessor provides fluorescent
lighting (fixtures only) and an appropriate air-conditioning unit.
The lessor is also willing to construct without charge a partition for
a storeroom--upon our convincing the agent that we will be what they
refer to as a "strong client."(11)

Initial Financing

Having decided on a location for the business and the amount of
rent to be paid, we estimated the total required investment and sought
bank financing.

Security Deposit. As already mentioned, the landlord requires a
security deposit of $1,625.00, the equivalent of two months' rent. The
landlord pays no interest on security deposits, which effectively
increases the annual lease expense by $162.50 (10 percent of $1,625.00).

Equipment and Fixtures. With the landlord providing a partition,
the lighting fixtures, and an air-conditioning unit, only the following
items are needed initially:

1.	Shelving on back well and two side walls	$ 350.00
2.	Deep-freeze unit (6 cu. ft.)	285.00
3.	Two refrigeration units (5 feet wide)	2,050.00
4.	Six standard-sized bread racks	438.00
5.	U-shaped checkout counter	225.00
6.	Juice bar	345.00
7.	Tiled floor at entrance (installed)	450.00
8.	Wall paneling (installed)	350.00
9.	Electronic cash register	1,150.00
10.	Outside sign (installed)	475.00
11.	Miscellaneous supplies	250.00

The total cost of the equipment and fixtures needed to start the
business is $6,368.00.

Beginning Inventory. The cost of stocking the store initially is placed at $14,500.00. Terms (initial order only) provide for payment of one third of this amount at the time of delivery, one third 30 days later, and the remaining one third 60 days from date of purchase. Terms of sale for the first order are F.O.B. delivered, which means that no transportation charges will be added to the vendor's invoice.

Working Capital. We will begin each month with $3,000.00 in a checking account. We anticipate, however, that our sales volume by the end of the third month of operation will have reached a level where working capital of only $2,000.00 will suffice. We plan to keep this figure as low as possible, because the bank does not pay interest on monies deposited in checking accounts.

Bank Loan. The security deposit, equipment and fixtures, beginning inventory, and working capital total $25,493.00. Because of a favorable Dun & Bradstreet, we can secure an $8,000.00 loan from Phoenix National Bank. The equipment, fixtures, and inventory will serve as collateral for the loan.

The loan agent at Phoenix National Bank advised that they will extend to us a $20,000 commercial loan for four years at 15 percent simple interest, which results in 48 monthly payments of $666.67. Having checked with other lending institutions and with officials of the Small Business Administration, we found this rate to be the lowest-cost loan available.(12)

Legal Obligations

The tentative name of the business is "Nutrition Corner," chartered as a separate corporation to begin with. As a domestic corporation, we must adhere to numerous government requirements.

Federal Taxes. The federal government requires the following forms:

1. Application for Employer Identification Number
2. Employee Withholding Allowance Certificate (Form W-4)
3. Income Tax Withheld and Social Security Taxes (Form 941)
4. Final Return (Form 941)
5. Deposit of Income and Social SecurityTax Withheld
6. Wage and Tax statement (Form W-2)
7. Unemployment Tax (Form 940)
8. Unemployment Tax Deposit
9. Self-Employment Tax (Form 1040-SE)
10. Estimated Tax (Form 1040-ES)

State Regulations. The following forms must be filed with the State of Arizona:

1. Application for Transaction Privilege
2. Combined Transaction Privilege Tax and Educational Excise Tax Return
3. Application for Employer's Identification Number
4. Report to Determine Liability
5. Contribution and Wage Report
6. Quarterly Report of state Income Tax Withheld (Form A-1)
7. Fourth QuarterReport
8. Federal and State Income Tax Withheld (Form A-2 or W-2)
9. Employer's Liability Insurance
10. Income Tax Return (Form 140)
11. Business Property Statement

County Requirements. The serving of juices for consumption in the store makes it necessary for us to comply with two county requirements:

1. Application for Health Permit
2. Health certificates for each employee who is to prepare and/ or serve food or beverages for public consumption

City Regulations. In addition to federal, state, and county regulations, all businesses within the City of Glendale must submit

1. Application for Privilege License
2. Monthly Privilege License Tax Return
3. Certificate of Occupancy

These requirements by the City of Glendale are in addition to periodic

building inspections and annual sign inspections.

Sales and Service

We have not yet accounted for all details of the business, but a

statement can be made concerning several aspects of the operation.

Buying Practices. We will purchase most of our products from Arizona

Wholesalers, which is located in Southwest Phoenix, about eight

miles from the store; and, except for the initial order, which is F.O.B.

delivered, we will use J&R Trucking to pick up our orders. Terms of sale

after the first order are 2/10, n/30, and delivery service by the vendor is

available when and if needed.

We will place orders directly with vendors, rather than through the

wholesaler, when we are able to order in a large enough volume to realize

lower per-unit costs. We will also order directly from vendors in Los

Angeles and have J&R Trucking pick up the merchandise when they have vehicles

in that vicinity.

Pricing Policy. markup will be based on cost, which is a common

practice within the health food industry, and our percentage markup will

be based on average markups of retailers in theRocky Mountain area as

reported periodically in Health Food Monthly. Our pricing policy will

be sufficiently flexible, however, to enable us to respond to competi-

tive practices within a ten-mile radius of the store, and we will run

weekly specials on selected "loss-leader" items.

Credit Card Sales. We are almost forced to follow the practice of accepting MasterCard andVisa credit cards. The cost to us for this privilege, based on an average ticket size of $10.50 (estimated) is 5 percent of all credit sales; and this cost is in addition to any charges that the banks may assess the credit card holders. The banks charge a nominal "set-up" fee for beginning this service, plus a charge for buying an imprinter—$27 new, $17 rebuilt.(10)

Store Hours and Employment. The store will be open for business from 10:00 a.m. to 7:00 p.m. on weekdays, and from 10:00 a.m. to 6:00 p.m. on Saturdays. We will close Sundays and all legal holidays.

The store manager will work weekdays andSaturdays to begin with, 53 hours per week. His or her efforts will be supplemented by two high school students, who will work approximately 16 hours apiece each week —stocking shelves, serving juices, assisting customers, and acting as manager during the manager's absences from the store. Part-time employees will be paid the prevailing minimum wage, with the store manager receiving approximately one and one-half times that rate.

Newspaper Advertising. Except for point-of-purchase advertising and displays, which are provided without charge by vendors, we will rely totally on newspapers for advertising our store and our products. Most vendors of health foods offer cooperative advertising programs, providing mats for newspaper advertising and paying 50 percent of the cost of local newspaper ads that feature their products.(3:441)

Summary andConclusions

We can lease a section of Lucky Center, a neighborhood shopping center in the northwest part of Metropolitan Phoenix, under lease conditions that parallel those for similar properties. Demographic patterns in this area and the traffic flows past the shopping center add to the attractiveness of Luck Center as the site for a health food store.

Initial financing will total about $25,500, and will include a security deposit, equipment and fixtures, beginning inventory, and working capital. Phoenix National Bank will extend a loan of 420,000, with the balance to come from the treasury of the parent company.

Our initial order and most orders for stock replenishment will be placed with a nearby wholesaler, under terms that are standard for the health food industry. We will place occasional orders directly with vendors, and will use a local drayage service to pick up most orders. Markup will be based on our costs in relation to industry averages and competitive actions, and Mastercard and Visa credit cards will be accepted.

Store hours will parallel those of competing stores and other retail establishments in the area, which will require, in addition to daily efforts of a store manager, the services of two part-time employees. Newspaper advertising will be our major promotional tool, most of which will be adapted to cooperative programs offered by vendors.

As a result of this study, and in consideration of favorable financial projections (separate report), we tecommend that the company proceed with the proposed business venture. Upon receipt of your approval, we are prepared to execute a lease, order fixtures and inventory, file the required reports with government agencies, and secure the necessary financing The grand opening could be set for June 21, a Saturday, which would allow sufficient time for arranging inventory, interviewing job applicants, ordering and shelving stock, and placing advertisements with local newspapers.

NUMBERED BIBLIOGRAPHY

A. BOOKS

1. Mercer, John W. How to Retail Dietetic Foods Successfully. San
      Francisco: Winston press, Inc., 1980.

2. Moore, Sarah P. and Benjamin Stewart. Health Fuide for Life. New
      York: Javitts Publishing Company, Inc., 1981.

3. Stein, Rosie S. and others. Marketing in the 80's. Boston:
      Business Publishers, Inc., 1980.

B. PERIODICALS

4. Binichi, Sylvia R. "Affluent Women are Health Conscious According
      to Survey." National health Guide 48 (January, 1980), 27-32.

5. Flood, Lean T. "You Aren't What You Don't Eat." The Health Food
      Store 181 (April 4, 1982), 23.

6. "Location is the Name of the Game in Retailing." National Health
      Guide 47 (December, 1981), 10-11.

7. Simon, Harold R. "Health-Food Retailing Brings High Returns."
      Health Food Monthly 34 (December, 1982), 12-15.

8. Yaw, Susan. "Some Interesting Statistics." Arizona Lifestyle 143
      (February 12, 1983), 21-22.

C. NEWSPAPER

9. "Glendale in Rapid Growth Area." Glendale Star, December 4, 1982,
      p. 5.

D. INTERVIEWS

10. Apley, Donald, First national Bank of Arizona, and Rose Anne Smith,
      Valley National Bank, Phoenix, Arizona, March 12, 1983.

11. Gonzales, Lydia, Commercial Agent, Milt Jackson andAssociates,
      Phoenix, Arizona, March 12, 1983.

12. Moreno, Delores, Commercial Loan Officer, Phoenix National Bank,
      Phoenix, Arizona, march 5, 1983.

SHORT REPORTS

Some reports are relatively short, making more than one level of headings impractical. When using only one level of headings, you may choose either the centered, unindented side-hanging, or indented form. The sample report that follows (Figure 20-3) carries indented headings, with the accompanying procedural information also being indented as a way of setting it apart from the general comments in the beginning and ending paragraphs. These headings are less prominent than unindented headings, which stand alone on separate lines, or the still more powerful centered headings.

The following short report (Figure 20-3) is not sufficiently extensive to justify a title page, contents page, or summary. The writer has utilized an interoffice memo format, instead, precluding the need for any type of transmittal. The report is single-spaced, for easier reading of this type information; and because the writer relies solely on primary data, with no references being made to outside sources (newspapers, magazines, books, interviews), no bibliography page is required.

CHECKLIST: BUSINESS AND ACADEMIC REPORTS

Transmittal
- Does your letter
  Indicate that the report is enclosed?
  Refer to authorization for the study?
  List all necessary comments about the study or report?
- Have you placed the report in a suitable envelope or folder with your name on it?

Title page
- Is the title concise (fewer than 15 words) and descriptive?
- Is the title centered on the 10th line and is it in all capital letters?
- Does it show the receiver's name, title, and location?
- Have you included your name and the date?
- Is the spacing attractive?

Contents
- Is the heading CONTENTS centered on the 10th line?
- Are the margins the same as those used in the body of the report?

(continued on page 259)

```
                    I N T E R O F F I C E   M E M O R A N D U M


DATE:  November 15, 1982

  TO:  Mr. R. D. Smith

FROM:  James Tyler

SUBJECT:  Credit Department Operations
```

On October 27, you instructed me to spend the first two weeks of my orientation program in the credit department, with the dual purpose of (1)out-
lining current procedures and (2) identifying possible areas for improvement.
As you know, this department is composed of three function areas: credit,
collections, and warehousing. This brief report concerns credit and
collection transactions, because they involve interdependent transactions,
with a separate report to follow on warehousing operations.

> New Accounts. Credit applications are required for all new accounts.
> Listed references are checked and Dun & Bradstreet credit reports
> are secured and analyzed. Final credit decisions are made by the
> credit manager, who either establishes credit limits or rejects
> the applications.
>
> Special Approvals. If an order is received for an account which
> has already reached or surpassed the established credit limit, special
> approval must be secured from the credit manager. Approval usually
> is extended routinely, however, providing the customer is not delin-
> quent in his payments.
>
> Remittances. Customer checks are compared with amounts reflected
> in the weekly open-item-file account. And customers are contacted
> immediately to clarify apparent variations between their checks
> and the invoiced amounts.
>
> Deposits. Checks are then entered on cash-receipts forms, one for
> each company; and bank deposit slips are issued. The accounts receiv-
> able manager takes the company deposits to the Arizona Bank, and
> subsidiary deposits are handed to the controller for recording and
> forwarding to the First National Bank of Arizona.
>
> Delinquent Accounts. A daily Customer-Account Summary reflects
> daily account balances as related to established credit limits.
> When an account is overextended, the phrase "EXCEEDS CREDIT LIMIT"
> appears on the computer printout to the right of the delinquent-
> account entry.
>
> Additionally, a monthly Accounts-Receivable Aging report categorizes
> all delinquent accounts as being either 30, 60, or 90 days past
> due. Efforts are made to effect collection of these accounts--by
> phone, by wire, and sometimes in person; and payments are noted
> in the aging printout in red ink as they are received.

Figure 20-3 Sample short report.

Monthly statements, reflecting all transactions for the past 30-day period, are mailed to all active accounts.

Accounts appearing on the aging printout, which cannot be collected in the interim, are entered on monthly C.O.D. lists—one for each sales department, including the branch offices. These lists include the names of customers which are handled presently, but not normally, on a C.O.D. basis.

Credit Insurance. All accounts are covered by American Credit Indeminity Insurance. Each account is automatically insured up to $5,000. Additional coverage is carried on certain accounts, in connection with which a monthly statement of delinquent accounts in excess of $5,000 is compiled and submitted to the insurance company.

You will recall from our earlier conversations that I expressed concern that too much reliance is being placed on the accounts receivable manager. What happens if this employee quits or becomes incapacitated? When additional clerical help is justified, therefore, I suggest that a back-up employee for this key position be considered. As in the accounts payable department at this very moment, receivables transactions should continue uninterrupted when the key employee is absent.

Too much reliance is placed on the aging printout for policing delinquent accounts. While this monthly report is useful in estimating bad-debt losses, the Daily Customer Account Summary should be used more extensively in the daily control of credit. This daily printout reflects daily account balances, as they relate to established credit limits; and overextended accounts are identified with the statement "EXCEEDS CREDIT LIMIT." This report is practically useless in its present form, because the listed credit limits for numerous accounts are unrealistically low.

It is imperative, therefore, that customer credit limits be reexamined and adjusted at once. And copies of monthly statements to customers could be utilized for this purpose.

Figure 20-3 continued.

- Did you leave two blank lines, triple-spaced following (below) the centered heading?
- Is your vertical spacing attractive, avoiding a crowded appearance?
- Are the dots in each of the dotted lines even with one another?
- Are the page numbers accurate?

Summary

- If your report is more than 15 pages, did you include a summary at the beginning?

- Did you keep it brief (not more than one page for a 20-page report or more than two pages for a 50-page report)?

Body of the report
- Are the margins consistent and correct?
- Are the pages numbered correctly?
- Did you include an unlabeled introductory section?
- Did you indent the first lines of all paragraphs five spaces?
- Are the first letters of all main words in *all* headings capitalized?
- Are the headings underscored?
- Are main headings preceded by an extra blank line and flush with the left margin? Do they stand alone on the lines, and are they without punctuation at the end (except for questions)?
- Are your subheadings indented and followed by punctuation?
- Does writing commence on the same lines—following each subheading?

Transition statements
- Does your introductory section end with a transition to all main (Roman numeral) sections of the report?
- Have you included transition statements between each main heading and the first subheading that follows each of them?

Documentation
- Have you quoted other people (used their exact words) only when paraphrasing would detract from the desired impact?
- Did you use quotation marks only with direct quotations?
- Did you use transition sentences to alert readers of impending quotations and their sources?
- Do your footnotes or endnotes (if used) follow some prescribed format?
- Are they consistent with one another throughout the report?

Writing style
- If you adopted a formal style, did you avoid using personal pronouns?

Bibliography
- Does the heading BIBLIOGRAPHY or NUMBERED BIBLIOGRAPHY begin on the 10th line of an unnumbered page, and is it followed by two blank lines (triple-spaced)?
- Are books, periodicals, and other types of documents placed in separate categories and labeled?

- Is the heading for each category preceded by a capital letter, a period, and two spaces?
- Are the headings for each category preceded by an extra blank line (triple-spaced) and centered on the page?
- Are the margins consistent with those in the body of the report?
- Are all but the first lines of each entry indented four spaces?
- If it is a numbered bibliography, is each entry preceded by a number (sequentially), a period, and two spaces?
- If the bibliography consists of more than one page, are page numbers shown on all but the first page?

Appendix

- If you placed materials in an appendix, are they preceded by a page with a centered heading APPENDIX?
- If there is more than one appendix, do the title pages for each specify the types of materials included?
- Are page numbers shown on all pages in the appendix, except the title page(s)?

Package

- Are all pages in the correct order?
- Are all pages of the report stapled in the top-left corner?
- Did you place the report and transmittal in an envelope or folder?

File copy

- Did you retain a copy (or at least a rough draft) for your file?

V
EMPLOYMENT COMMUNICATIONS

We have discussed many types of business communications in the preceding sections of this book, all of which have helped prepare you for what might be the most important communications of all—those that help you land a good job. This section of the book not only deals with some of the fine points in preparing for and conducting yourself during interviews but also shows you how to customize a resume, write attention-getting employment letters, and follow through on job offers, rejections, and noncommittals.

21

CREATING RESUMES

Because you are an educated person looking for an above-average job, potential employers will expect you to present them with a functional and attractive resume.* Resumes, which many people refer to as "data sheets" and "vitas" (short for Latin *curriculum vitas,* meaning "course of a life"), generally consist of three main parts: personal data, formal education, and work experience.

You may decide on the arrangement of these three categories of information. You may elect to list your education first, for example, because it is more impressive than your work experience. You list your work experience first, on the other hand, if it relates more closely to the job you are seeking than your education does. Or you may list personal data at the beginning because it improves the overall appearance of the resume. In addition to these three categories of information, you may include a career objective, personal references, or any other category of information that might interest employment managers in hiring you.

A resume should provide an overview of your past, so don't try to include every little piece of information. Accentuate the positive by listing only complimentary information, and leave questionable details for later explanation. Remember, a resume is not intended to reflect a complete record; that is the function of application forms provided by employers. The primary purpose of a resume, instead, is to secure an interview.

PERSONAL DATA

Don't consume valuable space at the beginning of the resume by using the title "RESUME"; employment managers and their assistants recognize resumes when they see them. Emphasize your

*Because most typewriters do not have accent marks, it is permissible to type *résumé* as *resume.*

name, instead, by placing it at the beginning in all capital letters, as illustrated in the sample resumes in Figures 21-1 and 21-2. Other personal data that usually appear at or near the top of resumes are your address (sometimes one for the present and another for the future) and telephone number (including the area code). Don't use the labels "Address" or "Telephone"; most people recognize addresses and telephone numbers when they see them.

You may place other personal details near the top of the page, such as your address to the left and personal data to the right; or you may follow the more current practice of placing such personal data near the bottom of the page, as shown in Figures 21-1 and 21-2. Job seekers often include their birth dates (not their ages, which would soon date their resumes), marital status, physical dimensions, general health, and special interests; but there is no need to label this information.

Unnecessary labeling	*Preferred form*
Birth date: June 5, 1959	Born June 5, 1959
Marital status: Divorced	Divorced
Height: 5'5"	135 lbs., 5'5"
Weight: 135 lbs.	Excellent health
Health: Excellent	Enjoy skiing and tennis
Hobbies: Skiing and tennis	

The preferred form eliminates the superfluous, leaving more white space (space without typing) on the page and less verbiage for the reader to deal with. Notice the different ways personal information is presented in the two sample resumes.

Most employment managers advise applicants *not* to include photos of themselves, but if you believe that your appearance might help you land a particular job, then by all means include a picture. Passport-type pictures are most appropriate, since they are small enough to fit in the top-right corners of resumes. When having the picture taken, dress in a manner appropriate for the position that you are seeking and assume a businesslike pose.

CAREER OBJECTIVE

A frequent complaint by the people who read resumes is that applicants do not indicate the types of jobs they desire. You may close this communication gap by stating a realistic career objective.

Example: To obtain employment as a legal secretary with a large company, where I can apply and expand my skills, efficiency, and knowledge of law.

Example: To work for Dun & Bradstreet in the area of research and development.

JULIA (JULIE) METZENDORF

Until May 16, 1983:   After May 16, 1983:
6035 North 21st Avenue   6395 Orange Avenue
Phoenix, Arizona 85015   Long Beach, California 90805
(602) 242-3807   (213) 423-9427

Employment Objectives

Initial: Any clerical position   Eventual: Accounting position

Formal Education

9/81 -   Phoenix College, Phoenix, Arizona 85013

                Accounting major (Earned A's in all accounting courses)
                Will graduate May 10, 1983, with Associate in Arts degree
                Dean's honor list two semesters

                Worked part-time (See Work Experience below)

9/77 - 6/81   Long Beach High School, Long Beach, California 90805

                Graduated in top one fourth of a class of 465
                Astronomy club three years (president, one year)
                Marching band four years (clarinet)

Work Experience

9/81 -   National Life Insurance Company, 1102 West Camelback Road,
                Phoenix, Arizona 85192

                Part-time file clerk in marketing department, reporting
                directly to Mr. Timothy Borman, Office Manager.

6/81 - 8/81   Desert View Resort Hotel, 1036 South Mountain Pass Road,
                Scottsdale, Arizona 85251

                Front-desk reservation clerk (full-time summer job). Also
                handled light bookkeeping chores and routine correspondence.

Special Skills

          Typist (60 wpm)   Filing systems and record management
          10-key calculators   Multilith and ditto machines
          Keypunch (IBM)   TELEX and TWX machines

Personal Data

          Born 5/11/60   Hobbies include reading, riding
          Single   horses, and gardening
          Excellent health   Active in community social programs

Figure 21-1 Sample resume.

```
                    MICHAEL R. SCHULTZ
                    3231 North 53rd Drive
                    Phoenix, Arizona 85031
                    (602) 247-8560
```

career objectives	Seeking a position as data-processing manager, a position that will not only permit me to demonstrate my creative and administrative abilities more fully, but one that will also enable me to expand my knowledge of sophisticated computer systems and business management.

computer experience	**Data Processing manager** Wholesale Distributors, Inc.
	1/81 - present 6322 North 34th Avenue
	     Phoenix, Arizona 85005
	
	Manage the activities of five employees: two computer
	  operators and three keypunch operators.
	Schedule production runs and consult with the Controller an
	  other key management personnel regarding current problems
	  and future informational requirements.
	Determine data requirements (format and timing), design forms,
	  and plan file layouts and program specifications.
	Write, rewrite, and test programs.
	Major accomplishment: Designed and implemented programs
	  for the complete automation of inventory-control systems.
	
	Computer Operator J & R Electronic Systems
	6/79 - 12/80 713 University Drive
	     Tempe, Arizona 85281
	
	Ran scheduled jobs, checked validity of output, distributed
	  printouts, and maintained a log of computer utilization.

related education	**Business Administration Major** Arizona State University **9/79 - 5/81** Tempe, Arizona 85281 Strong emphasis on computerology and economics Graduated with high distinction Member Beta Gamma Sigma (honorary business fraternity) **General Business Major** Phoenix College **9/77 - 5/79** Phoenix, Arizona 85013 Data processing curriculum Dean's honor list every semester Cumulative grade point average of 3.65 (3.50=A)

Personal	Born 10/3/58 . . .married, 2 children. . .5'7" . . . 150 lbs. excellent health . . .avid sports fan and dedicated jogger.

Figure 21-2 Sample resume.

The first example narrows the applicant's interests to the legal field, which probably was his or her exact intention. The second example not only narrows the applicant's interest to a particular field of business but also to a specific company; the resume is useful only when applying to Dun & Bradstreet. In contrast, the employment objective in the sample resume in Figure 21-1 states the applicant's long-term objective while effectively leaving the door open for any clerical position that might now be available. If you would accept almost any type of job to begin with, don't include a career objective that is unnecessarily restrictive.

FORMAL EDUCATION

Try to maintain the reader's interest by listing your most recent education first. Forget about grade school, unless you were some type of whiz kid, and mention your high school education only if you had an outstanding record or if you are younger than 35 years of age.

Show the dates of attendance (months and years) in a prominent place, so the reader doesn't have to search for them, along with the name and address of the institutions. Specify your major areas of study at each school, and list any accomplishments of merit, such as being included on the Dean's honor list, belonging to an honor society or fraternity, and maintaining a respectable grade average. In deciding whether to mention your grades, you should realize that employment managers hire many, many more average people than they do Einsteins. If you graduated from a school, say so; and if you ranked in the top half or higher of your graduating class, now is the time to mention it.

Employment managers are especially interested in activities that reflect an inclination and ability to get along well with people. Respond to this interest in any way possible. Did you belong to a club? The newspaper staff? A sports team? A debating team? The band? Student council? ROTC? Did you direct the activities of others in any way? Group leader? Office holder? Team captain or co-captain?

You may include separate categories such as Leadership Experiences and Honors and Awards, but only if you have rather impressive lists. Otherwise, list your educational and extracurricular activities along with other information about the high school or college where they occurred, as shown in Figures 21-1 and 21-2. If you don't have much information to include under Education, you might add a list of Related Courses Taken. If you are seeking a sales job, for example, list marketing, math, speech, and other classes that reflect preparation for that type of work. If you are applying for a clerical position, on the other hand, list such courses as typing, filing, and business machines. You may also list any special education, such as training programs provided by companies where you have worked and business-related education received in the military.

WORK EXPERIENCE

Outline your work history by showing your most recent experiences first. You may follow any of several formats, including those shown in Figures 21-1 and 21-2, so long as you show the names and addresses of the places where you were employed, positions held, duties entailed, and dates of employment.

One of the first details that people consider when reading resumes is the continuity of dates, so place the beginning and ending dates of employment (months and years) in prominent positions on your resume and explain any gaps that might exist. If there was a period when you were unemployed, provide an explanation.

Example: Attended college full time during this period.

Example: Devoted full time to my role as wife, mother, and homemaker.

Unexplained gaps in employment often exclude applicants from further consideration for employment.

Many women return to school and to work following "interrupted" careers. If this is your situation, be sure to mention any involvement that you might have had in community affairs during that time, such as being active in politics, working for charitable organizations, and helping manage church affairs.

If you have worked several jobs during school or during interruptions in your career, avoid the appearance of instability by lumping the experience into a single statement.

Example: Worked in numerous part-time jobs while attending school, including employment as a service-station operator, construction worker, and salesman.

Example: My husband was transferred to five different cities in this four-year period, during which time I performed a variety of clerical duties for several manufacturing and retailing firms.

Potential employers are interested in the job functions where you are presently working and those in earlier positions. Notice in the sample resume in Figure 20-2 that each of the statements in the first position (this applicant's current job) begins with an action word in present tense: *manage, schedule, determine,* and *write.* For the Computer Operator position (an earlier job) the applicant uses action words in past tense: *ran, checked, distributed,* and *maintained.*

List different jobs that you have held with the same company, especially when you have assumed more responsible positions with each job change.

Example: Promoted to stenographer after working just six months as file clerk.

Example: In my first position as <u>Claim Agent,</u> I was responsible for the compilation and presentation of OS&D claims to transport and insurance companies. After just one year in that position, I was appointed <u>Office Manager</u> of the West Coast division, where it was my responsibility to run the office and coordinate procedures and personnel with all other divisions.

Notice in the second example that the positions are underscored for emphasis. If you use complete paragraphs in your resume, as in the second example, keep them brief (no longer than eight short lines) and guard against overuse of the pronoun *I*. Consistency in your resume is important also; use either phrases or complete sentences, but not a mixture of the two; and maintain parallelism in your sentences and paragraphs.

Potential employers are especially interested in major accomplishments by applicants. Did you design or introduce any new procedures? Did you solve any problems? Did you establish any performance records? Were you directly involved with any special programs? Did you receive any type of recognition for your contributions? If you can answer "yes" to any of these questions, now is the time to brag a little.

Example: When my supervisor needed legal documents prepared right away, she routinely assigned them to me.

Example: The division manager frequently called upon me to rearrange disorganized offices and, on occasion, sent me to large offices for the main purpose of abolishing unneeded positions and reducing or completely eliminating overtime work.

Note the "major accomplishment" listed in the sample resume in Figure 21-2 (first computer position). This statement provides evidence that the applicant's contributions exceeded the minimum effort that his employer might have expected.

How far back should you go when listing jobs? You should account for all work-related activities for at least the last ten years, if you have worked that long. You may show positions that you held beyond a ten-year period, if you believe the information will make the record appear more comprehensive and impressive. But you should devote less space to earlier positions. Notice in the sample resume in Figure 21-2 that the applicant has devoted five times as much verbiage to his current position as to the previous one. If you have had absolutely no work experience, on the other hand, omit the Work Experience section and dwell on your preparation for the job that you are seeking.

If early positions would emphasize advancing age, which you might see as a negative factor, don't list them. The same advice applies to your date of birth; if you believe that knowledge of your age might work against you in the employment decision, don't list it. Employers cannot legally request this information, even in employment applications or during interviews.

Do not consume valuable space or introduce negative thoughts by explaining why you left earlier jobs; save this information for the formal application form that you will be asked to complete. And don't list the salaries earned in previous positions. Employment personnel might view a high salary as an indication that you are overqualified for the position that you are seeking; if the salary appears low, they might have the opposite reaction. Also, with present rates of inflation, a salary that was impressive a couple of years ago might be relatively unimpressive in today's labor market.

Employment personnel talk of "creative" resumes, those in which job seekers lie. Applicants have been known to list degrees they haven't earned, positions they haven't held, and achievements that were never realized. Their fabricated resumes sometimes open doors for interviews, but the truth invariably catches up with them. Most companies automatically reject (some even fire) people they expose as having made dishonest statements in resumes and applications.

Be truthful in resumes, but not to the point of being naive. If you are trying to secure a job with an accounting firm, for example, do not mention in your career objective that you actually wanted to be a doctor but failed chemistry. If you ranked fifth in your high school graduation class, don't reveal that there were only sixteen students in the class; and, if you were fired from a job, even if through no fault of your own, don't even bring up the subject in your resume. If you introduce potential problem areas in the resume, you may never receive an interview and a chance to explain your side of the story.

Businesses don't advertise the unfavorable features of their products unless the government forces them to do so, and neither should you. Emphasize the positive instead, including only information that might cause others to view you as a promising candidate for the type of job that you are seeking. This is the name of the game; this is the approach that employment managers have come to expect.

MILITARY SERVICE

Do not go into great detail about your military experiences unless directly related to the particular job that you are seeking. Avoid the use of military jargon and any mention of retirement status. Even more important, perhaps, do not use the guidelines that the military provides for resume preparation, because they are widely recognized as "military." Many employment managers are unreceptive to people with extensive military backgrounds, on the theory that such people have never had to assume responsibility for earning profits, so plan your resume to establish yourself as a business-oriented person.

If you directed the activities of others, even one other person, be sure to provide details. Also provide details of any foreign travel that may be relevant to the target position. If any of the knowledge that you received through military training programs can be transferred to business situations, relate the experience in a way that will help the reader make the connection. Also list any honors and awards received.

If you wish to deemphasize any military service you have had, simply enter under Work Experience the dates of service, branch of service, terminal rank, and the fact that you were honorably discharged. You may devote a separate section of your resume to your military background, on the other hand, if it was extensive or if you have several experiences to list that in any way relate to the type of job that you want.

PERSONAL REFERENCES

Most employment managers, the people who actually read resumes, advise against listing references on resumes. To do so is redundant, because most companies have job seekers complete application forms before they actually begin checking references; and all standard application forms have sections for listing several personal references. Besides, if potential employers should check references from the information provided in resumes, the people listed would soon tire of responding to requests for information. Knowing this, most applicants add one line to their resumes indicating that references will be provided on request, or they simply avoid mentioning references altogether.

You will want to show references on your resume, however, if they are influential people; but be sure to secure their permission beforehand. Also, if you are without extensive education or work experience, you may add from two to four references to help balance your resume on the page. Type complete references at the end of the resume, so that employment managers will not have to search for street addresses or zip codes.

Example:

> Professor Rhonda Rhodes-Hanna
> CAL POLY—Room 242
> 3801 West Templer Avenue
> Pomona, California 91768

Example:

> Mr. Michael Gonzales, Manager
> Plaza Shoe Center
> 1177 Berea Road
> Cleveland, Ohio 44111

Notice in the first instance that the addressee uses both her maiden and married names, an increasingly common practice.

References should *not* include previous employers; if you want the people who are analyzing your resume to contact a particular person at a company, list the person's name under Work Experience as illustrated in the sample resume in Figure 21-1 (in the current position). You should also distinguish the references as educators, business people, government officials, or clergy—not just pals of yours. Without this clarification, references are valueless.

GOOD APPEARANCE

Employment managers claim that a resume has only 30 seconds or so to bring success or failure to the applicant. Because of the hundreds of resumes received each day, they must select promising candidates through process of elimination. In other words, they look for reasons to exclude applicants from consideration. And an unattractive appearance can eliminate a resume from consideration before they even begin to read its contents.

So how can you create an attractive resume? Begin by planning an appealing layout. When the people at advertising agencies create advertisements, they place parts of ads on separate pieces of paper and then position the pieces (pictures of products and printed matter) in different arrangements on a page of paper until they identify the best arrangement. You should take the same approach with your resume, determining whether to center your address at the top with your name or place it alone to the left, whether to use centered headings for each category of information (Figure 21-1) or side headings (Figure 21-2), whether to show personal data at the beginning of the resume or at the end, and to answer a host of other questions concerning indentations and spacing.

Although you should leave sufficient white space to avoid a cluttered appearance, most people with fewer than ten years of work experience can easily confine their resumes to a single page. If you must use a second page to include essential detail, rearrange your information to balance it evenly on both pages. Don't use a three- or four-page resume, unless you are a very high-level employee with extensive managerial experience, because most busy employment managers will not take the time to read it.

Employment managers can easily recognize professionally prepared resumes, and they respond more favorably to resumes that have been prepared by the applicants themselves. So plan your own resume, and, if at all possible, type it yourself. High-quality paper, a good typewriter, clean type, and a fresh ribbon will contribute significantly to the appearance of your resume. Properly spelled words and good grammar are essential also, so check and double-check your wording before typing; and have a knowledgeable person appraise the final product before actually putting it to use.

No, you do not need to prepare a separate resume for each potential employer, because resumes are relatively difficult to type. Instead, take the original to a local duplicating service, where they will use a multilith or regular copy machine to produce copies that will be difficult or impossible to distinguish from the original. The cost will depend on the quality of paper requested and number of copies ordered. Do *not* use resumes that have been reproduced with a ditto machine or carbons.

The information in your resume will change from time to time as you acquire more education and work experience, but it is much easier to update a resume than it is to start from scratch, especially at a time when you are under pressure to secure a job. As you put forth the considerable effort that is required to develop a functional resume, therefore, remember that a resume is not just another page of information; it is a document that is likely to influence your business career and life for many years to come.

CHECKLIST: RESUMES

Personal data
- Did you avoid use of the word "resume"?
- Did you include your name, address, and phone number near the top of the page?
- Did you include in a separate place on the page your birth date (not your age), and marital status?

• Did you decide to add or omit a photograph or any reference to your health, physical dimensions, or hobbies?
• Did you avoid the use of unnecessary, space-consuming labels?
• Did you exclude any reference to your social security number?

Career objective

• If you included a career objective, is it sufficiently broad to encompass a wide range of potential jobs?
• Is the statement appropriate for more than one company?
• Is the objective realistic in terms of your preparation and experience?
• Did you consider a two-part objective, one for your initial objective and another for long-range goals?

Formal education

• Did you begin with and emphasize your most recent education?
• Did you show the dates of attendance, names of schools, their locations, and your major areas of study?
• Did you list any honors and awards received? Your grade average? Honorary groups? Social groups?
• If you had difficulty completing a full-page resume, did you consider listing classes taken that relate to the type of job that you are seeking?
• Was there a need for separate categories such as Leadership Experience, Honors and Awards, and Special Skills?
• Did you list school activities in which you participated?
• Did you identify any leadership roles that you fulfilled?
• If you are under 35 years of age, did you include information about your high school education and related activities?
• Did you mention that you worked part-time while attending school?

Work experience

• Did you begin with your most recent job?
• Did you show the beginning and ending dates, the names and addresses of companies, and the positions held?
• Did you list your duties and accomplishments?
• Did you emphasize the positive, omitting any detail that might cause employers to question your attitudes and abilities?
• Did you use action words to describe your duties and accomplishments, using present tense for current activities and past tense for previous activities?
• Did you use short phrases (the preferred form) or complete sentences and paragraphs, avoiding a mixture of the two forms and avoiding or minimizing use of the word *I*?

- Did you include part-time and summer employment, if any?
- If you held many jobs during high school or during interruptions in your career, did you avoid the appearance of instability by grouping them?
- Did you provide an employment record for at least the last ten years, omitting any earlier references that would emphasize advancing age?
- Are your comments truthful, but not to the point of naivete?

Military experience

- Did you use a separate section (if your military service was extensive) or place this information under Work Experience?
- Did you show the branch of service, your terminal rank, and the fact that you were honorably discharged?
- Did you outline your activities, if business related, and especially those involving leadership roles?
- Did you avoid the use of military jargon, any mention of retirement status, and the military format for dates and resumes?

Personal references

- Did you include references only of people with recognized and impressive positions or titles? Or only if you needed them to complete a full-page resume?
- Did you avoid using previous employers as references?
- If you listed references, did you place them in address format, showing each person's complimentary title (Mr., Miss, Ms., Mrs., Dr.), complete name, position or title, street address, city, state, and zip code?

Good appearance

- Did you place all parts of your resume in the most attractive arrangement possible?
- Does the resume contain a liberal amount of white space?
- Did you confine your resume to one page (if fewer than ten years' work experience) or two pages at most?
- If you used two pages, did you balance the information evenly on both pages?
- Is the resume well typed?
- Is the paper of high quality and without smudges?
- Are the words correctly spelled?
- Is your grammar in good form?
- Are the copies clear and on high-quality paper?
- Does the finished product represent you accurately and positively?

22

WRITING APPLICATION LETTERS

If you decide to approach companies directly by showing up at their employment offices and asking for interviews, it won't be necessary for you to write application letters. You will simply present your resume in person. Many people have landed their present jobs this way, knocking on one business door after another until the right one opened for them.

Realizing that the direct approach requires a lot of time, effort, shoe leather, and gasoline, and knowing that employment managers don't always respond positively to unannounced visits, you may decide to rely on the U.S. mail. Rather than actually knocking on doors, you may decide to mail copies of your resume to several companies, briefly describing your potential contributions to each company and requesting interviews. But which companies should you contact? What should you include in your letters? How long should your letters be? What should they say? These next few pages will answer these questions and others that you may not have considered.

TARGET COMPANIES

You may select companies randomly in your search for employment, but the chances of finding the "right" job through such a hit-or-miss approach are not favorable. The probability of your finding a suitable job will be much greater if you respond to the challenge systematically.

Campus services

If you are currently enrolled at a college or university, or if you are a recent graduate, check with the campus placement office to see what jobs are available and which companies have scheduled interviews.

Most placement offices use bulletin boards to post information about local job offers. They also invite students to complete standard application forms and to submit letters of recommendation and personal resumes. They present copies of this information to representatives of companies in which applicants express interest before the representatives grant interviews to students during their scheduled visits to the campus.

Also take the time to inform business instructors of your search for employment. Many companies contact business faculty directly rather than relying on placement offices. When an employment manager is seeking recruits for an accounting position, for instance, he or she might telephone an accounting instructor. Although faculty members generally pass such information to placement offices, they might give you a running start toward the job by telling you about it first. And such a recommendation from an instructor, someone who is personally aware of your performance record and abilities, often results in employment.

Employment agencies

Local governments in large cities provide employment services without charge to applicants or employers, but many are understaffed and most focus on the placement of unskilled or semiskilled applicants. You will also find many private employment agencies listed in telephone directories. Private agencies usually specialize in stenographic, secretarial, and relatively low-level clerical positions; and their fees range anywhere from 10 to 25 percent of the annual salary earned in the new positions.

Newspapers
and trade journals

Many employers place employment ads in the classified sections of city and neighborhood newspapers, and they usually invite those who are interested to respond by submitting resumes to listed box numbers. Many employers also advertise in nationally distributed newspapers such as the *Wall Street Journal* and the *Christian Science Monitor*. Other popular vehicles for employment offers are trade journals—magazines directed at specific segments of society such as people who work in the food, electronics, aviation, and auto industries; and there are thousands of such publications.

Yellow Pages

If you are interested in working locally for a specific type of company, you should "let your fingers do the walking through the Yellow Pages." These annual publications place local businesses in categories ranging from accounting to insurance and heavy machinery to X-ray equipment. And with the use of maps at the front of the directory, you can avoid running from one side of town to the other on the same day by categorizing the target companies geographically. For a broader approach, you may visit the telephone company and consult the Yellow Pages for other cities.

Industrial directories

Most state governments regularly publish industrial directories, categorizing different types of businesses according to geographic location and types of products manufactured. Complete addresses are provided, as well as names of key officials and number of people employed.

National directories

If your search for employment is national in scope, a visit to a local library will enable you to consult one or more national directories such as the following:

1. *Dun & Bradstreet Million Dollar Directory*
2. *Poor's Register of Corporations, Officers, and Directors*
3. *Thomas Register*
4. *Moody's Manual*

These directories differ in amount of information provided, but they all list companies alphabetically, geographically, and by product line or services offered. Looking in the alphabetical section under C, for instance, you will find a listing for Coca-Cola. You will also find Coca-Cola listed under Atlanta, Georgia (and many other geographic locations) and in product classifications under "Soft Drinks." These directories provide the name, address, and telephone number for each company—along with the names, functions, and backgrounds of key management personnel. As you know from our discussion in Chapter 18 (page 215), *Moody's* is published annually for industrial, financial, transport, and other categories of business activities; and it includes extensive biographical and financial information for each company listed.

If you are interested in working in a particular industry (advertising, cosmetics, grocery, marketing research, soft drinks) in a specific area (Chicago, Denver, Los Angeles), you can use directories to pinpoint target companies and to learn something about the companies and their managements. Consult the contents pages at the front of these directories for details about the specific types of information included and methods of locating the information.

Government publications

The federal government issues three directories that may assist you in your search for a specific type of employment. The Department of Labor publishes the *Dictionary of Occupational Titles,* which groups occupations into occupational classifications (based on job tasks and requirements) for nearly all jobs in the U.S. economy. Included also are comprehensive descriptions of job duties and related information for more than 20,000 different occupations.

The Department of Labor's *Encyclopedia of Careers and Vocational Guidance* catalogs opportunities in major industries such as advertising and retailing, and includes detailed information about the nature of work in different occupations—educational and special requirements, methods of entry, conditions for advancement, employment outlook, earnings potential, working conditions, and additional information concerning the social and psychological factors involved. You may also study the current and projected demand for employees in different employment categories by consulting the *Occupational Outlook Handbook,* an annual publication by the Department of Labor.

Personal leads

Many jobs, perhaps most of them, are found by word of mouth. Before going to the trouble and expense of advertising new or vacant positions, many employment managers first make the information known to their own employees. Rather than keeping your search for employment a secret, therefore, ask friends, relatives, and acquaintances to inform you of any job leads they encounter. Provide them with copies of your resume, and keep in touch.

Mass mailings

You may entertain the idea of mailing your resume to dozens or even hundreds of companies, hoping to increase the probability of early employment. Although many job seekers have landed desirable positions in this manner, business people generally respond more favorably to resumes that are accompanied by separately prepared cover letters, especially letters that are addressed to specific persons within their companies.

PSYCHOLOGICAL CONSIDERATIONS

The S*T*A*R (service, time, audience, reason) approach presented in Chapter 5 is extremely important in all types of employment communications.

Service

Employment managers are human, just like the rest of us, and they often identify with job seekers—remembering when they, too, were mailing resumes, calling on prospective employers, and being interviewed. But these people who do the hiring, if they are doing their jobs correctly, strive to employ people they believe will contribute more to the welfare of their companies than they will cost the companies in wages, salaries, and fringe benefits. Correspondingly, self-centered statements about the applicant's personal goals and ambitions generally make an unfavorable impression.

When applying for a job, therefore, dwell on the employer's interests and the welfare of the companies they represent. Adopt a service attitude by outlining those aspects of your education and experience that will make you a valuable employee—an employee who will make a greater contribution to the company than other applicants would be able to do. Such an approach will enable you to minimize use of the self-centered pronoun *I,* as illustrated in the following examples.

Self-centered	I read your advertisement in the morning paper on July 5, and am interested in such a position because I like the benefits, the pay, and the chance of advancement that your company offers. I am seeking a job with a future.
Service-oriented	The position that you advertised in the *Denver Star* on July 5 seems to match my qualifications exactly. My typing speed and knowledge of legal terminology, as outlined in the enclosed resume, should enable me to complete all types of legal documents for you with only a minimum of on-the-job exposure.

On the basis of these two statements alone, can there be any doubt about which applicant will capture the interest of the people who placed the ad in the newspaper?

Time

As with all types of communications, pay close attention to the time element when you are writing employment letters. If you mention your activities at a previous job, keep your writing in past tense (*performed, directed, participated, handled, improved*). Use present tense (*perform, direct, participate, handle, improve*) when discussing your current activities. Use future tense (*will, plan to, expect to, going to*) when discussing events that are yet to occur, and use the subjunctive mood (*would, could, should*) when dealing with uncertainty (events that you hope will take place).

Audience

Before you begin writing an employment letter or any other communication, identify your audience. Do you consider it best to direct your remarks to one person (the employment manager, the personnel manager, the vice-president of marketing) or to more than one person (all persons involved in the hiring process)? If you are addressing just one person, is the individual a male or a female? By identifying your audience, you will find the correct choice of words almost automatically.

Reason

Identifying and remembering the main reason for your communication will help you keep your thoughts on track, and the main reason for writing application letters is to secure interviews which might lead to employment. Correspondingly, you should phrase every statement in your employment letters to persuade readers that you are a likely candidate for the position you seek. Such an orientation will help you write concise and convincing letters.

UNEXPECTED LETTERS

Many job seekers mail copies of resumes each week to several companies hoping that at least a few will result in interviews. These unexpected letters, the ones that businesses have not solicited from applicants, should follow a three-part format: attract attention, provide evidence of qualifications, and request action.

You are trying to sell a product that is dear to your heart (your own services), and, in a very real sense, you are competing with many other products (the qualifications of other applicants seeking the same job). To compete successfully, you must phrase the opening statements in your application letters so that they will capture the attention of employment managers. Try to arouse their interest in the letter, in the resume, and (eventually) in the person.

Example: WORK WANTED! ONLY COMPANIES SEEKING SOMEONE WITH MIDDLE MANAGEMENT EXPERIENCE NEED APPLY.

Example: Is your company in need of a competent, mature secretary? A person who has the ability to follow instructions, as well as exercise good judgment in independent work?

Be sure to indicate the type of position you desire, and do not overstate your qualifications. Don't apply for a high position if you are without experience, for example, and don't suggest that all of their problems will disappear soon after your arrival.

Another effective way to begin an unexpected employment letter is to indicate that some recognized person has suggested that you apply. If trying to secure a job as ticket agent with an airline, for instance, drop by a ticket office or the airport and talk with a company employee. Make a note of the individual's name and learn the name, position, and address of the person who hires ticket agents. This information will enable you to begin employment letters with attention-getting statements.

Example: Margaret Jones at your Rosemead office suggested that I write directly to you concerning employment as a ticket agent.

Example: After discussing my ticket-selling experience with me at some length this morning, Mr. Beech at your Palm Springs office recommended that I submit a resume for your consideration.

Such opening statements imply that a company employee has seen and talked with you and was favorably impressed. Accordingly, recipients of these types of communications tend to be receptive to what applicants have to say about themselves.

Once you have attracted the attention of readers, you must maintain their interest by presenting evidence of your qualifications.

Example: A glance at the enclosed resume will reveal that I have had five years experience as Operations Manager for a medium-sized distributor of air-conditioning units and replacement parts. This experience included regular participation in new-product workshops presented by the company each month.

Example: As shown in the accompanying resume, my academic training and actual work experience have provided me not only with knowledge of standard accounting procedures, but have also given me a comprehensive overview of an entire manufacturing operation. Don't you agree that this experience, coupled with the business courses that I have taken in college, qualifies me for a clerical position with your firm?

When writing application letters, don't just copy a lot of information from the resume. Call attention to specific highlights of your background instead, making sure to mention the accompanying resume at some point in your letter.

End your application letters with appeals for action. If you want an interview, ask for one. Phrase your request as a question, rather than giving the impression that you *expect* a positive response.

Example: If you are favorably impressed with my qualifications, Ms. Teng, will you please call me for an interview?

Example: May I have an interview, please?

Don't detract from your request for action by tacking on an afterthought or a plea for consideration. End your letter with the question; and if you have not mentioned the person's name elsewhere in the body of the letter, include it in the closing sentence as shown in the preceding example.

Sample application letters

Having considered the three parts of unexpected application letters, let's put the pieces together to form two completed letters. The following letter is related to the sample resume in Figure 21-1 on page 267.

Unexpected application letter

Attract attention	Several accounting courses in college and some actual work experience! Would a young person with these qualifications be able to make a positive contribution to your clerical staff this summer?
Provide evidence	In addition to outlining my formal education and work experience, the enclosed resume lists several skills that I possess which may be directly applicable to your office procedures. Notice also that I am seeking any type of clerical work to begin with, even though my greatest contribution will eventually be in the area of accounting.
Ask for action	If you have a need for such a person, Mr. Reuter, will you please invite me in for an interview?

As a second example, the following letter is based on the sample resume in Figure 21-2 on page 268, and was written by an applicant who has considerable experience in data processing.

Attract attention	**DATA-PROCESSING PROBLEMS?** Are there obvious gaps in your information system? Are you paying too much money for the information you are receiving? Are you experiencing recurring problems in the data processing area? If you answer "yes" to any of these questions, you should consider my application for employment as <u>Data Processing Manager</u>.
Provide evidence	The enclosed data sheet presents evidence of my qualifications as an experienced and creative data processing manager. You will notice, for example, that I write and test my own programs—including the designing and implementation of a sophisticated inventory control system for my present employer.
	My managerial potential with your company is further enhanced by several academic achievements. My education has continued following graduation, moreover, because of an insatiable desire to continue learning as much as I can—not just in the field of data processing, but about all areas of business management.
Ask for action	Shall we discuss my potential contributions to Westco Corporation?

Brevity is essential in unexpected application letters, just as it is in advertisements. Two paragraphs were judged necessary in the middle section of the second letter, because more explanation was called for in connection with this managerial position. Both letters are sufficiently brief, nevertheless.

EXPECTED LETTERS

Expected letters are those that potential employers have asked you to submit. Maybe you have talked with employers in person or on the telephone, and they have asked you to send a resume. Or maybe you are responding to a help wanted ad in the local newspaper or a magazine.

Expected letters differ from unexpected ones in one major respect: The attention-getting statement at the beginning of the letter is replaced with a reference to the employer's request for information.

> Example: The enclosed resume is in response to your ad in today's <u>Washington Post</u>.
>
> Example: Here is the resume that you requested during our telephone conversation this morning.

One other way that expected letters sometimes differ from those not expected by employers is that they are longer. When an employer has requested job-related information, you may include a considerable amount of data in your letter without risking a loss of interest. You must still exercise good judgment, however, avoiding the temptation to include every little bit of available information and, in most cases, confining your letters to a single page. A good rule of thumb concerning the length of application letters is to include just enough information to arouse the interest of employers, but to withhold enough information to make them want to learn more through interviews.

The sample application letter in Figure 22-1 is "expected," since the campus recruiter for the company asked Roslyn Petre to write to R. Ronald Becker, the employment director. In fact, the recruiter probably submitted a report to Becker, presenting his impressions of the applicant from having interviewed her. Correspondingly, Roslyn begins the letter with a reference to the interview rather than a different type of attention-getting statement. She then interprets her training and experiences by relating them to the needs of the company—instead of simply repeating what has already been stated in the accompanying resume.

She does not include her address in the letter (above the date line), because to do so would repeat information that is prominent in her resume. She uses a modified block format, as described on pages 103–106, and she notes at the bottom of the page that two items are being enclosed with the letter (a resume and a list of courses and grades).

When preparing application letters for yourself, follow the same advice that was given about the appearance of resumes: high-quality paper, a good typewriter, clean type, and a fresh ribbon. Unlike the resume, however, you should not send the same letter to more than one company. If you are writing to similar companies (15 oil companies, for example), you may use similar wording; but each letter should be an original and, if at all possible, each should be addressed to a specific person. You are using the same resume for all companies; your application letter serves to customize each presentation.

February 6, 1983

Mr. R. Ronald Becker
Director of Employment Services
Melbourn Industries, Inc.
3546 N.W. 58 Street
Oklahoma City, OK 73112

Dear Mr. Becker:

As the conclusion of a very informative interview yesterday with James
Mason, your campus representative in this area, he asked that I write
to you concerning my interest in your management training program.

If you will take a moment to consider the enclosed resume, Mr. Becker,
you will see that my academic achievements in high school and in college
reflect a capacity to master complex materials. Just as important,
perhaps, the nature of my participation in extracurricular activities
throughout school is indicative of a strong leadership potential and
an ability to relate well to diverse groups of people.

The part-time job that I have held for the last two years has enabled
me to apply several of the managerial concepts that I studied in college,
and my personal supervision of several people for three months this
last summer provided me with additional leadership experience.

From what I learned of your training program from Mr. Mason, and based
on information about your company that is available in our school
library, it appears that much of my curriculum is closely related to
the type of merchandising that is your specialty. In addition to the
accompanying resume, therefore, please see the attached list of related
classes taken and the grades earned.

I believe that I could do well in the Melbourn environment, during the
training program and in the field, and would welcome an opportunity to
discuss that possibility with you.

Sincerely,

Roslyn W. Petre

Roslyn W. Petre

Enclosures (2)

Figure 22-1 Sample of an expected application letter.

CHECKLIST:
APPLICATION LETTERS

Target companies

- Have you checked all employment possibilities?
    Campus employment services?
    Employment agencies?
    Newspapers and trade journals?
    Yellow Pages?
    National directories?
    Government publications?
    Personal leads?

Psychological considerations

- Did you apply the S*T*A*R approach?
    Adopt a service attitude?
    Maintain consistent time frames?
    Communicate with specific audiences?
    Focus on the primary objective?

Unexpected letters

- Did you open with an attention-getting statement?
- Did you identify the type of work wanted?
- Are your objectives and claims realistic?
- Did you follow with evidence of your qualifications?
- Did you refer to the enclosed resume?
- Did you refer to the addressee by name?
- Did you end with a request for action?

Expected letters

- Did you open with a reference to their request for information?
- Did you identify the type of work you want?
- Are your objectives and claims realistic?
- Did you follow with evidence of your qualifications?
- Did you refer to the enclosed resume?
- Did you provide sufficient information, without trying to include every detail?
- Did you refer to the addressee by name?
- Did you end with a request for action?

Other considerations

- Did you use your own words, rather than copying?
- Did you keep a file copy of each letter?
- Did you enclose a copy of your resume?
- Did you attach sufficient postage?

- If writing to more than one company, did you type a separate letter for each? Did you double-check to make certain that you placed the letters in the correct envelopes?
- Did you confine your letter to one page?
- Is your letter attractive (see Chapter 7)?

23

PREPARING
FOR INTERVIEWS

Okay, an employer is favorably impressed with your letter and the qualifications outlined in your resume and has asked you to come in next Tuesday for an interview. Now what?

After first learning as much as possible about the company, identify elements in your education and work experience that relate to company operations. Prepare answers to probable questions and plan ways to support your statements. You should then approach the interview with a high degree of confidence that what you are selling (your services) is what they are seeking.

ANALYZE THE COMPANY

One sure way to please interviewers is to demonstrate extensive knowledge of company organization and operations. If you are to be interviewed for possible employment at The Greyhound Corporation, for example, you can use a *Moody's* manual to learn that this business is now much more than a bus company; Greyhound is a holding company with controlling interest in or full ownership of more than 100 subsidiary companies. You would also learn that Greyhound employs nearly 55,000 people, divides operations into six distinct product or service groups, and generates sales in the billions of dollars each year. Notice that the correct name of this company, as shown in *Moody's,* is "The Greyhound Corporation," not just "Greyhound Corporation"; such detail is sometimes important to the people who would be interviewing you.

A glance at *Moody's* or *Standard & Poor's* (two leading financial publications that are available at most brokerage offices and libraries) will also give you an indication of the financial condition of the company. You may learn, for instance, that the company you are considering is very profitable, or, at the other extreme, on the verge of bankruptcy. Knowledge of such conditions is essential before the interview rather than after the fact—after you have already accepted employment.

But what if the company is not listed in either of these publications? You may approach the company directly for information by simply writing or telephoning and requesting a copy of the most recent annual report. Annual reports usually include financial data and summary statements about the firm's plans, profitability, products, and services; but the information will probably be less objective than the coverage by *Moody's* or *Standard & Poor's*.

A company's suppliers, customers, employees, and even its competitors often represent candid sources of information. Ask anyone who relates to the company in any of these capacities what they think of the company and what kind of place it would be to work. You may find that the company is known for excellent employee relations or, conversely, that it is not what you would consider an acceptable work environment.

RELATE YOUR BACKGROUND
TO THE JOB

It isn't enough to be a well-qualified person; you must demonstrate that you are prepared for the specific job you are seeking. Having learned as much as you can about the company, therefore, identify those parts of your education and work experience that relate to the type of work that you would be performing as a newly hired employee.

Next, try to anticipate questions that interviewers may ask. Using your resume as the basis for questions, they may suggest that you elaborate on your major areas of study: Why did you decide to major in marketing? What type of marketing position would you eventually like to hold? Which college courses did you enjoy the most? Which ones did you like the least?

Interviewers often ask very direct questions about past employment: Are you still employed at National Insurance Company? Why are you thinking of changing jobs at this particular time? How do you like working for the people there? Why did you leave your job at Desert View? Would the people there be willing to provide you with a letter of recommendation? What made you look to us for employment?

If you already have a job, try to hang onto it until you find a better one, because it is widely accepted knowledge that employment managers prefer to hire people who are presently employed. The implication is that the employed are ambitious people who are probably seeking employment as a way of improving their situations; those who are unemployed, by this way of thinking, probably experienced difficulty in their previous positions and are more apt to represent future problems.

After questioning applicants about their education and work experience, interviewers often discuss the applicant's preparation for the job at hand: In what ways has your education prepared you for this job? Did any of your tasks with other employers involve this type of work? What makes you think that you can relate well to our customers? These are the types of questions that will enable you to tie your specific skills and knowledge directly to the position being sought, providing you are well prepared with answers.

If the job involves some degree of teamwork with other employees, cite evidence from your past that illustrates an ability to perform well in group efforts. If the job calls for leadership ability, mention any leadership roles that you played in school or at work. If the job involves clerical work, call attention to your knowledge of office equipment and procedures.

As a very young man being interviewed for his first clerical position, the author was just one of many people seeking the job—until he mentioned that he could type well. As it turned out, the job didn't involve much typing, but the mere mention of this one skill gave him enough of an edge over other applicants that he landed the job. Such skills as typing and the operation of various types of office equipment, no matter how basic they may seem to you, often gain important points with employment managers.

After you have practiced answering questions that interviewers are likely to ask (in front of a mirror, perhaps), ask someone to role-play an interview situation with you. Have the person sit on the opposite side of a desk or table, the usual setting for interviews, and assume the role of interviewer. Direct the surrogate interviewer to ask questions that you have prepared and to interject unplanned questions during the role-playing session. Although the sessions may seem strained (even a little corny) at the beginning, the experience can add significantly to your confidence when you engage in actual interviews.

GO PREPARED

Now that you have your thoughts organized for the interview, begin organizing the materials that you are to take along. Don't take just one pen; ballpoints seem to run out of fluid at the times you need them most. Equip yourself with two pens and two or three well-sharpened pencils and some paper.

When employment managers decide that you are a likely candidate for employment, they usually have other managerial personnel interview you, so take along additional copies of your resume for their use. Also prepare a list of important personal data so that you will be able to complete application forms accurately and quickly:

1. Details of your education (including dates, courses, and extra-curricular activities)
2. Names and addresses of previous employers (zip codes and all)
3. Dates of employment
4. Military records (DD-214)
5. Beginning and ending salaries
6. Reasons for leaving earlier jobs
7. Addresses and dates of previous residences
8. Social security number (self and spouse)
9. Marriage and divorce dates
10. List of references (including their titles, complete addresses, and phone numbers)
11. Financial data

Some application forms request financial information such as additional sources of income, lists of debts and assets, and insurance coverage—information that may be impossible for you to provide if not included in the type of data sheet recommended here.

You will want to convince interviewers that you did more than just "float along" during your schooling and work experience, so include samples of your work—copies of reports that you prepared in school or at work, letters and other documents that you wrote, computer programs that you designed. And be sure to include copies of any commendations received from college instructors and employers.

Where will you put all these materials? Place the samples of your work and letters of commendation, if any, in a separate folder, so that you can easily find them to present to interviewers at opportune times during interviews. Place this folder, along with your pens and pencils, resumes, data sheets, and other materials in a folder or large envelope. A briefcase would appear too formal unless you are applying for a position as middle manager or higher.

SELL YOURSELF

You've gone to a lot of trouble so far—developing a resume, writing an application letter, researching the company, preparing a personal data sheet, role-playing. With the interview now at hand, put the finishing touches on the package by presenting a favorable appearance, being punctual, and conducting yourself properly during the person-to-person exchange.

Check your appearance

Numerous studies have shown that interviewers tend to make up their minds about applicants during the first two or three minutes after meeting them—often using the time remaining in the interviews to justify their first impressions. Cater to this tendency by playing the part; dress at least as well as they would expect for the type of work you are seeking. Strive for a businesslike appearance by avoiding extremes in dress and hair styles, and make sure that your shoes are clean, that your clothes are fresh and well pressed, and that you are well groomed. Remember, companies hire people, not resumes or application letters. The main purpose of interviews, in fact, is to provide employment personnel with opportunities to observe applicants before deciding which ones will "fit in" best with the people who already work there.

Arrive ahead of time

Don't arrive on time; arrive at least 30 minutes before the scheduled interview. Allow time for traffic delays, mechanical failures, and parking hassles. If everything goes smoothly en route to the interview, use the extra time to organize your thoughts and to observe as much of the company facilities and as many employees as possible.

Be pleasant to the help

Be courteous to all employees that you encounter. While waiting for the interviewer, you may have an opportunity to converse with a secretary or receptionist; pleasant exchanges at this time might bring important rewards later. These are the people you may later be telephoning to check on the status of your application. Also, interviewers often ask assistants for their impressions of certain applicants. In other words, people other than the interviewer may be interviewing you without your even realizing it.

Use care with the application

You will be asked to complete an application early in the employment process, usually before the interview, the result of which will be part of that critical first impression that you make on the interviewer. So provide complete information, in printed form if possible. A high school junior with outstanding qualifications applied for summer employment at one of the country's leading corporations. He was extremely disappointed and puzzled when two less-qualified acquaintances were hired and he wasn't, until later learning that the employer had viewed his application form as being "sloppy." He worked the entire summer in a menial position instead, at about half the pay he would have received—a high price to pay for a few minutes carelessness.

Providing complete information can be potentially damaging if the questions on the application ask about physical problems or limitations, arrest or prison records, or mental illness. An honest answer is usually the best response, because the discovery of untruthful answers may result in rejection or termination. As an alternative, you may respond to sensitive questions by entering an asterisk (*) instead of an answer, to flag it for explanation during the interview.

Also in advance of the interview, you should decide what your response would be to a request that you take a polygraph (lie detector) test as a condition of employment. Many companies now use polygraphs to check the accuracy of statements made by applicants during interviews and on applications and resumes.

Examiners typically discuss the questions to be asked before beginning polygraph tests, sometimes rephrasing these questions during the actual testing. Honesty is the best policy, most experts agree, especially concerning whether you have ever taken relatively inexpensive property (such as pencils, stationery, stamps) from previous employers or whether you have ever cheated with respect to hours or expenses claimed. Such practice is not uncommon, it seems, and inaccurate answers to such questions may work to your disadvantage with respect to overall test results. Applicants usually learn the results immediately upon completion of the tests, at which time they are given an opportunity to explain any responses that may have been viewed as questionable.

Make an impressive entrance

Those critical first impressions do not depend entirely on your appearance; behavior is equally important. If you are sitting when the interviewer approaches, rise and prepare yourself for the traditional handshake. Respond to an offer to shake hands by looking the interviewer directly in the eye and shaking hands firmly. If the interviewer doesn't initiate a handshake, which is sometimes the case, you must decide if you are to take the initiative. The best advice for this situation is to do what seems natural to you at the time.

Be yourself

During the initial encounter, and after the interviewer has offered a chair to you, be pleasant and courteous. And, if at all possible under these trying conditions, try to smile a little. Interviewers expect a certain amount of nervousness from applicants, even experienced ones, because they realize that anxiety is a natural reaction to having other people analyze your background, preparation, and potential. So relax and act natural. Keep reminding yourself that these people believe you to be the right person for the job or they wouldn't have called you in for an interview in the first place. This outlook should allow you to contribute to an intelligent discussion of the job you are seeking and your qualifications for it, to reinforce their belief that you are the best possible candidate for the job.

Be responsive

As stressed throughout this book, the ability to communicate well is very important in business. Employment managers at one or more companies have already observed samples of your written communications by reading your resume and application letters; interviews will now enable them to judge your ability to communicate orally.

They usually begin interviews by engaging in small talk. Sure hot out today, isn't it? Did you find our building without too much difficulty? Can I offer you a cup of coffee? Try to relax and be friendly during these first few moments, realizing that interviewers generally do not spin their wheels long before delving into the topics that you are so eager to discuss.

Interviewers not only seek answers to specific questions; they also want to hear how you convey the information. So don't be reluctant to talk; answer each question as accurately and tactfully as possible, keeping your answers brief and to the point. Try to respond naturally—not as if you were on a witness stand in a court of law, but as though you were engaging in cordial conversation with a respected friend. Think before you answer, and if you realize at any point that you do not have an acceptable answer to a specific question, admit your lack of knowledge in that area. Interviewers generally react better to candid responses than they do to bluffers and "know-it-alls."

But don't talk too much

Be enthusiastic, but don't overdo it. Come up for air occasionally to give the interviewer an opportunity to control direction of the discussion. Be sensitive to the other person's wishes; if the interviewer appears to be losing interest in what you are saying, pause and seek new direction: Do you want me to comment further on this subject? Does that answer your question, Mr. Green? I never tire of discussing frazitts, but maybe you are eager to move on to another question? Such comments gain a lot of points, because they demonstrate a high degree of tact and empathy.

Be positive

The dialogue in interviews typically centers on past interrelationships of applicants with other business people. No matter how frustrating your experiences with other employers might have been, do not dwell on the negative. Negative comments imply not only that you have experienced difficulty with others, but that other people have also experienced difficulties in their relationships with you; and your main objective during interviews should be one of demonstrating your ability to relate well to people.

Postpone discussions of money

Don't bring up the subject of money during the initial interview. A direct question about salary will typically result in a counterquestion about how much money you expect to earn, and expectations that are either too low or too high will have an adverse effect on your chances of landing the job.

But what if the interviewer introduces the subject? Try to postpone any discussion of money at the beginning of the interview with statements such as, "I believe that I will be in a better position to discuss salary after learning more about the job," and "Can't we talk about money after we determine that I am the right person for the job?" The risk of jeopardizing a job opportunity will be reduced considerably if the discussion of money is postponed until later in the hiring process, when you begin to sense that you are the chosen candidate.

Interview the interviewer

After preparing and mailing many resumes and application letters, the name of the game by the time you reach the interview is "Land that job." Such an orientation often causes applicants to overlook valuable information during their visits to companies. When the author was being interviewed for a middle-management position with a food-processing company, for example, he was so intent on securing the job that he might as well have been blindfolded during his entry and exit to the interview.

Try to avoid being so goal oriented or self-conscious that you stop seeing or hearing what is going on around you. Take an inquiring look at the facilities and the people, and keep asking yourself if it is a working environment in which you could be reasonably content and productive. Go one step further by interviewing the interviewer. Ask questions about company operations, programs, and products; and listen closely to what is said. Ask for a look at the department where you would be working and, if practical, a tour of related facilities. Such an introduction to the company isn't too much to expect, considering the fact that you might end up spending

250 working days each year at the company for the rest of your productive life. Moreover, interviewers are usually favorably impressed with applicants who have the knowledge and foresight to ask discerning questions.

Watch nonverbal clues

Try to read the feelings of interviewers by observing their facial expressions, voice inflections, and posture. Comment favorably on items in their offices that appear to be cherished status symbols. Monitor their body movements for signs of interest, acceptance, rejection, and impatience. When you respond to nonverbal cues by altering the length or content of your responses, your success ratio should increase significantly.

—here is another person at every interview whom you should watch even more closely—yourself. Broadcast the desired signals of interest, honesty, reliability, and intelligence by monitoring and controlling your own nonverbal behavior. Arrive at the interview freshly groomed and in appropriate clothing, as advised earlier, and make certain that your body language conveys the intended messages. This advice includes several no-nos such as not picking at or biting your nails, not chewing gum, not talking with your hand over your mouth, not playing with your pen or pencil, not giggling, and not smoking (unless the interviewer lights up and invites you to smoke also).

Exit strategically

When the comments or nonverbal activities of an interviewer suggest that the interview is nearing an end, tactfully interject any points that you consider relevant to your chances of landing the job. This moment may represent your final opportunity to sell the interviewer on the importance of your potential contributions to the company.

Try to extract a commitment from the interviewer at this time, or as you both rise and prepare to end the conversation. If the interviewer does not provide such a commitment but does indicate that you are still in the running for the job, ask when you may telephone for a progress report. Thank the interviewer for having taken the time to visit with you, and, if you truly want the job, say so.

PERSEVERE

Many applicants express shock and dismay when employers do not respond warmly to their initial efforts to find employment. But wouldn't it be unusual for applicants to land the desired jobs on the first try—or even the second, third, or fourth attempt? The job market doesn't even become aware of their presence until they begin introducing themselves with resumes, application letters, and interviews.

So keep trying until the right door swings open. You may do poorly the first few interviews; most people do. But the only way to improve your performance during interviews is through more interviewing. Accept every interview that is offered to you, therefore, by on-campus recruiters and by employment managers in their offices. Your feelings will not be so easily bruised after a few rejections, and you will learn to settle down during interviews and do a better job of selling yourself. Remember, you are not alone in this endeavor. Almost all business people, even those who will be interviewing you, have experienced a similar challenge at least once in their lives. This year just happens to be your turn.

24

FOLLOW-UP LETTERS

Don't just fade away after an interview, no matter how well or how poorly you may have presented your case. Follow the interview with a letter, a telephone call, and maybe another visit to the company. A job offer, when it comes, often requires a letter of acceptance or rejection; and, if you take the job, you should present a letter of resignation to your current employer and send brief notes of thanks to those people who provided job leads or references for you.

FIRST A LETTER

You have been interviewed and have put forth your best effort in relating your qualifications for the job. But don't stop now! In your competition with other applicants who are seeking the same job, a follow-up letter might be the extra input that tips the employment scales in your favor.

Send a letter to the interviewer within the first day or two following the interview. As illustrated in the following examples, express your gratitude for the time taken to interview you, mention your qualifications for the job, and ask for further consideration.

Follow-up letters

| Express gratitude | Our discussion on Monday was very interesting, and I thank you for the time that you spent with me. | I appreciated the opportunity to talk with you yesterday concerning my application for employment. |
| Allude to your qualifications | After hearing your description of the duties of an inventory clerk, I am even more certain that my qualifications match the | Although my educational background was discussed at some length, I cannot recall our having talked about my actual work ex- |

	position. Correspondingly, another glance at my resume (copy enclosed) may convince you that I am well prepared to undertake this type of work.	perience. My extensive dealing with the public (see the attached resume) and the part-time position that I presently hold seem to relate directly to the type of duties that I would be performing for you.
Request further consideration	I will appreciate any further consideration that you may give me for this position, Ms. Jones, because I am even more eager to work for Bell Enterprise than before talking with you.	Will you please take this experience into account, Mr. Roberts, when selecting someone for the clerical position that you presently have open?

Notice that the applicants are including copies of their resumes, making it very convenient for the interviewers to review the mentioned qualifications.

THEN A PHONE CALL

When four or five working days have passed with no word from the company, give them a call. Beginning a telephone conversation with the interviewer is especially easy if you mentioned such a follow-up during the interview.

> Example: Good morning, Ms. Jones, this is Ron Cox. You suggested that I phone you a few days following the interview last Monday about the position in inventory control.

When Ron Cox has introduced himself and the situation in this manner, the remainder of the conversation will depend largely on Ms. Jones's response. At some point in the conversation, however, he should seek a commitment on the current status of his application and when the employment decision is to be made. He should briefly restate his interest while avoiding any indication of desperation.

If you are unable to get through to the interviewer in your follow-up call, attempt to question whoever answers the telephone. Try to coax as much information from the person as possible, using all the tact and persuasive abilities at your command. A good impression on the office help often results in favorable comments passed to the interviewer about your continuing efforts to land the job. And at this point in the employment process, you need all the help you can get.

But how long should you wait before abandoning the effort as hopeless? If two or three weeks pass with no encouragement, telephone and ask for a status report.

Example: Am I still being considered for the job?

Example: When is a decision to be made?

Example: May I provide you with additional information?

Your patience may be nearly exhausted by this time, because days often seem like weeks when you are waiting for job offers, but don't be too demanding. The wheels of business turn slowly sometimes, and you may still be a prime candidate for the position.

A TIMELY VISIT

While you await the employment decision, consider the practicality of dropping by the company on your own volition. If you judge the interviewer to be fairly accessible and receptive, go directly to his or her office. The people there may consider this action a little atypical, but they will probably admire your initiative and perseverance. Just tell the interviewer or the assistant that you are concerned that you haven't heard from them and that you want to do everything within your power to secure the job.

The final decision about hiring you is usually left to the person who would be your immediate superior, the person who would be directly over you. If you have already been interviewed by this individual, consider a follow-up visit. You may catch the person at an inopportune time, but you can always offer to come back at a time that *is* convenient. A visit of this type will not cause them to label you as a nuisance but instead will make them realize that your interest in the job is sincere; and employers would rather hire people who are eager for employment than those who are lackadaisical about the whole process. Of 53 applicants who recently applied for a position as administrative assistant with a manufacturing firm in Phoenix, Arizona, for example, the person who landed the job was the only one who took it upon herself (a female in this instance) to drop by the office and ask the receptionist if a follow-up meeting could be arranged.

Also consider the possible benefits of talking with rank-and-file employees, the people you would be working with if hired. Upon learning of your plight, they might be able to provide you with insight into the hiring process. You might learn, for example, that the best approach in dealing with the employment people at this particular company is to keep contacting them. Conversely, you might discover that a subtle approach will be more effective. Of course, the amount of time and effort you expend on this type of follow-up depends on how badly you want the job.

ACCEPTANCE OR REFUSAL

Sooner or later you are bound to hit the jackpot; someone will offer you a job. But an offer that comes early in the search, especially if it is of only marginal interest to you, can present problems. Do I really want this job? Could I command a higher salary elsewhere? Should I wait until I hear from all those other companies?

Don't panic and accept the first offer that comes along, unless you are convinced it is a good one. If the company directs you to respond to the offer by a certain date, you might be able to delay acceptance (or rejection) until you receive responses from other companies where you have applied. This is also the time to mention a higher salary if you plan to, and to discuss reimbursement for moving expenses and other conditions of employment, because you will have much less leverage in such negotiations once you accept the job offer.

Because of the federal laws that now regulate their actions, many employment managers present job offers in writing to establish a record of when and to whom the offers are made. If you receive an offer that is satisfactory, you should respond with a written response—a letter or a telegram, whichever they sent to you. Begin your communication by indicating your acceptance of the job. Continue with a discussion of the starting date and other relevant details, and end with a "thank you" and an optimistic comment about the future.

Acceptance letters

Accept the offer	I am very pleased to accept your offer of employment.	Yes, I do accept the position that you have offered me.
Provide necessary detail	Allowing a two-week notice to my present employer and about five days for traveling and locating an apartment, I should be prepared to begin work on November 6; and, unless you instruct differently, I will report directly to Mr. Hedges at 8:00 a.m. on that date.	The hours stated in your letter will be perfect, and I have already arranged transportation with a neighbor who works at your McDowell facility. I will report to the personnel office promptly at 8:30 a.m. on January 27, as you suggested.
Express gratitude	Thank you for selecting me from among the several applicants for the job, Ms. Green. I will do my best to prove that your choice was a wise one.	Thank you very much.

Although most acceptance letters are brief, like these, you may find it necessary to extend the middle paragraph (or add another paragraph or two) to include additional information. If you could not begin employment at the agreed date, for example, you should include a detailed explanation of your circumstances. Employers seldom resent delays that result when employees continue in their old jobs until replacements can be found, because they realize that such employees may some day extend the same consideration to them.

If you receive a job offer after already beginning work at some other company, tactfully refuse the offer in a brief letter. Use the deductive approach by stating your refusal in the first paragraph. Provide some detail in the middle paragraph, and end with an expression of gratitude.

Refusal letters

Decline the offer	Although I appreciate the chance to work for Esquire Sporting Goods, I must decline your offer of employment.	I certainly appreciate your very pleasant letter, but cannot at this time accept your offer of employment.
Provide an explanation	Since discussing the clerical position with you last month, I have accepted employment elsewhere.	Because of the very intense competition for summer jobs this year, I felt it prudent to accept one of the earliest offers. Therefore, I have already begun work with another company.
Express gratitude	Thank you for the time that you spent with me, Mr. Lyons. I enjoyed talking with you and was very impressed with your offices.	I thank you for the offer, and hope that you will be receptive to my application for employment next year.

Avoid any temptation to brag about the position you did accept, and do not burden the reader with excessive detail about your employment decision. Be brief, courteous, and appreciative. If you are upset with the offer or their delays in making the offer, do not express your true feelings, because you may look to them for employment again someday.

LETTER OF RESIGNATION

Once you have the new job well secured, present your current employer with a letter of resignation. This communication establishes a permanent record of the fact that you resigned, rather than being fired, and it sets forth the conditions of your departure. The most frequent pattern, and probably the best one is to (1) break the news in the first sentence, (2) provide some detail in the middle paragraph, and (3) express appreciation in the final paragraph.

Resignation letters

Break the news either directly or indirectly	The main purpose of this letter is to inform you of my impending departure. I have accepted employment with Rodgers Manufacturing Company as a data processing supervisor—an opportunity that is too attractive to pass up.	Miss Kingston, my immediate supervisor, knows that I have been taking evening classes in business administration and will soon receive my bachelor's degree in office management. When offered a position as assistant office manager for Western Products, therefore, I accepted.
Provide details of departure	I am prepared to continue working here until November 10 or to assume the new job immediately, whichever arrangement you prefer.	The position at Western begins June 15, so that I may continue in my present job for two more weeks—if you wish.
Express appreciation	The experience that I have gained with this company contributed greatly toward my preparation for the type of work that I will be performing in the new position, and I am very appreciative of the fine treatment that I have received from Mr. Lambert and all of my co-workers here.	My responsibilities as stenographer have related well to my educational and career interests, for which I am grateful. In addition to this invaluable learning experience, I have enjoyed working with all members of this fine organization.

Don't gloat over your success in landing a better job, and don't tell anyone off. You may succeed in making other employees envious and in humiliating your superiors, but they will have the last and loudest laugh if things don't go well for you in the new position. Many employees leave companies each year to take "better jobs" only to return a few months later in pursuit of their earlier positions. So don't slam the door too abruptly or too permanently when you depart.

INFORM REFERENCES

When friends, relatives, or business acquaintances have provided references or assisted you in any way, be sure to notify them promptly of your successful conclusion of the job search. Send them an informal letter, but one that is attractive and well written. Begin by conveying the good news. Provide some details in a middle paragraph, and end the letter with a direct expression of gratitude.

Reference thank-you letters

Convey the good news	You asked me to let you know how things turned out with my job search, and the news is positive.	SUCCESS AT LAST! I finally landed the job.
Provide some detail	In fact, I am already working in Warcor's legal department—in a paralegal capacity. I love it.	Thanks to you and others who helped me, I am now the data processing supervisor at Rodgers Electric. The job suits me perfectly, and I am certain that my letters of reference (like the very impressive one that you wrote) were an important consideration in the selection process.
Express gratitude	Thank you so much, Professor Martin, for following through so promptly on your offer to write a letter of recommendation for me.	I thank you very much, Clarence, and look forward to taking you to lunch sometime soon for a mini-celebration. Okay?

Rewarding the people who helped you secure employment is good business, because you never know when you may need their support again. A luncheon at a fancy restaurant, a family get-together, some type of small gift, or just a sincere "thank you" will help to maintain these invaluable relationships.

REFERENCE LETTERS

Once settled in a job, you may be asked to write reference letters for former employees who are seeking employment elsewhere. References are a pleasure to write when they relate to employees who have performed well. When employee performance has not been commendable, on the other hand, we should avoid potentially damaging statements that cannot be supported with detailed, objective evidence.

Reference letters

Refer to their request	We are delighted to be called upon as a reference for Susan L. Scott.	In reply to your letter of December 15, James Randolph began work in our product-distribution department on May 1, 1980, and left our employment on August 31, 1982.
Provide only positive or	During her three years with us, Susan worked in various positions. She started as a	During this period, he was responsible for processing all incoming sales orders

neutral infor- mation	teller and advanced within the accounting department to become an investment counsellor. As can be determined from her promotions, she is high- ly intelligent, capable, and dependable. We consider her performance to be ex- emplary, in that she has the ambition and initiative to begin new projects while still being reliable and con- scientious in routine tasks.	from our California custom- ers. This task involved cred- it checks, inventory commotments, pool-car com- pilations, and all related correspondence.
Close with a positive or neutral statement	Based on Susan's perfor- mance and our association with her, we are confident that she will do well in al- most any job situation.	We hope that this informa- tion proves helpful.

While the second letter may seem unnecessarily brief and noncommital, such letters are standard policy at many companies today. In fact, some employers provide only the starting dates of employment, regardless of the amount or kind of information requested or how well or poorly the employees performed. Their main concern is to protect their companies against potential lawsuits initiated by former employees. For superior results, keep the S*T*A*R approach in mind (page 75). The *Service-Time-Audience-Reason* orientation is just as applicable to employment letters as it is to other types of business correspondence.

GOOD WRITING!

Abbreviations, 3–5, 34
addresses, 5
business terms, 3
company names, 4
days, months, holidays, 4
geographic areas, 5
government agencies, 3–4
metric prefixes and units, 4
person's name, 5
school subjects, 5
self-check, 5
state codes, 4
time expressions, 4
titles with names, 4
Accept-except, 49
Acronyms, 33
Active voice, 68–69
Addresses, 5, 7, 11
Advertising (*see* Persuasive
    communications)
Advice/advise, 49
Affect/effect, 49
Ages of people, 9
Air mail, 115
Almanacs, 215
Amount/number, 53
All ready/already, 49
All together/altogether, 49
Among/between, 50
Anxious/eager, 51
Apostrophes, 23–26
Appendixes, 242
Application letters, 278–90
Articles, 6, 27
Articles in magazines, 7, 27, 31
Atlases, 214–15
Attention line, 98–100
Authorization for research,
    209–11

**Bad-news communications,
    167–75**
checklist, 174–75
examples, 171–74
Balance/remainder, 50
Bar graphs, 223
Better/best, 50
Between/among, 50
Bibliography
card system, 217–19
entries, 232–35
pages, 231–32
sample page, 259
Books, titles of, 7
Business Periodicals Index, 216

Cablegrams, 134
Canned letters, 126
Capital/capitol, 51
Capitalization, 6–9
addresses, 7
complimentary closes, 8
days, months, holidays, 6
directions, 6

family relationships, 7
historical events, 6
important documents, 6
language courses, 7
occupational positions, 7
person's title and name, 7
publications, names of, 7
quotations, 8
self-check, 8–9
titles of magazine articles, 7
titles of books, 7
words relating to numbers, 8
Carbon copies, 102–3
Card catalog, 214
Card system for reports, 217–19
Cartoon cards, 188–89
Certified mail, 115
Charts, 228
Checklists
application letters, 289–90
bad-news communications,
    174–75
collection communications,
    192–93
good-news communications,
    165–66
interoffice memos, 91–92
letter styles, 117–19
persuasive communications,
    184–85
routine correspondence,
    158–59
reports, 259–61
resumes, 275–77
Circle graphs, 223–25
Cite/sight/site, 50
Clauses, 2–3
Cliches, 43
Collection communications,
    186–93
appeals for action, 190
cartoon cards, 188–89
checklist, 192–93
inquiry, 189–90
reminder, 187–89
telephone, 187
ultimatum, 191–92
Colons, 21–22
Commas, 16–19
Commendation letters, 194–95
Communicate
getting ready to, 1
naturally, 76–77
promptly, 77
Communication levels, 73
Communications
electronic, 129–37
employment, 263–308
media, 73–74
planning the, 72–74
techniques of, 151–97
Company names, 4
Complex sentences, 59–60
Compliment/complement, 50

Complimentary close, 8, 100–101
Component graphs, 225–27
Compound sentences, 59–60
Computers (*see* Data banks)
Conjunctions, 6
Consolation messages, 195
Contents page(s), 242
sample of, 245
Continuous/continual, 50
Cover letters (*see* Letters,
    transmittal)
Credit letters (*see* Collection
    communications)
Credit terms, 10

Dashes, 30
Data/datum, 51
Data banks, 135
Date collection, 211–19
card system, 217–19
primary data, 211–14
secondary data, 214–19
Datagrams, 134
Datelines
in interoffice memos, 82–83
in letters, 93
in reports, 231–44
Dates, 18
Dictation guidelines, 147–50
Dictionaries, 12
Directions, 6
Direct quotations (*see*
    Quotations)
Documentation (*see* Reports,
    documentation)
Double negatives, 64–65

Each other/one another, 51
Eager/anxious, 51
Effect/affect, 49
Electronic communications,
    129–37
Ellipsis, 31
Elite type, 106
Eminent/imminent, 52
Employment agencies, 279
Employment communications,
    263–308
acceptance of job offer, 304–5
application letters, 278–90
checklist, 289–90
expected letters, 286–88
following up, 301–8
Government publications, 281
industrial directories, 280
interviews, 291–300
personal leads, 281
psychological considerations,
    281–83
reference letters, 307–8
references, letters to, 306–7
refusal of job offer, 304–5
resignation, letter of, 305–6
resumes, 265–77

Employment communications (*cont.*)
  sources of job information, 278–81
  target companies, 278–79
  unexpected letters, 283–86
  Yellow Pages, 279–80
Enclosures, 102–3
Encyclopedias, 215
Endnotes (*see* Footnotes)
Envelopes, preparation of, 112–14
  advertising on, 116–17
  attention lines, 113
  checklist, 118–19
  inserting the letter, 114
  mailing instructions, 114–15
  receiver's address, 112–13
  return address, 112
  sample of, 113
  (*see also* Postal services)
Euphemisms, 42
Exaggeration, 41–42
Except/accept, 49
Exclamation marks, 35
Experimental research, 211
Express mail, 115

Facsimile communications, 136–37
Farther/further, 52
Faster/fastest, 50
Feedback, 73–74
Fewer/less, 53
Figures, 248–49
Firm names, 4
First-class mail, 115
Footnotes, 233–35, 238–40
Foreign words, 31
Form letters, 124–26
  sample of, 125
Fractions, 9, 29
Fragments, 57–58
Full block, 103–5
Further/farther, 52

Gender, 44–45
Generalities, 39–40
Good-news communications, 160–66
  checklist, 165–66
  examples of, 163–65
Goodwill close, 155–56
Government agencies, 5
Graphic illustrations, 220–29
  bar graphs, 223
  charts, 228
  circle graphs, 223–25
  component graphs, 225–27
  line graphs, 221–23
  tables, 220–21
  visual aids, 227–29

Handshaking, 296
He/him, 54

Headings in reports, 237–38
Her/she, 54
Him/he, 54
Holidays, 4, 6
Hyphens, 28–30
Hypothesis, 202–3

I/me, 54
Ibid., 239
Illustrations (*see* Graphic illustrations)
Imminent/eminent, 52
Imply/infer, 52
Indentation of paragraphs
  in letters, 106
  in reports, 237
Indexes, 216–17
In/into, 52
Inductive reasoning, 160–61
Infer/imply, 52
Initials
  on memos, 84
  typist's, 86, 103
Interoffice memos, 81–92
  carbonized forms, 87
  checklist, 91–92
  copies of, 86
  date line, 82–83
  examples (pictorial) of, 83, 87, 210, 243, 258–59
  guidelines for writing, 89–90
  ICE lines, 86
  interoffice mail, 90–91
  purpose of, 81–82
  round-trip forms, 88–89
  short form, 86–87
  standard format, 82–89
  subsequent pages of, 85
Interviews, employment, 291–300
  research for, 291–92
Into/in, 52

Jargon, 45–47
Job applications (*see* Application letters)

Later/latter, 52
Lay/lie, 52
Less/fewer, 53
Letterhead, 106
Letters
  appearance, 103–11
  application, 278–90
  attention line, 98–100
  bad news, 167–75
  body of, 100
  canned, 126
  carbon copies, 102–3
  checklist, 117–19
  collection, 186–93
  commendation, 194–95
  complimentary close, 100–101
  consolation, 195

  copies of, 102–3
  cost of, 122–23
  date line, 93
  employment, 263–308
  enclosures, 102–3
  envelope preparation, 112–14
  examples (pictorial) of, 94, 104–5
  folding, 114
  form letters, 124–26
  format, 103–10
  full block, 103–6
  good news, 160–66
  letterhead, 106
  margin stops, 106
  minimizing, 120–28
  modified block, 103–6
  multipage, 110
  parts of, 93–103
  personal, 94
  persuasive, 176–85
  placement on page, 103–10
  postscripts, 103
  reasons for writing, 120–21
  reasons for not writing, 122–23
  receiver's address, 95–96
  reference, 307–8
  resignation, 305–6
  return address, 93–94, 112
  routine, 153–59
  salutation, 96–98
  sender's address, 93
  sender's name, 101
  sender's position, 101–2
  sender's title, 101–2
  simplified format, 110–11
  state codes, 96
  style of, 103–6
  subject line, 98
  substitutes for, 124–28
  thank-you, 195–96
  typist's initials on, 102
  vertical spacing, 106–10
  welcome, 196–97
Letter style, 93–119
  full block, 103–6
  modified block, 103–6
Letterhead, 106
Levels of communications, 73
Library references, 215–17
  atlases, 215
  Business Periodicals Index, 216
  card catalog, 214
  Christian Science Monitor, 217
  encyclopedias, 215
  financial services, 215
  government publications, 215
  New York Times Index, 216
  Reader's Guide to Periodical Literature, 216
  reference books, 215
  Statistical Abstract of the United States, 215

Wall Street Journal Index, 216–17
Lie/lay, 52
Line graphs, 221–23
Listings, 250, 252–53
loc. cit., 239
Loose/lose/loss, 53

Magazines, 7, 27, 31
Mailgrams, 133–34
Mailing instructions, 113–14
Mail services, 115–16
  electronic, 136–37
  interoffice, 90–91
Margin stops
  for letters, 106
  for reports, 235–36
Marketing, Four P's of, 177
Me/I, 54
Mechanics, 3–15
Media, selection of, 73–74
Memos (*see* Interoffice memos)
Metered mail, 116–17
Metric prefixes, 4
Micrographics, 143
Modified block, 103–5
Money, 10
Months, 4, 6

Names of people, 5
National directories, 280
Negatives, double, 64–65
New York Times Index, 216
Newspapers, 216–17
None (the word), 62
Number/amount, 53
Numbers: words or figures, 9–12,
  19, 29, 34
  addresses, 11
  ages of people, 9
  beginning a sentence, 9
  credit terms, 10
  days and years, 10
  fractions, 9
  money, 10
  number of units, 10
  percentages, 10
  periods of time, 10
  self-check, 11–12
  time of day, 11

Objectivity, 41–42
On/onto, 53
One another/each other, 51
op. cit., 239
Oral/verbal, 53
Ordinals, 10
Outlining reports, 203–8
Overused expressions, 43–44

P's of marketing, 177
Pagination in reports, 236
Paragraph
  indentation, 106, 237
  structure, 70–71

Parallelism, 64–66
Parentheses, 33–34
Passive voice, 68–69
Percent sign, 12
Percentages, 10
Periodicals, 216–17, 234–35, 256
Periods, 74
Persuasive communications,
  176–85
  checklist, 184–85
  samples of, 181–84
Phrases, 17–18
Pica type, 106
Pie charts (*see* Circle graphs)
Planning the communication,
  72–74
Possessives, 24–25
Postal services, 114–16
  electronic mail service, 136–37
  metered mail, 116–17
  postage equipment, 116–17
Postcards, 126–28
Postscripts, 103
Predicates, 57
Prepositions, 6
Pretesting questionnaires,
  212–13
Primary data, 211–14
Principle/principal, 53
Pronouns, 54
Psychological techniques of communication, 151–93
  bad-news communications,
    167–75
  collection communications,
    192–93
  good-news communications,
    160–66
  persuasive communications,
    176–85
  routine correspondence,
    153–59
Publications, 7, 31
Punctuation, 16–36
  apostrophes, 23–26
  colons, 21–22
  commas, 16–19
  dashes, 30
  ellipsis, 31
  exclamation marks, 35
  hyphens, 28–30
  minimizing, 68
  parentheses, 33–34
  periods, 34
  question marks, 35
  quotation marks, 26–28
  semicolons, 20–21
  underscore, 30–31
  (*see also* Self-checks)

Question marks, 35
Questionnaires, 212–13
Quotations, direct
  elipses, 31

  indented, 246
Quotation marks, 26–28

***Reader's Guide to Periodical Lit-
erature,* 216**
References, personal (*see* Resumes, Personal references,
  273–74, 306–8)
Registered mail, 115
Remainder/balance, 50
Repetition, avoidance of, 66–67
Reports, 199–261
  appendix, 242
  bibliographic entries, 231–35
  bibliography page, 231, 256
  body of, 235–36
  card system, 217–19
  checklist, 259–61
  contents page(s), 242, 245
  documentation, 238–40
  example (pictorial) of, 244–56
  experiments, 211
  figures, 248–49
  file copy, 242–43
  footnotes, 233–35
  guidesheet, 240
  headings, 238
  hypothesis, 202–3
  indentations in, 237
  interviews, 211
  introductory section, 237,
    246–47
  key steps, 201
  lists in, 250, 252–53
  margins in, 235–36
  organization of ideas, 204
  outline preparation, 203–8
  page numbers, 236
  parts of, 230
  placement on pages, 235–36
  planning the study, 201–8
  preliminary investigation,
    202–3
  preparation of, 244–61
  primary data, 211–14
  questionnaires, 212–13
  quotations in, 240–41
  reference books, 214–17
  researching the topic, 209–19
  research, 202–3
  research proposal, 209–11
  sample report, 244–56
  scientific method, 203
  secondary data, 214–19
  sequencing of parts, 230
  short report, 257–58
  spacing, 235–36
  statistical analysis, 213–14
  summary of, 242
  survey, 212–13
  terminal section, 241
  time schedule, 219
  title page, 231, 244
  topic selection, 201–2

Reports (*cont.*)
  transition statements, 238, 240
  transmittal, 243
  writing style in, 241
  (*see also* Library references)
Research, 202–3, 209–19
Resignation letters, 305–6
Resumes, 265–77
  appearance of, 274–75
  career objective, 268–69
  checklist, 275–77
  education, 269–70
  examples (pictoral) of, 266–67
  military service, 273
  organization of, 265
  personal data, 265–68
  personal references, 274–75
  photographs with, 268
  work experience, 270–72
Return address, 93–94
Routine correspondence, 153–59
  checklist, 158–59
  examples of, 156–59

**Sales messages (*see* Persua-
  sive communications)**
Salutations, 96–98
Sampling, 213–14
School subjects, 5
Scientific method, 203
Secondary data, 214–19
Self/selves, 55
Self-checks
  abbreviations, 5
  apostrophes, 25–26
  capitalization, 8–9
  colons, 22–23
  commas, 19–20
  correct word usage, 55–56
  dashes, 31–32
  desexing communications, 45
  economizing on words, 48–49
  exclamation marks, 35–36
  fresh terminology, 44
  hyphens, 31–32
  interesting sentences, 69–70
  jargon, 47
  numbers, 11–12
  objective words, 42
  parallel construction, 66
  parentheses, 35–36
  positive emphasis, 43
  question marks, 35–36
  quotation marks, 27–28
  semicolons, 22–23
  sentence structure, 60–61
  simpler words, 38
  sincere words, 40

subject-verb agreement, 63–64
tact, 40–41
underscore, 31–32
Secondary data, 214–19
Selling (*see* Persuasive
  communications)
Semicolons, 20–21
Sentence structure, 57–69
  active, 68–69
  complete, 57–58
  complex, 59–60
  compound, 59–60
  fragments, 57–58
  interesting, 66–70
  parallel construction, 64–66
  passive, 68–69
  self-check, 60–61
  simple, 59–60
  subject-verb agreement, 61–64
Series, 17, 21, 34
Service attitude, 75
Short report, 257–58
She/her, 54
Signature, 101–2
Simple sentences, 58–61
Site/cite/sight, 50
Slang expressions, 26
Spelling, 12–15, 28
S*T*A*R approach to commu-
  nication, 75–76
State codes, 96
*Statistical Abstract of the United
  States,* 215
Statistical analysis, 213–14
Studies (*see* Reports)
Styles of letters, 93–111
Subheadings in reports, 237–38
Subjunctive mood, 209–10
Subject line, 98
Subjects of sentences, 57–60
Subject-verb agreement, 61–64
Surveys, 212–13
Symbols: words or signs, 12
Synopsis (*see* Reports, summary)

Tables, 220–21
Table of contents (*see* Contents
  Page(s))
Telegrams, 129–31
Teletypes, 131–33
Telex service, 131–32, 135
Tenses, 61–64, 75–76, 209–11
Term papers (*see* Reports)
Terminology (*see* Word choice)
Thank-you letters, 195–96
That/who/which, 55
They/them, 54
Time expressions, 4, 11

Time periods, 10
Title page, 231, 244
Titles, 4
Transition statements, 238, 240
Transmittal letters, 243
Type size, 106
Typist's initials, 86, 102
TWX service, 132–33, 135

Underscore, 30–31
Us/we, 54

Verbal/oral, 53
Verbs (*see* Subject-verb
  agreement)
Visual aids, 227–29
  chalk boards, 227–28
  charts, 228
  movie projectors, 229
  overhead projectors, 228–29
Vitas (*see* Resumes)
Voice, active vs. passive, 68–69

Wall Street Journal Index,
  216–17
We/us, 54
Welcome letters, 196–97
Western Union, 129–135
  cablegrams, 134–35
  datagrams, 134
  mailgrams, 133–34
  telegrams, 129–31
  Telex service, 131–32, 135
  TWX service, 132–33, 135
  other services, 135
Who/which/that, 55
Who/whom, 54
Word choice, 37–56
  cliches, 43
  correct usage, 49–56
  desexed communications,
    44–45
  economize on words, 47–49
  euphemisms, 42
  fresh terminology, 43–44
  jargon, 45–47
  objective words, 41–42
  positive approach, 42–43
  simple words, 37–38
  sincere words, 39–40
  tact, 40–41
Word divisions, 29–30
Word processing, 138–50
  centers, 138–47
  dictation guidelines, 147–50
  plan of action, 144–47

Zip codes, 96